imaginary ethnographies

IMAGINARY ETHNOGRAPHIES

Literature, Culture, and Subjectivity

GABRIELE SCHWAB

COLUMBIA UNIVERSITY PRESS   *New York*

COLUMBIA UNIVERSITY PRESS
Publishers Since 1893
NEW YORK   CHICHESTER, WEST SUSSEX
cup.columbia.edu

Library of Congress Cataloging-in-Publication Data
Schwab, Gabriele.
  Imaginary ethnographies : literature, culture, and subjectivity / Gabriele Schwab.
     p.   cm.
  Includes bibliographical references and index.
  ISBN 978-0-231-15948-7 (cloth : acid-free paper)—ISBN 978-0-231-15949-4 (pbk. : acid-free paper)—
ISBN 978-0-231-53080-4 (ebook)   1. Literature—History and criticism—Theory, etc.   2. Literature
and society.   3.   Social science literature.   I. Title.

PN51.S3196 2012
809'.93358—dc23

                                                                        2012017415

∞

Columbia University Press books are printed on permanent and durable acid-free paper.
This book is printed on paper with recycled content.
Printed in the United States of America

c 10 9 8 7 6 5 4 3 2 1
p 10 9 8 7 6 5 4 3 2 1

Cover Image: © Brion Gysin, untitled, courtesy of Galerie de France

To my sons, Manuel and Leon

Contents

Acknowledgments

I *maginary Ethnographies* has evolved like a mutant creature moving slowly toward an ever-changing future. Initially I conceived the book as a sequel to *The Mirror and the Killer-Queen*, where I first developed a theory that looked at reading as a form of cultural contact. In one of the chapters, titled "Haunting Legacies," I wanted to include an auto-ethnographic reflection, analyzing the transgenerational transmission of violent histories with a focus on my own history of growing up in Germany in the wake of World War II. Soon it became clear, however, that this topic could not be handled in a single chapter but required an entire book. For several years I worked on both projects simultaneously, and during that time published several chapters of *Imaginary Ethnographies* in essay form. Eventually *Haunting Legacies* took over and demanded to be completed first. Once I returned to the more encompassing *Imaginary Ethnographies*, its organization into two discrete sections and a coda suggested itself almost naturally. I had written an essay on Lévi-Strauss, Derrida, and the Nambikwara that provided a productive opening for the book since it dealt directly with ethnography, writing, and aesthetics. I then added two chapters on literature, culture, and ethnography, one on "traveling literature," and the other on exoticism and the vicissitudes of cultural transference. The second section of *Imaginary Ethnographies* focuses on close readings organized around iconic cultural figures, namely the cannibal, the child, and the alien, followed by a coda on the posthuman.

Different institutions supported *Imaginary Ethnographies* during its various stages, and colleagues and students—too many to name individually—contributed in myriad ways and with remarkable engagement and generosity to the development of the project into a book. Over the years I taught several graduate seminars on *Imaginary Ethnographies*, not only at the University of

California, Irvine (UCI), but also in Munich, Santiago de Compostela, and at Rutgers University. My deepest gratitude goes to the students in those seminars, whose involving, imaginative, and sophisticated discussions helped me in shaping the final version of *Imaginary Ethnographies*. First and foremost, my heartfelt thanks go to my research assistants: Clara McLean is one of the most careful and skilled editors I have ever met, and Travis Tanner, one of my most attuned readers, put the greatest care into preparing the initial manuscript for the press. I owe them a million thanks. It was most fortuitous that Shambhavi Prakash was assigned to me as my research assistant during my semester at Rutgers. We share an interest in the relationship between literature and ethnography, and I thank her for the many unforgettable discussions, not to mention helping me survive the practical challenges of teaching in a new place. Philip Anselmo, my research assistant during the final editing, helped me immensely not only with his feedback but also with saving me precious time by making me more computer literate.

Special thanks go to the numerous institutions and colleagues who hosted lectures at their home universities. Over the years I have presented more than thirty lectures on *Imaginary Ethnographies* in the United States, Germany, Australia, Bulgaria, China, England, Canada, Israel, and New Zealand. Introducing the project, or specific chapters, in these places kept the momentum going, even during the times I had to put the book on hold because of other obligations. A few instances were seminal for the current shape of the book: I am indebted to Mihai Spariosu for inviting me to teach a summer seminar on *Imaginary Ethnographies* at the School for Theory and Criticism in Santiago de Compostela, where I had superb discussions with students and colleagues from different parts of the world, many of whom I am still in touch with. They helped me tremendously in getting the project launched. During the summer in Santiago, I discussed initial ideas about the project with my friend and mentor, Wolfgang Iser, and his wife, Lore. While they were both somewhat shocked about the fact that I seriously considered including a chapter on science fiction and the figure of the alien, our friendship and collegiality survived as we shifted our discussions to what they considered to be "more serious" aspects of my research. I will always be grateful to Wolfgang for supporting my work even when, rather than merely following in his footsteps, I deliberately chose a different path. At Santiago de Compostela, I met Dimitar Kambourov, who later came to work with me at UCI, hosted various lectures of mine in Bulgaria, and became a translator of my work. I also met

Iping Liang and Hanping Chiu at Santiago de Compostela, both colleagues from Taiwan, who were unbelievably generous and intellectually stimulating hosts when I lectured in Taipei on *Imaginary Ethnographies*. Murat Eyuboglu came to Santiago with a dissertation project on music, using the theory I had developed in *Subjects without Selves*. He became so involved with our discussions on the Nambikwara that he began a collaboration with Marcelo Fortaleza Flores on a most interesting ethnographic film titled *Claude Lévi-Strauss: Return to the Amazon* (2009). I thank Dimitar, Iping, Hanping and Murat for their loyal friendship and the many creative exchanges about our common interests.

I also thank my colleagues at UCI, where I first presented my ideas on *Imaginary Ethnographies* at the Distinguished Faculty Lecture sponsored by the Irvine Division of the Academic Senate, and later at various conferences in the Department of Anthropology. I was truly fortunate that George Marcus joined UCI and hosted a series of exciting events about experimental ethnographies at the Center for Ethnography. He, together with Michael Fischer and James Clifford, originally inspired my project in its earliest stages during the "writing culture" debates. I thank George and Michael for their wonderful support and feedback over the years.

My colleagues at the University of Constance invited me on various occasions to present from my project. Special thanks go to Aleida Assmann and Renate Lachmann, whose continued support keeps my ties with my alma mater alive. I am grateful to Florian Sedlmeier for our inspiring discussions at Irvine and for his invitation to present "Imaginary Ethnographies" at the Graduiertenkolleg in Constance. Ross Morris couldn't have known what a special gift she offered me with her invitation to lecture on *Imaginary Ethnographies* at Columbia University. The wonderful discussion that ensued with her and other colleagues, including Gayatri Spivak, Andreas Huyssen, Marianne Hirsch, and Paul Kockelman (who later wrote me an ingeniously insightful letter addressing my presentation) gave me the extra push I needed during the final stages of writing.

I thank Bernd Ostendorf for the invitation to give the commencement speech at the University of Munich in 1998, where the idea for my chapter on Lévi-Strauss, Derrida, and the Nambikwara was born. Ulla Haselstein, who had arranged for my yearlong visiting professorship at Munich, offered me the pleasurable experience of many long and involved discussions as well as of coteaching a seminar on primitivism. My chapter "Another Writing Lesson" profited immensely from discussions with Jacques Derrida, who was at the time I wrote the first version, still my colleague and friend at UCI.

My chapter "Traveling Literature, Traveling Theory" was inspired by my first lecture tour in China, and I am especially grateful to Huimin Jin for taking me to see Kaifeng and arranging interviews with the remaining members of the Jewish Diaspora community. Unfortunately I had to cancel my lecture at Pusan National University in South Korea because of complications related to September 11, 2001, but I thank the university for publishing a shorter version of "Traveling Literature, Traveling Theory" in its journal *Studies in the Humanities*.

I wrote the first version of "Restriction and Mobility" for a conference on "Literature and Anthropology" at the University of Constance and am indebted to the Graduiertenkolleg for its continued support of interdisciplinary research in literary studies and anthropology. "The Melancholic Cannibal" was inspired by initial discussions with Gabriel Riera and Laura Garcia and then conceived during my research fellowship at the Australian National University. I am grateful for the inspiring feedback I received from my colleagues in Canberra and Melbourne, especially John Cash, Phillip Darby, Michael Dutton, and Leila Ghandi. I thank Ann Kaplan, director of the Humanities Institute at Stony Brook, for her continued support and for inviting me to present a later version at her conference on psychoanalysis after Freud.

Thanks to my colleagues at Tel Aviv University for inviting me to present on Richard Powers's *Operation Wandering Soul*. The ensuing discussion with Zephyra Porat on our way back to Jerusalem convinced me to include a chapter on Powers in my book. I also thank Katrin Springer and Simona Sitkov for bringing me back to Rutgers University to present the keynote lecture on Powers at their graduate student conference on "Writing the City." It was a sheer stroke of almost unbelievable luck that I met Richard Powers when we were both guest researchers at the Free University of Berlin. Richard and I became friends almost instantly, and I will always most fondly remember the wonderful walks, talks, and dinners we had, together with his wife, Jane, in that sunny summer in Berlin a few years ago. Richard's response to my chapter on *Operation Wandering Soul* is the greatest gift a literary critic could ever receive from an author, and I am happy he gave me permission to quote him: "You do so many remarkable and right-hearted things with this thorny and difficult book, the "problem child" of all my work. . . . And at its best, this chapter makes me wonder whether OWS might be the one book that I would save from the bonfire, if I could only rescue one." I can only add that if this were the only response I would ever get to *Imaginary Ethnographies*, all the work that went into the book would still have been worthwhile.

The chapter on Octavia Butler was inspired by Donna Haraway's path-breaking work on Butler. I cannot say how highly I value her long friendship, her unfailing support, as well as her astute feedback to an early talk version on the topic. I first presented on Butler as part of the Irvine Lectures in Critical Theory, which was then published in *Accelerating Possession: Global Futures of Property and Personhood*, a volume I coedited with Bill Maurer. I thank the members of the Critical Theory Institute, especially Mark Poster, John Rowe, Steven Mailloux, Jim Ferguson, Liisa Maalki, and Lindon Barrett for invaluable feedback. Lindon continued discussions on *Imaginary Ethnographies* as well as on his own projects with me at the Zinc Cafe before he passed away. Those times belong to my fondest memories of him. Thanks also to Renate Hof and Klaus Millich for engaging discussions when they invited me to give a presentation on Octavia Butler as part of the Du Bois Lectures at Humboldt University.

The chapter on Beckett's *The Lost Ones* was inspired by Jean-François Lyotard's *The Inhuman*. Its conception reaches back to Steven Connor's invitation to present the keynote address at his conference on "New Approaches to Beckett" at Birbeck College and owes much to the ensuing captivating discussions I had with him and Kyoo Lee. I had shared my initial idea with Jean-François Lyotard while he was still a colleague at Irvine, and when, after his death, *Parallax* solicited a piece from me for their memorial issue on Lyotard, I couldn't think of a better occasion to write the essay on Beckett and Lyotard that had already formed in my mind.

Among the many colleagues and friends from different universities in the United States and other countries, I must at least mention those who have read or heard parts of my work and supported me with lucid feedback: Kathleen Woodward, Herb Blau, Michael Levine, Shahla Talebi, Ileana Orlich, Claudia Sadowski-Smith, Sally Kitsch, Martin Matustik, Dirk Hoerder, E. Ann Kaplan, Dragan Kujundzic, Meera Lee, Larry Bogad, and, last but not least, my former students, who remain faithful and supportive readers: Gregg Lambert, Naomi Mandel, Natalie Eppelsheimer, Lini Chakravorty, Leila Neti, Holli Levitsky, and Yvonne Reinecke. Friends and colleagues in English and Comparative Literature and in Anthropology at UCI gave me invaluable feedback on specific chapters, and my heartfelt thanks go to all of them. Special thanks go to Ackbar Abbas, Ngũgĩ wa Thiong'o, Alex Gelley, David Goldberg, Nasrin Ramihieh, Annette Schlichter, and Etienne Balibar in Comparative Literature, and to Julia Elyachar, George Marcus, Kaushik Sander Ranjan, Bill Maurer, Tom Boellstorff, Kris Peterson, and Angela Garcia in Anthropology. In the Institute of Postcolonial Studies in Melbourne, I profoundly thank the director, Phillip Darby, and John Cash, with whom I have collaborated for many years. I also received challenging and supportive feedback from my colleagues in Germany: Irene Albers, Aleida and Jan Assmann, Vittoria Borsò, Anselm Franke, and Reinhold Görling.

I want to express my gratitude to the many people who helped with the production of the book at Columbia University Press. As always, my first thanks go to my editor, Jennifer Crewe, for her support of many years. This is the fourth project I have done with her, and I cannot say how highly I value her collegiality, professional integrity, and friendship. I thank her for the fruitful discussions both at UCI and in New York. I also thank Kathryn Schell for her assistance in seeing the manuscript through its final stages to publication, as well as Mike Ashby for his care and insightful suggestions during the copyediting process and Ron Harris for taking care of the proofs.

As always I thank my two sons, and those close friends I consider my extended elective family, for the many years of encouragement and support of my work: Manuel continues to be one of my sharpest readers, and Leon always surprises me with sudden unfailing deep insights in our discussions. I thank Charmian for the many hours during which we silently worked next to each other, and for sharing our mutual passion for our work and for keeping our spirits high. The collaboration with Simon Ortiz on *Children of Fire, Children of Water* continues to keep my creative energies in balance with my scholarly work. I thank Leon, Lucia, and Anthony for keeping me company this past summer during the tedious stages of the final editing. Ackbar Abbas, Sola Liu, Ngũgĩ wa Thiong'o, Njeeri wa Ngũgĩ, Alex and Mieke Gelley, Julia Elyachar, Tomaz Mastnak, and Martin Schwab have all inspired the work that went into *Imaginary Ethnographies* by not only their lucid intellectual engagement but also their emotional presence. Finally, I thank Aijaz Ahmad for unforgettable discussions during his time at Irvine.

Earlier versions of several chapters of *Imaginary Ethnographies* have been previously published, in English and other languages. A shorter version of "Restriction and Mobility" appeared in German in Stefan Rieger, Schamma Schahadat, and Martin Weinberg, eds., *Interkulturalität: Zwischen Inszenierung und Archiv* (Gunter Narr Verlag, 1999). The essay also appeared in Portuguese in Amelia Sanz Cabrerizo, ed., *Interculturas/Transliteraturas* (Arco Libros, 2008). An early version of "Ethnographies of the Future" appeared, with a different emphasis, in German in Vittoria Borsò and Björn Goldammer, eds., *Moderne(n) der Jahrhundertwenden* (Baden-Baden: Nomos, 2000). The essay was included in Bill Maurer and Gabriele Schwab, eds., *Accelerating Possession: Global Futures of Property and Personhood* (Columbia University Press, 2006). An earlier version of "Cosmographical Meditations on the In/Human: Samuel Beckett's *The Lost Ones*" appeared, with a different emphasis, as "Cosmological Meditations on the In/Human: Lyotard and Beckett" in *Parallax* (2000). A Chinese translation of the essay appeared in *Cultural Studies* 6 (2007). An earlier, shorter version of "Another Writing Lesson: Lévi-Strauss, Derrida, and the Chief of the Nambikwara" appeared as "The Writing Lesson: Imaginary Inscriptions in Cultural Encounters" in *Critical Horizons* (2003). A Bulgarian translation of the essay appeared in 2002. An earlier, shorter version of "Traveling Literature, Traveling Theory: Imaginary Encounters Between East and West" appeared as "Traveling Literature, Traveling Theory: Literature and Cultural Contact Between East and West" in *Studies in the Humanities* 29, no. 1 (2002). I thank the editors of those journals for their permission to reprint the essays.

imaginary ethnographies

Introduction

Still now, and more desperately than ever, I dream of a writing that
would be neither philosophy nor literature, nor even contaminated by
one or the other, while still keeping—I have no desire to abandon this—
the memory of literature and philosophy.[1]
—Jacques Derrida

A rgentine writer Juan José Saer once defined literature as a "speculative
anthropology."[2] Envisioning the particular role of literary production in
the *writing of culture*, Saer locates literature in a transitional space between
anthropology and cultural philosophy (*Kulturphilosophie*). After the rhetorical turn in anthropology, however, ethnographies borrowed more freely from
narrative and literary devices, and therefore the boundaries between the two
genres became more porous. We may ask what specific difference there still
is between literature and recent ethnographies, and how we can theorize
the specificity of literature in light of its cultural function. Perhaps the most
distinct aspect involved in literature's writing of culture is its appeal to the
psyche, the emotions, and the unconscious. The psychological dimension of
literature belongs as centrally to its cultural function as do the anthropological and philosophical dimensions. In *Imaginary Ethnographies*, I therefore
focus on how in literature *writing culture* is enmeshed with and mediated by
writing psychic life.

I thus use the term "imaginary ethnographies" with the triad of anthropology, philosophy, and psychoanalysis in mind as contextual disciplines for
the study of literary writings of culture. While this project is interdisciplinary
in scope and relevance, it is grounded in literary studies. Instead of blurring
the boundaries between the disciplines in question, I am rather interested

in working out the specificity of literature in contrast but also in relation to them. Literature is a medium that *writes culture* within the particular space and mode of aesthetic production. It therefore uses discursive and figurative modes, regimes of knowledge, and structures of appeal that are specific to literature and related aesthetic practices.

I restate the single most persistent question in literary studies—why literature?—by highlighting the ways in which literature relates to, produces, or intervenes in culture. Saer's term "speculative anthropology" highlights literature's imaginary ways of remaking language and the world, shaping not only culture but also, and more directly, the cultural imaginary. In a similar vein, I read a paradigmatic selection of literary texts as imaginary ethnographies, that is as texts that *write culture* by inventing a language that redraws the boundaries of imaginable worlds and by providing *thick descriptions* of the desires, fears, and fantasies that shape the imaginary lives and cultural encounters of invented protagonists. But imaginary ethnographies do more than write life stories; they also rewrite cultural narratives. They use alternative signifying practices and bold refigurations to undo cultural iconographies and unsettle the status quo of habitual cultural codes. In this respect literatures, and aesthetic practices more generally, can also be seen, as Jacqueline Rose insists, as discourses and practices of cultural resistance.[3] In reading literary texts as "imaginary ethnographies," I am, of course, putting forth a certain reading practice. In principle, any text can be read as an imaginary ethnography to the extent that all texts make a cultural intervention. I am, however, selecting texts in which the focus on cultural intervention is more prominent and often accompanied by a metatextual reflection on particular cultural moments, turns, or iconic figures in the cultural imaginary.

Within the framework of reading literary texts as imaginary ethnographies, I further expand my theory of reading as cultural contact that I developed in *The Mirror and the Killer-Queen: Otherness in Literary Language*.[4] In that book I analyze how literature and reading impact the boundaries of and between cultures. I emphasize that, more than simply "writing culture," literature is also "making culture." In *Imaginary Ethnographies*, I expand this perspective, borrowing Hans-Jörg Rheinberger's notion of "experimental systems"[5] to define literature as an "experimental system" that uses language to explore, shape, and generate emergent forms of subjectivity, culture, and life in processes of dialogical exchange with its readers.[6] Trained as a molecular biologist, Rheinberger has shifted his recent work to the history of science and philosophy. Focusing on what it means to explore something new and unknown and insisting that research is a search that moves along the boundary between knowledge and the unknown, Rheinberger's epistemological theories also cross the boundaries between the sciences and the humanities. Initially, it was Jacques Derrida's *Of Grammatology* as well as art historian George Kubler's *The Shape of Time*[7] that inspired his shift from molecular biology to epistemology. Kubler emphasizes that every artist works in the dark, guided only by the tunnels of earlier works. Accordingly, the creative process anticipates a knowledge that can be understood and articulated only a posteriori.

Rheinberger uses a similar notion of "playing in the dark" as the basis for his exploration of experimental systems. Experimental systems, according to Rheinberger, are spaces of emergence that invent structures in order to grasp what cannot yet be thought. Experimental systems function as generators of surprise and machines for the production of the future.[8] In this context, Rheinberger also addresses the relevance of his notion of experimental systems for the arts and humanities. Drawing on *Of Grammatology*, Rheinberger emphatically asserts that the single most important source for emergence is writing itself. He proposes to view writing as an experimental system, emphasizing that it is by giving thought a material condition that writing facilitates the emergence of something new, including new systems of meaning and, as Michael Fischer proposes in extending Rheinberger's concept, new forms of life.[9]

It is in this sense that *Imaginary Ethnographies* explores literature as an experimental system able to generate emergent forms of language, subjectivity, culture, and life. I use "forms of life" in a double sense here: for one, literature *is* a form of life in the sense in which Wittgenstein defines a linguistic form as a form of life.[10] But in another sense, literary texts are also relational objects that generate forms of life in interactions with readers. Literature as an experimental system comes to life only in concrete writing and reading experiences and therefore necessarily includes the reader. Emergence is then facilitated not only by the anticipatory potential of writing but also by a reader's intuitive grasp of something that is experienced before it is understood.

Rheinberger's notion of "experimental systems" became productive for my theoretical framework for various reasons. My theory of literature and reading has been inspired by encounters with either highly experimental texts or texts that are foreign to my own cultural and literary formation. In both cases the reading experience is marked by creative disruptions of familiar uses of language and the need to cope with and to make productive use of this disruption. Texts that appear unfamiliar and strange force one to deal with their otherness or foreignness. According to Rheinberger, experimental systems create "epistemic things." Could we define one of literature's cultural functions as the production of "epistemic things" in the form of a particular literary knowledge? But what could an "epistemic literary thing" be and how would it differ from an epistemic scientific thing? Rheinberger defines epistemic things as "material entities or processes—physical structures, chemical reactions, biological functions—that constitute the object of inquiry.... Epistemic things *embody what one does not yet know*."[11] We could describe the literary text as a "language object" that performs a speech act that, in turn, becomes the generative matrix for the reading process by anticipating a knowledge that is not yet available discursively.[12] Like material scientific objects this "language object" embodies what one does not yet know.

If we see the reading process as an engagement with this epistemic literary thing, we may assume that literary knowledge has the capacity to anticipate understanding. Accordingly, literary knowledge includes, but cannot be reduced to, literature's referential function. A historical or ethnographic novel may undoubtedly impart knowledge—and even some concrete information—about the historical period or cultural site it portrays. But this type of knowledge is embedded in and impacted by the "knowledge" that emerges from a particular literary use of language and the experience of reading this particular use facilitates. It is this latter I call literary knowledge. It is knowledge in the sense of a memorable and transformational experience of something that at this point still escapes a full understanding or conceptual grasp.

In trying to define the "particularity" of literary knowledge, we must expand the notion of the epistemic to include more than informational knowledge. Literary knowledge in the strict sense is less "about" something than it is an embodied experience of something. It relies on intangible forms of knowing and, as I have argued elsewhere, unconscious forms of knowing.[13] For example, Patricia Grace's *Baby No-Eyes*[14]—a Maori novel that deals with the new biocolonialism and the indigenous land rights movement in New Zealand—is certainly a form of "writing culture" that imparts knowledge about the Maori. But the "literary knowledge" proper emerges from the reader's encounter with and processing of a polyvocal composition that includes the voice of a ghost and the mosaic of a transgenerational memory that disrupts the linearity of time and narrative, creating a polytemporality that includes past, present, and future.[15] It is in processing these polytemporal and polyvocal voices that readers are made to feel the impact of the traumatic silencing of the violation of a dead child's body and the displacement of the mother's grief onto another child.[16] The novel thus conveys a literary knowledge of trauma that may, but does not need to, become the object of conscious reflection. Rather, it is imparted in the form of an experiential and emotionally processed form of knowing, closer to a "knowing how" than to a "knowing that." Moreover, it is possible that for some readers the novel's mood of grief may resonate with a hidden personal grief that has never become conscious. This experience of resonance may be transformational in the sense that an unconscious mood has found a symbolic expression and thereby entered a communicative space.[17]

In more general terms, I argue that the most fundamental role of literary knowledge consists less in providing information than in facilitating the emergence of new forms of being in language, thought, emotion, and ultimately life, including the emergence of new subjectivities, socialities, communalities, and relationalities. What literature brings forth could not emerge or be conceived in quite the same ways otherwise. While the particular form of "emergence" facilitated by literature thus includes "epistemic things," literature's primary function is less epistemic than transformational. It is as a transformational object that literature contributes to the (re)shaping of subjectivities and cultures. This transformational power of literature is not confined to the actual reading experience. Rather, the latter functions as a catalyst for transformations that unfold beyond the narrower confines of specific literary encounters. These transformations extend over time and unfold in close relation to other experiences, including aesthetic ones.

This does not mean, however, that texts lose their epistemic dimension. The latter enters into the transformational frame in different ways: as virtual textual knowledge, as knowledge activated in the reader, and as knowledge generated by and left as a trace of the reading experience. Finally, the knowledge that emerges from individual reading experiences facilitates the emergence of new cultural forms or structures of feeling such as, for example, the emergence of passionate love or romantic love that Niklas Luhmann analyzes as an effect of literary codings of intimacy in bourgeois society.[18]

In the development of my own literary theory, I have explored in different stages and from different angles how literature impacts the boundaries of subjectivity and culture. Reading as a process of transformational and generative experiences and activities contributes to the emergence of new forms, including new forms of subjectivity, culture, and life. This begins already in infancy when listening to the first stories, fairy tales, and nursery rhymes becomes part of a word-forming experience. In this early environment, the voice not only transmits a rudimentary experience of language and story; it simultaneously functions as a relational object that transmits an affectively structured holding environment.[19] Even this early encounter with literature operates at both an individual and a cultural level. While these early stories function as a central vehicle for the social transmission of culture, the infant also receives them within a culturally colored, but nonetheless individually inflected, aesthetics of care that is expressed in the storyteller's rhythms, tone of voice, mood, and affective connection. Later in life, readers may encounter in poetry, prose, or dramatic dialogue ways of being in language that facilitate a breakthrough of cultural knowledge and affect. In *The Power of the Story: Fiction and Political Change*,[20] Michael Hanne shows that in particular instances and historical circumstances such affective engagement can generate dramatic political effects. One of his examples is Harriet Beecher Stowe. Hanne points out that "many politicians and historians attributed to *Uncle Tom's Cabin* a major role in bringing about the war and thereby hastening the abolition of slavery."[21]

At a more subliminal level, readers may also encounter ways of being in language that are so radically unique and unfamiliar that it appears as if one were temporarily transported into a different mode of being or had slipped into another form of life. Working via indirection and detour, these experimental texts disrupt the smooth operations of referentiality, enfolding their otherness into formal and rhetorical choices, thus almost forcing readers into close encounters with literary materiality and craft. Reading Samuel Beckett's later agrammatical and asemantic prose, for example, may induce a dizzying oscillation between a radically disruptive and a hypnotically close encounter. On the one hand, Beckett goes so far in defamiliarizing language that his texts may induce an almost schizoid state of dissolution. On the other hand, his meticulously crafted rhythms and cadences of speech exert a hypnotic pull that draws readers into the very fabric of the text. For readers open to the alterity of Beckett's texts, this experience may impact the very boundary between discursive conscious thought and unconscious mental production.

By contrast, reading science fiction, such as, for example, Octavia Butler's *Xenogenesis*, may induce an almost corporeal reaction to the alien species' radically different and changing forms of embodiment. This reaction will, in turn, become the affective foil for experiencing the aliens' imagined otherness as a species and culture. In this process, Butler not only reorganizes cultural knowledge about racism and colonialism; she also draws her readers affectively into experiencing the "work of death"[22] performed by these violent cultural formations. Both Beckett and Butler thus impact their readers' scope of understanding, perception, and affective disposition, albeit in different ways. Where such challenges to habitus occur, the experimental system has induced a reorganization of both epistemic knowledge and structures of feeling or affect.

In my own work I have so far particularly emphasized the emergence of new ways in which language impacts psychic life, conscious and unconscious. It is via the detour of the psychic life of language, I argue, that literature processes and affects both cultural and political life. In this process, literature engages our entire mode of being in language and, mediated through language, the world, including unconscious ways of knowing and remembering.[23] How is this engagement with the most fundamental modes of being in language related to literary modes of *writing culture?* Proposing to read literary works as "imaginary ethnographies," I am interested in how literature records, translates, and (re)shapes the internal processing of culture. This internal processing of culture is closely tied to what I have earlier called the psychic life of language. My examples suggest that the transmission of affect and its relation to unconscious knowledge, or what I call the process of literary transference, plays a crucial role in literary forms of writing and making culture. Literary transference relies strongly on what Wolfgang Iser has emphasized as the most generative feature to solicit readers' active participation in the constitution of meaning, namely "indeterminacy."[24] Although Iser addresses mainly informational gaps, other indeterminacies such as linguistic, conceptual, situational, or generic ones may have more impact. Conceptual indeterminacy is, according to Rheinberger, the essential quality of experimental systems because it facilitates emergence. In literature, conceptual indeterminacy generates transformational effects and becomes a precondition for the emergence of new forms. Indeterminacy operates like a virtual blank screen that generates a free flow of projection, affect, and unconscious transference, thus engaging readers in the co-construction of virtual textual spaces.

In order to grasp these dialogical processes between text and reader, we need to account for the epistemic and transformational functions of literary texts as well as the epistemic disposition of readers and their openness to transformation. Before indeterminacy can become productive in the reading process, it is first experienced as perturbation. How readers react to such perturbation opens questions of a politics and ethics of reading. Readers who try to reduce indeterminacy by imposing a predetermined framework on a text obviously produce very different readings from those who attune themselves to what appears as new, strange, or incommensurable. The choices we make in reading and interpreting belong to an ethics of reading that concerns a text's alterity, be it linguistic, historical, cultural, or psychological.

How then do these considerations bear more specifically upon my exploration of literary texts as imaginary ethnographies? In a certain sense, I am "ethnologizing" the process of reading. I supplement the perspective of literature as a form of writing culture (with epistemic effects) with a perspective of reading as an active form of transformational cultural contact. Juan José Saer's *The Witness*, for example, can be read as an imaginary ethnography about the *colastiné*,[25] an indigenous tribe in the Amazonian rain forest Saer invented by using a bricolage of cultural knowledges and fantasies about indigenous peoples, including intertextual references ranging from Herodotus and Jean de Léry to Freud and Lévi-Strauss. In positioning his readers, however, Saer emphasizes largely the transmission of affect, orchestrating the entire novel around the narrator's grief and guilt about his own involuntary participation in the destruction of the indigenous people. Readers are thus scripted into both understanding the violence of colonialism (epistemic function) and experiencing it indirectly through the transference of guilt and grief (transformational function).

While Saer's text works through both a layered transference of affect and a sustained philosophical reflection on radical alterity, other texts convey alterity more immediately and materially through disruptions of familiar uses of language and through the creation of what we could perceive, through the lens of Rheinberger, as strange linguistic and epistemic objects. Literary objects, I argue, move freely across the boundary of epistemic and psychic or internal objects. Generated in the transitional space between external and internal objects, strange literary objects emerge from a language that is in the process of renegotiating the boundary between self and world. In extreme cases, these objects may resemble the "bizarre objects" Wilfred Bion (Samuel Beckett's analyst) has theorized as psychotic objects created through the projection of unwanted psychic elements.[26] An ethics of reading that grants priority to unfamiliar or strange linguistic, epistemic, or psychic objects privileges the challenge of familiar frameworks. It encourages new patterns of reading or relating to otherness and promotes openness to emergence. Literary objects are then used as vehicles for emergent ways of thinking, reading, and experiencing.

Of course, we are unable ever to experience literary objects with a pure or empty mind, that is, in the epistemological position obsessively aspired to and never attained by so many Beckett characters. Without some sort of preconception or apprehension, we could never be surprised by something new. Inevitably, we bring to a text not only an entire arsenal of previous experiences, including aesthetic ones; we also mobilize the theories and philosophies that form our (implicit) archive. Using literature as an experimental system requires openness to a process of dialogical exchange in which the traces of cultural experiences—including the traces of one's theoretical formations—become retraced and rewritten in the encounter with a text's alterity. Such retracing has both epistemic and material effects. After all, the abstract theoretical ideas we carry (mostly unconsciously) shape our ways of thinking and being in the world. The practice of a deliberate temporary bracketing of preconceived theoretical knowledge, however, is the basis of a truly generative reading experience that can be called an event. At stake is a certain relationship of literature to theory that, rather than reducing literature to a mere "representation," illustration, or affirmation of a theory or a world as we have come to know it, allows literature to make an intervention at the cultural, linguistic, and epistemological levels. Only then can it function as a catalyst for transformation and emergence in systems that ground and form experiences.

Psychoanalysis argues that psychic emergence requires a mode of attention that circumvents the constraints of habitual conscious censorship. States of *reverie* or freely flowing attention are conducive to such psychic emergence. Supplementing Freud's notion of a repressed unconscious with that of a "structural unconscious," or, as Christopher Bollas calls it, a "receptive unconscious," psychoanalytic art critic Anton Ehrenzweig shows that such unfocused attention or syncretistic vision is the basis of emergence in creative processes more generally.[27] According to Ehrenzweig, freely flowing attention facilitates "unconscious scanning," that is, a mode of aesthetic apprehension and judgment rooted in primary process thinking. In this vein, reading may mobilize the freely flowing attention theorized in psychoanalysis as a pathway to unconscious knowledge.[28] We may even deliberately approach a literary text in the same manner as we would approach a dream, namely, as Bion suggests, beyond memory and desire.[29] For Bion, the suspension of memory and desire honors the fact that a dream—and we could add a literary text—forms an autopoietic system that generates its own rules.

I am not suggesting, of course, that unconscious scanning is the only or even the primary mode in which to create or receive a literary text or, for that matter, any work of art. Rather, I am suggesting that it is a mode that operates unconsciously alongside and in interaction with our conscious modes of reception and our focused attention to processes of signification and figuration, the development of narrative or poetic voice, or even to the referential contexts of specific works. It is this mode of reception, I argue, that has the most subliminal impact on the boundaries of subjectivity and, by extension, culture and life. In this capacity, it also has profound epistemological implications and constitutes a prime modus operandi for experimental systems. Unconscious scanning works by temporarily dedifferentiating, if not dissolving, familiar modes and structures of perception and reception. Many writers and artists productively use a temporary dissolution and subsequent reorganization of mental and psychic processes in the act of creation. They often position their recipients in ways that invite a similar mental dedifferentiation and reorganization. Think, for example, of the impact of a Beckett text, a Francis Bacon or Jackson Pollock painting, or a musical composition by Schoenberg. All of them create what Bion calls bizarre objects, that is, artistic forms that induce a fragmentation of the surface structures of consciousness by breaking down the "contact barrier" between consciousness and the unconscious, particularly between conscious and unconscious fantasy life.

Using literature as an autopoietic experimental system implies foregrounding receptiveness to the unknown, and, I would argue, to the unconscious and the "unthought known."[30] Autopoiesis furthermore suggests that in order to creatively process a literary text, we may begin to develop a reading by trying to focus on what the text offers us within its own permeable boundaries. Even in interpreting a text's imagined and imaginable referentiality to a phenomenological world, we find guidance in the particular artistic translation and transformation of referential material. Bion's ideal mode of a reception divested of memory and desire furthermore suggests that privileging the signifying apparatus of writing on its own terms may be helpful in moving beyond conscious reception and gaining access to the textual unconscious.

Whereas unconscious scanning partakes in artistic reception in general, it may be more or less pronounced depending on the degree of strangeness or bizarreness of the literary object in question. Partly under the historical impact of psychoanalytic theories of the mind and a concomitant increased cultural awareness of unconscious processes, experimental texts and artistic works since modernism have shifted the emphasis of aesthetic production toward a higher valuation of unconscious production and scanning. We may even assume that culturally the contact barrier between consciousness and the unconscious has become more permeable, generating a shift from representation and referentiality to transformation and invention and a related shift from linear narratives to complex, fuzzy, and multilayered or multivoiced narratives. In *Acts of Literature*, Derrida argues that modernist texts have forced such a shift: "These texts operate a sort of turning back, they *are* themselves a sort of turning back on the literary institution. Not that they are only reflexive, specular or speculative, not that they suspend reference to something else, as is so often suggested by stupid and uninformed rumor. And the force of their event depends on the fact that a thinking about their possibility (both general and singular) is put to work in them in a *singular* work."[31] In a similar vein, unconscious scanning does not suspend other modes of reading but creates a supplementary mode that works in tandem with others. But if unconscious scanning temporarily brackets the priority of referentiality, this process follows the logic of the supplement in which the bracketing impacts the entire reading process, including how references to an imagined phenomenological world are received.

I place so much emphasis on the supplementarity of unconscious scanning because I take it to be the mode most conducive to emergence. If "experimental systems," according to Rheinberger, are "machines for generating the future,"[32] this raises the issue of temporality, the temporal structure of retroactive literary memories, and the paradox of memories of the future. I propose to understand the reading process within a temporal logic of *Nachträglichkeit* (Freud), supplementarity (Derrida), and polytemporality (Latour). Rheinberger's notion of experimental systems is predicated on the a posteriori quality of knowledge formation (*Erkenntnis*). The same holds true for the constitution of meaning in the reading process. Adding the dimension of a belated construction of memory and recognition in traumatic experiences, Freud's concept of *Nachträglichkeit* becomes particularly relevant in traumatic writing that works against the boundaries of memory and language. *Nachträglichkeit* for Freud highlights the paradoxical temporality of unconscious inscription, that is, a retroactive (traumatic) ascription of meaning. This temporality partakes in a certain episteme of things to come, or a mode of being in which the inscription or the trace carries an anticipated knowledge of the future.

Wittgenstein's famous dictum that the boundaries of language define the boundaries of our world[33] raises the question of how we define the boundaries of language in relation to this paradoxical temporality. We must be able to grasp within the notion of language the infant's preverbal modes of being and relating as well as the corporeal, sensorial, and experiential memories that remain inscribed as traces and can be recalled through certain moods, rhythms, colors, or forms.[34] If one defines language in this larger sense, one can say that unforeseeable ways of being in language generate unforeseeable forms of life and ways of being and thereby profoundly impact the boundaries of our world. Literature and the arts with their emphasis on figuration, rhythm, color, form—what Kristeva calls the semiotic[35] or what Derrida calls a lithography before words[36]—reactivate these earlier modes of "unthought knowledge" (Bollas) in order to make this knowledge culturally and interpersonally available. This processing of modes and moods of being before the actual acquisition of language may be one of literature's most subliminal and undertheorized functions. Derrida's notions of the trace and supplementarity may once again help to understand unconscious inscription in writing. In his essay "Freud and the Scene of Writing,"[37] Derrida develops his concept of the trace by linking psychoanalysis to the neurobiology of memory, where memory appears as encoded in corporeal and sensorial inscriptions. Rheinberger, we recall, draws on Derrida to define experimental systems as "machines for generating the future." Derrida writes, "The structure of the psychical apparatus will be represented by a writing machine" and later asks the question, "What apparatus must we create in order to represent psychical writing?"[38]

Similarly, we may define literature as an apparatus or machine for psychical writing that generates the future in the sense that it continually works on the shaping of emergent subjectivities. Emphasizing the intricate intertwinement of writing and memory, Derrida further defines memory as the "very essence of the psyche."[39] But it is not conscious memories Derrida is interested in. In his theory of writing, he responds to Freud's view that "consciousness . . . is a surface exposed to the external world"[40] by arguing that "the labor of the writing . . . circulated like psychical energy between the unconscious and the conscious."[41] It is in this sense that Derrida understands psychical writing as a machine that produces the future. Derrida reiterates Freud's assertion that in the unconscious nothing is ever lost because a memory trace is left in our psychical apparatus of the perceptions that impinge on it. Those traces, Derrida argues with Freud, cannot but permanently modify the elements of the entire system.[42] Derrida, in turn, elaborates the notion of the trace and its location in a transitional space between neurological trace and memory: "This impression has left behind a laborious trace which has never been *perceived*, whose meaning has never been lived in the present, i.e., has never been lived consciously."[43]

This concept of the trace inverts the conventional relationship between consciousness and the unconscious or between psychic life and psychic writing: "Unconscious experience . . . does not borrow but produces its own signifiers; does not create them in their materiality, of course, but produces their status-as-meaningful (*signifiance*)."⁴⁴ Derrida thus systematically emphasizes Freud's notion of the productivity and generativity of the unconscious in order to highlight psychic writing and the entire mnemonic apparatus on which it depends as a machine that inscribes, writes, and generates the future. At the same time, the temporality of the unconscious is marked by "belatedness," that is, *Nachträglichkeit*, or, as Derrida recasts it, supplementarity. Time supplements and rewrites what has never been perceived or lived consciously but has been retained as a trace in the psychic apparatus. It is in this sense that the psychic apparatus can be compared to a machine that writes the future. Dare we compare the psychic writing machine to a continually morphing experimental system? And what would the relationship be between the experimental system of the psychic writing apparatus and the experimental system of the literary apparatus? Finally, wouldn't the literary apparatus constitute a particular episteme in the form of unconscious knowledge?

Perhaps it is helpful to explore these hypotheses by looking at forms of writing that have traditionally been perceived as the most referential writings: autobiography and ethnography. Autobiography is a form of literary writing that is closely connected to the mnemonic apparatus and to psychic writing. In "This Strange Institution Called Literature," Derrida speaks of his "adolescent dream of keeping a trace of all the voices which were traversing me."⁴⁵ Both specular and speculative, this dream, he adds, engages both "the archive of the 'real' and the archive of 'fiction.'"⁴⁶ Derrida locates the autobiographical impulse in "an interminable 'internal' polylogue" that refuses to give up "the 'culture' which carries these voices."⁴⁷ It is in this context that he restates the fundamental question—why literature?—and defines its power as residing in its "economy of exemplary iterability."⁴⁸ Yet this iterability, he continues, cannot be dissociated from writing as an "*absolutely* singular event, an *absolutely* singular signature, and therefore also of a date, of a language, of an autobiographical inscription."⁴⁹ Derrida insists that the entire impact of literature rests on this paradoxical intertwinement between singular autobiographical inscription and exemplary iterability: "In a minimal autobiographical trait can be gathered the greatest potentiality of historical, theoretical, linguistic, philosophical culture—that's really what interests me."⁵⁰

This statement facilitates the transition to exploring the status of ethnographic writing, including the concept of imaginary ethnographies. Derrida's insistence on the "autobiographical inscription" in literature highlights its traces of psychic writing or, as one could call it, the writerly unconscious. Literature as an experimental system that writes and (re)makes culture includes the traces of psychic writing. In "Autobiographical Voices (1, 2, 3) and Mosaic Memory," Michael Fischer coins the term "experimental *sondages*"[51] to describe efforts to listen to the many kinds of voicings we find in autobiographical forms. Such experimental *sondages*, or "soundings"—or, to invoke the French connotation that emphasizes the epistemic dimension, such acts of probing or surveying—may also be needed to attune one to literature more generally, and perhaps particularly to its experimental forms that often inscribe what Derrida calls the internal polylogue.[52] With Derrida's expanded notion of the autobiographical trace in mind, we can understand why literary writing more generally is inscribed by traces of psychic writing even when it locates itself at the opposite end of autobiography by eclipsing personal reference.

Viewing literature as an experimental system to write the future must, as I argued earlier, include the reader since a text in itself is nothing but a generative matrix, frozen in a mode of virtuality. It is the dialogical process between text and reader that composes the experimental system. Not unlike the Heisenbergian scientific object, a literary object is highly sensitive to what readers bring to it. At the same time, literary objects create spaces and assemblages of attunement and resonance to cultural, psychological, and affective dispositions. In this context, it is the reader's capacity for unconscious scanning that facilitates the perception of and responsiveness to emergent new forms in language, culture, or life.

Literary experience is thus located in a transitional space between reader and text. In "The Location of Cultural Experience," D. W. Winnicott writes, "The place where cultural experience is located is in the *potential space* between the individual and the environment."[53] Culture, in turn, circulates within this potential or transitional space in an open and fluid process in which aggregates from both the text's and the reader's different cultural systems interact with one another, creating new amalgams and myriad emergent forms. While literary texts are saturated with virtual cultural materials, readers approach a text saturated with the traces of previous cultural experiences. The transformative power of such encounters generates new cultural forms that, in turn, facilitate a more general cultural transformation.

Literature, we could then say, invites readers to practice a willful engagement in artifices of psychic writing, cultural memory, and future-oriented speculation. Fischer speaks of "mosaic memory" "layered in differently structured strata, fragmented and collaged together like mosaics in consciousness and in unconscious maneuverings, all of which takes hermeneutical skill to hear and unpack."[54] Given that there almost is, as Fischer points out, a consensus that social relations, culture, and psychology are structured in significantly new ways, we long for imaginary maps or, if you like, imaginary ethnographies that help us navigate the unfamiliar terrain. Haunted as these imaginary ethnographies may be by the ghosts of the past and the graphics of absences and silences, the mute images and traumatic eclipses, which bear the traces of such hauntings, their direction is always toward an emergent future. We could, in fact, read experimental literature as a form of imaginary ethnography of the future.[55] It is in its disjunctive uses of language and figuration, its resistance to constituted powers (Derrida calls this the duty of irresponsibility[56]), that literature is able to provide what Fischer calls counterintuitive challenges[57] to extend the human sensorium in a virtual and experimental space. And it is in this sense that the history of literature can be read as "the narrative of a memory which produces the event to be told and which will never have been present."[58] This paradoxical temporal disjuncture reveals most succinctly the dimension of literature as an experimental system to write the future: literature provides us with the supplementarity we need to cope with the traumatic belatedness of human temporality.

In my opening reflections, I have emphasized generativity and emergence as particular effects of the ways in which literature writes and makes culture. This complex exchange between cultural and psychic processes includes the transference between reader and text that, in turn, enables literature's transformational effects.[59] A culture's literature and arts generate a certain cultural idiom, providing abstract shapes that resonate with particular culturally sanctioned emotions, moods, tastes, values, and mental structures. It is in this sense too that literary texts operate as imaginary ethnographies. Providing continually changing forms for emotions, moods, tastes, and values, literature does cultural work that crosses the boundaries between politics and psychology and takes part in the continual reshaping of the historically changing notions of the human and of emergent forms of psychic life.

Imaginary Ethnographies is organized into three parts: "Writing, Desire, and Transference," "Cannibals, Children, and Aliens," and a "Coda" on the posthuman. "Writing, Desire, and Transference" deals with writing, transference, and the cultural imaginary from a range of different perspectives, including the advent of writing in indigenous oral cultures, the vicissitudes of traveling literatures, and fantasies of cultural otherness. "Cannibals, Children, and Aliens" focuses on a series of cultural iconotropes used to delineate human liminality.

The three chapters in this section unfold their theoretical reflections from within close readings of specific authors, including Juan José Saer, Marianne Wiggins, Richard Powers, and Octavia Butler. The last part opens up the framework with a metatheoretical reflection on the posthuman in Samuel Beckett.

"Writing, Desire, and Transference" investigates the notion of "writing culture" from three different angles. Chapter 1, "Another Writing Lesson: Lévi-Strauss, Derrida, and the Chief of the Nambikwara," revisits Lévi-Strauss's key intervention in anthropology, namely his claim in "A Writing Lesson" that he introduced writing to the oral culture of the Nambikwara. Lévi-Strauss's essay inspired the well-known chapter in Derrida's *Of Grammatology* on structural anthropology. Derrida's critical engagement with Lévi-Strauss constitutes a seminal intervention regarding ethnographic writing that challenges conventional anthropological assumptions about orality and writing. Engaging both Lévi-Strauss and Derrida, I give the debate a new turn by highlighting the Nambikwara chief's agency and his performative, playful, and ironical use of writing that escape the attention of both Lévi-Strauss and Derrida. This performativity is crucial, I argue, in expanding the notion of writing to include performative modes of indirection as a communicative device. The latter are not unlike literary uses of irony that invoke what cannot be spoken directly. In fact, one could even argue that the chief uses writing in the manner of an "epistemic thing."

Chapter 2, "Traveling Literature, Traveling Theory," explores the implications of Edward Said's notion of "traveling theory" for the boundary crossings facilitated by traveling literature. The essay highlights the crucial role of literature and the cultural imaginary in the fashioning of cross-cultural encounters. In travels to and contact with different countries and cultures, we routinely bring along the baggage of a cultural imaginary formed by literary or artistic accounts of the culture we encounter. In this sense, the first time we travel to a different country is never the first time. I draw on examples from my first travels to China and the literature that formed my eclectic cultural imaginary of China, including my childhood readings of the novels of Pearl S. Buck and Marco Polo's travel narratives. I then turn to more contemporary explorations of the Chinese imaginary, specifically Italo Calvino's literary response to Marco Polo in *Invisible Cities* and Ulrike Ottinger's experimental film *Johanna d'Arc of Mongolia*. Both play with artistic constructions of polytemporality, blending past, present, and future visions in an eclectic pastiche of geopolitical imaginaries about encounters between the East and the West. While Calvino constructs a fictional dialogue between Marco Polo and Kublai Khan in order to reflect on the role of maps and mapping, the politics of territorialization, and the emergence of future cities, *Johanna d'Arc of Mongolia* stages a satire of the Orientalist imaginary in which a nomadic tribe of Mongolian women kidnaps a group of travelers on the Trans-Siberian Railroad. Ottinger's exuberant and carnivalesque mixing of genres ranges from documentary and ethnographic film to costume dramas of ancient China and Western-style kidnapping stories. The film can be read as a metareflection on the ways in which in today's global world both Orientalism and Occidentalism overdetermine the imaginaries of cross-cultural encounters since they are inevitably marked by the traces of an entire history of travel literature, ethnography, fiction, and film. A true visual "imaginary ethnography," this film's celebration of alternative encounters between East and West recalls, yet undermines, scripted codes of Western Orientalism. I end with a piece of an almost coincidental fieldwork experience. When I lectured in Beijing on my childhood reading of Pearl Buck's *Peony*, which is about the Jewish Diaspora in Kaifeng, I received a spontaneous invitation to Kaifeng and, with the help of a translator, I was able to interview some of the remaining Jewish community there. In this case, reflecting on the power of imaginary ethnographies provided the rare chance of a life encounter with members of the imagined community of a fictional narrative read decades earlier in my childhood.

Chapter 3, "Restriction and Mobility," expands the reflections on cross-cultural encounters by looking at two specific literary instances that complicate the familiar primitivist script of a fascination with exoticized Others, namely Franz Kafka's "Der Wunsch, Indianer zu sein" (The Wish to Be a Red Indian) and Leslie Marmon Silko's "Yellow Woman." By highlighting the dynamic of cultural transference in the desire for the Other, these texts point to a marked difference between literary and ethnographic explorations of cultural otherness. Rather than focusing on the materiality of cultures, on culture as a social and economic formation, or on kinship and communal organizations, these texts pointedly mobilize and transform the fantasies and phantasms that aggregate around cultures and form the cultural unconscious. Both texts employ and critically reflect on the vicissitudes, illusions, and ruses of a human desire for otherness, if not cross-cultural mobility. These authors' emphasis on fantasy places emergence and cultural transference rather than cultural representation at the center of the imagined cross-cultural encounters, even though the latter also play with referential attributions.

In "Cannibals, Children, and Aliens," I develop a sequence of close readings of literary texts. I choose texts that allow me to focus on prominent iconic figures in the cultural imaginary, namely the cannibal, the child, and the alien. Within literature, these figures function less as icons than as iconotropes. Robert Graves defines iconotropy as a practice of creatively misreading the visual representation of an icon by weaving a verbal picture that changes it.[60] Literature, I contend, reworks cultural icons in similar ways. Each of the figures I analyze marks a particular boundary that reconfigures notions of the human in the cultural imaginary, conveying literary visions of human liminality in the culture at the turn of the millennium. In this vein, the cannibal, the child, and the alien serve as iconotropes that shape contemporary notions of the human in light of the emergence of what we have come to call, with a slight taint of nostalgic pathos, the posthuman. These iconotropic figures provide an ideal ground from which to explore the specific contribution literature makes as a form of *writing culture*. Compared with ethnographies proper, the imaginary ethnographies under consideration link their exploration of culture to the question of the human. But rather than taking up the preoccupation of Enlightenment anthropology with the universalizing question "Was ist der Mensch?" (What is man?), they explore how specific historical conditions impact the boundaries of the human, leading to new epistemological and aesthetic formations as well as emergent subjectivities and socialities. In this context, they also emphasize how the imaginary, the "unthought," and the literary or the aesthetic contribute historically to construct notions of the human. These imaginary ethnographies resemble Rheinberger's "experimental systems" in the sense that they use language and artistic form to reshape iconic figurations in order to generate emergent forms of subjectivity, culture, and life.

In four interrelated chapters I then read literary reconfigurations of the above-mentioned cultural icons—the cannibal, the child, the alien, and the posthuman—in light of other discourses drawn from anthropology, philosophy, psychoanalysis, and popular media culture. Focusing on how literature intervenes in and (re)shapes the cultural construction of such icons, my readings address the particular function of aesthetic practices in the context of other discursive practices. In each case I show how poetic languages, literary forms, or aesthetic practices may generate an anticipatory vision of an emergent future.

In *Heterologies: Discourse on the Other*, Michel de Certeau argues that the term "savage" marks the genesis of a language of culture, difference, and cultural alterity.[61] Cast as the most savage of savages, the figure of the cannibal embodies the core phantasm that haunts the so-called discovery of the

New World. In "The Melancholic Cannibal," I perform an intertextual reading of Saer's *The Witness* (*El entenado*) and Wiggins's *John Dollar* through the lens of critical readings on cannibalism ranging from Montaigne, Voltaire, and Rousseau to Freud, Lévi-Strauss, Derrida, de Certeau, and Kristeva. In the flourishing of postcolonial cannibal narratives, I argue, the cannibal gains new prominence as a melancholic icon, and the phantasm of eating the Other reemerges in a transference based on postcolonial guilt.

In the regime of colonial knowledge production, the figure of the cannibal was intimately tied to the emerging discipline of anthropology. Saer scrutinizes the philosophical, political, and psychological implications of phantasms of cannibalism in the ethnographic imaginary through the story of the *colastiné*, an imaginary cannibalistic tribe modeled on an eclectic bricolage of colonial narratives depicting Amazonian Indians. He invents a narrator who lived among the *colastiné* for fifteen years after they had chosen him as a "witness" to their culture, an agent necessary for the creation of an outside. After his return, he tries to write down the *colastiné*'s cosmology based on the ontological construction of externality—the outside, the Other, the foreign— as the basis for a sense of an inside or a center. At a metalevel, the novel traces the history of cannibal narratives from an obsessive phantasm of colonial self-fashioning to its postcolonial emergence as the core of a psychological discourse on melancholia and incorporation.

Modeled after William Golding's *Lord of the Flies* as well as after a rich set of intertexts ranging from Leonardo da Vinci to Freud, Marianne Wiggins's *John Dollar* further develops the connections between cannibalism, melancholia, and incorporation. Stranded on an island after a cannibal raid, a group of British schoolgirls witnesses a quasi-totemic meal in which the girls see their own fathers being eaten alive. In a compulsive traumatic repetition, two of the girl protagonists perform nightly cannibalistic rituals during which they consume the flesh of the paralyzed John Dollar, the only surviving male protagonist. Like Saer, Wiggins explores melancholia as a self-devouring condition she identifies with "the failure of community that comes with grief."[62]

The readings of Saer and Wiggins in "The Melancholic Cannibal" illustrate how from its inception in the ethnographic imaginary, the figure of the cannibal had not only anthropological but also psychological valence. Whereas political discourses on savagism and civilization portray the cannibal as the dark side of humanity's childhood, psychological discourses on incorporation and abjection figure the cannibal as a psychic object of transference. Freud uses this overdetermination of the political and the psychological to construct his myth of origin in *Totem and Taboo* and in *Moses and Monotheism*, both of which could be read as imaginary ethnographies. The brother horde's devouring of the father in a cannibalistic meal originates civilization through melancholic guilt. Postcolonial cannibal narratives refigure mourning, melancholia, and incorporation in their contemporary political and psychological valence.

This enmeshment also expresses itself in the construction of national narratives, recalling Homi Bhabha's notion of "double time."[63] The civilized subject of the modern nation-state is fashioned by encapsulating or encrypting the cannibal within the self as an abject Other from a remote time. The cannibal hibernates in a time capsule that denies, yet also recalls, the double time of the modern fashioning of self and nation. If cannibal narratives return with a vengeance in the postcolonial imaginary, it is because global literatures are working through colonial legacies, generating new visions that intervene in the politics of nostalgia, mourning, and melancholia.

Like the cannibal, the child is an iconic figure in the cultural imaginary subject to the "double time" of cultural and psychic self-fashioning. But while the cannibal is figured as belonging to an abject prehistory, the child becomes a placeholder for both prehistory and the future, phantasmatically casting humanity in a process of becoming. Recalling the ambivalence of cannibal visions, the child's status in the cultural imaginary is also deeply ambivalent. Oscillating between hagiography and savagism, figurations of the child as either little angel or savage, as innocent or polymorphously perverse, are enfolded in a complex pedagogy that controls the child's becoming adult.

In the chapter "War Children in a Global World," I look at disenfranchised children as heralding the changing culture of childhood under the forces of globalization and global warfare. Drawing on the work of Sharon Stephens[64] and that of Nancy Scheper-Hughes and Carolyn Sargent,[65] I reconsider the profound changes of childhood—increase in child labor, child migration, child soldiers, child prostitution, and the emerging criminalization of childhood in legal discourses—that have led critics to diagnose the disappearance of childhood. I explore this cultural imaginary of a vanishing childhood through the lens of Richard Powers's *Operation Wandering Soul*, a novel that views the current global displacement of children in light of a geopolitical and polytemporal imaginary. Juxtaposing the global histories and geographies of cities such as Los Angeles, Beirut, Jerusalem, Saigon, and Bangkok, Powers constructs a monumental palimpsest of the world history of migrant and displaced children. He uses a historical arsenal of stories of disappearing children that invoke different historical times through a layering of present experiences over faded pasts. In this context, I read *Operation Wandering Soul* as a critical intervention in narratives of apocalypse that proliferated at the turn of the millennium. Powers's story of the departure of children from planet Earth challenges the finality of apocalyptic narratives, engaging readers in a complex transference in which the figure of the disappearing child is embedded in a future-oriented ethics concerned with warfare and planetary survival. In this process, the apocalyptic narrative is transformed into an imaginary ethnography of the future that explores changing notions of the human in a palimpsest of polytemporal global cultures.

Narratives about aliens have always been transcoded as discourses on the boundaries of the human. The focus of my chapter on Butler's trilogy *Xenogenesis* is on science fiction as a particular literary genre concerned with the imagination of alien life. The *Xenogenesis* trilogy also constitutes a literary intervention in discourses on colonialism, racism, imperialism, and ecology, with profound implications for cultural changes in the relationship between property and personhood in late capitalist global cultures. In particular, I read *Xenogenesis* in light of current debates on genetic engineering and the new reproductive technologies. At a political level, *Xenogenesis* explores the boundaries of human reproduction as a new "frontier" at century's end. Butler's aliens, the Oankali, are gene traders who value genetic diversification and transspecies reproduction. The imagined human reproduction with extraterrestrials is cast as a literary metareflection on the ethical implications of reproductive biopolitics, especially since the Oankali's engineered gene trade plays on a deep-seated species anxiety.

In *Xenogenesis*, the politics of human reproduction has become inseparable from the danger of planetary destruction. The Oankali are both gene traders who promote transspecies reproduction and ecologists who pursue a politics of survival. Octavia Butler's experimental fiction presupposes this irreducible intertwinement of planetary destruction and genetically engineered reproductive politics. In conjunction with Butler's reflections on racism and colonialism, these biopolitical futuristic interventions in debates about reproductive politics and biogenetic engineering also lucidly prefigure current debates about a new biocolonialism, especially in indigenous communities. Butler's trilogy can accordingly be understood as an "experimental literary system" that compels readers to mentally inhabit a world of transspecies reproduction while looking at the precarity of terrestrial existence from the perspective of a posthuman future.

In recent decades, we have witnessed the emergence of discourses on the posthuman that question the boundaries of the human from within rather than by exclusion. Ending the book with a reading of Samuel Beckett's *The Lost Ones*, I approach the notion of the posthuman through an author who explored its philosophical premises decades before its emergence as a new episteme. Unparalleled in its philosophical radicality, *The Lost Ones* can be read as an imaginary ethnography of the future under conditions of life at its vanishing point. In minimal life everything depends on the "vibration of difference."[66] Suspended in outer space, a small population of humans lives in an enclosed cylinder. We witness a world much stranger than simply alien. Zones are "separated by clear-cut mental or imaginary frontiers invisible to the eye of flesh."[67] Naked, desiccated bodies brush together with a rustle of dry leaves.[68] The ear distinguishes "a faint stridulence as of insects which is that of the light itself.[69]

This universe is described by an anonymous narrator who at times sounds like an alien ethnographer, and whose voice extends between a "thinking being coldly intent on data"[70] and a poetic language of rare beauty. In his short piece "Scapeland," Jean-François Lyotard develops a vision of the posthuman along the trajectory of a Western philosophy of space ranging from Aristotle to Kant and beyond. Drawing on Kant's reflection upon the transference of the soul to a standpoint of difference, Lyotard explores a condition of the soul that he calls *vesania*, or "systematic" madness.[71] *The Lost Ones* seems to induce a similar condition.

Challenging any merely referential or allegorical reading, Beckett increasingly pushes readers into the very materiality of poetic language. It is as if language and imagination have been cut loose but keep running on empty, inspired like automatic writing. The primacy of a uniquely singular language that obeys nothing but its own code prevents the ethnographic fallacy of appropriating a radically alien culture to familiar conditions. In order to attune ourselves to the singularity of Beckett's text, we must learn to listen to the narrative voice with a child's primordial auditory capacities. It is in this sense that I read *The Lost Ones* as an experimental literary system par excellence. We are partaking in the emergence of something entirely unfamiliar yet deeply resonant that we are able to experience but cannot fully understand with the means at our disposal. Beckett thus initiates a nonappropriative approximation to what we cannot yet know.

The alien space of the cylinder with its virtual boundaries, its ruptures and folds, functions as an experimental literary system that induces a particular form of *vesania*, "systematic madness." It is the madness felt when one faces the collapse of familiar coordinates and categories to map the world. As if to save us from this madness, Beckett offers us a poetic space of resonance. Instead of a psychotic breakdown, this systematic madness therefore induces the emergence of the unthought, the *impense*, in the form of an imaginary posthuman from which we may finally intuit the vast expanse of the human *if that notion were maintained*. Beckett suggests that this is perhaps the most subliminal transformational use of literature—a form of *soul making* that reconfigures the primordial imprints of the human.

Part I
Writing, Desire, and Transference

1 Another Writing Lesson
Lévi-Strauss, Derrida, and the
Chief of the Nambikwara

What else, indeed, have I learned from the masters who taught me, the philosophers I have read, the societies I have visited and even from that science which is the pride of the West, apart from a few scraps of wisdom which, when laid end to end, coincide with the meditation of the Sage at the foot of the tree?[1]
—Claude Lévi-Strauss, *Tristes tropiques*

In *Tristes tropiques*, Lévi-Strauss includes a chapter entitled "A Writing Lesson" in which he reflects upon the emergence of writing in the hitherto oral culture of the Nambikwara, an Indian tribe in the Amazon rain forest. This piece has become a cornerstone of Derrida's theory of writing and his arguments about epistemological, linguistic, and metaphysical phonologism and logocentrism. In part 2 of *Of Grammatology*, Derrida dedicates a whole chapter to a scrupulous reading of "A Writing Lesson" in which he targets Lévi-Strauss's libertarian ideology of ethnocentric assimilation/exclusion. In particular, he faults him on the grounds of "an ethnocentrism *thinking itself* as anti-ethnocentrism, an ethnocentrism in the consciousness of a liberating progressivism."[2] It is well known that in response to Derrida's critique, Levi-Strauss wrote a letter in which he points out that Derrida has read him with the "delicacy of a bear."[3] Interestingly, Levi-Strauss targets Derrida's misrecognition of the aesthetic dimension of his discourse on the Nambikwara, namely his particular use of philosophy in a style comparable to that of painters or musicians. This charge is all the more interesting because the aesthetic quality of writing and the question whether the aesthetic is intrinsic or extrinsic to writing is at the very heart of the controversy Derrida opens with Levi-Strauss. And it is in the question of the aesthetic that I will anchor my own argument.

Derrida addresses the problem of aesthetic value in the context of the Nambikwara word for writing. Lévi-Strauss had drawn attention to the fact that the Nambikwara called the act of writing *iekariukedjutu*, a word that literally translates as "drawing lines." He concludes from this choice of word that writing, for the Nambikwara, had primarily an aesthetic signification. Derrida, in response, criticizes Lévi-Strauss for presuming "that one can isolate aesthetic value"[4] and, more important, for implying that in writing aesthetic value is extrinsic.

It is precisely the question of the aesthetic that interests me here. While I fully agree with Derrida's insistence on seeing the aesthetic as an intrinsic value of writing that cannot be isolated, I would like to give the debate a different spin by exploring the role the aesthetic plays as an instance of intercultural transference. I use "transference" in the psychoanalytic sense of an unconscious displacement of affects or ideas. Transference occurs whenever unconscious desires, fantasies, or patterns of being and relating are enacted in an interpersonal or intercultural encounter, including the indirect encounters between literary or artistic objects and their recipients. It emerges as a largely unconscious operation designed to bridge, close, fill, or deny the inevitable gaps in knowing another person or another culture, and to manage the affects such gaps bring forth. Transference therefore relies on imaginary constructions that reduce or transform otherness by giving it a familiar shape. Such constructions may range from highly creative and empathic apprehensions of the other to projective identification, and to foreclosure or paranoid rejection of difference. The imaginary fashioning of others, including cultural others, according to one's own frame of reference and organization of affect may thus reduce anxieties that emerge in the face of otherness more generally. But often such imaginary operations entail projections of fear, hostile impulses, or even illicit desires and come therefore at the high price of distortion and misrecognition, not only of the other but also of oneself and one's own role in the encounter.

In intercultural encounters more specifically, transference is stimulated by the mutual unfamiliarity with the other's cultural codes and rules of communicative behavior as well as the other's culture of emotions. Transference is, in fact, the very process that grounds what we have come to call the cultural imaginary or the cultural unconscious. The gaps in cultural competence and knowledge and the indeterminacy of performative interactions function analogously to what Freud envisioned as the "empty screen" in the psychoanalytic situation that facilitates projection. We know, of course, that neither in interpersonal nor in intercultural encounters we will ever find a truly "empty screen." We encounter rather a nebulous or blurred screen replete with gaps and hieroglyphic encodings of unfamiliar signs. Strangers to each other, the protagonists try to read these unfamiliar signs, each according to their own cultural codes, in an attempt to fill those gaps with projections based on their own personal and cultural knowledge. The ensuing projective dynamic can be understood as a transference both because it activates interiorized patterns of cultural contact that have become habitual or unconscious, and because it inevitably entails an imaginary element. The role of the imaginary is, of course, highly ambivalent in that it may facilitate access to the other, or foreclose it by ignoring, denying, or resisting difference. There is also a conscious or unconscious struggle for power at work around the question of which culture will ultimately prevail in providing the framework and values of the interaction.

As "A Writing Lesson" illustrates, fieldwork situations are intensely cathected by the psychic energies of both the anthropologist and the indigenous people and therefore constitute hotbeds of intercultural transference. Let me briefly mention what Lévi-Strauss highlights as the "extraordinary incident" that turned into the writing lesson. The scenes that immediately precede and follow the writing lesson are, in fact, a stunning, highly self-ironical travesty in which the anthropologist exposes himself as a *culturally* illiterate dupe among the *alphabetically* illiterate indigenous tribe. Lévi-Strauss's hilarious report on his expedition into the rain forest with his indigenous Utiarity friends borders on slapstick. The anthropologist had arranged this enterprise to meet and receive information about the Tarundé, who are, like the Utiarity, a subgroup of the Nambikwara. Lévi-Strauss's choice of a highly self-ironical comic tone stems from a retrospective working through of the intense affects that accompanied his initial experience. His narration in fact barely conceals his strong fear during the event that, at times, borders on paranoia.

The story begins when Lévi-Strauss virtually coerces the chief of the Utiarity to assist him in this expedition to the Tarundé, despite the fact that the two tribal groups had been living in a rather precarious balance. Reluctantly, the chief finally complies after limiting the expedition to four oxen for carrying the presents. Immediately after their departure on the journey, which Lévi-Strauss retrospectively calls a "grotesque interlude,"[5] his Brazilian companion notices the absence of women and children. "In travel books, such circumstances mean that an attack is imminent,"[6] writes Lévi-Strauss, thus exhibiting his cultural *illiteracy* in his utter reliance on the extrinsic literary knowledge of travel books, that is, his own culture's imaginary construction of indigenous cultures and encounters with the New World. Lévi-Strauss continues the trip in utter apprehension; yet as soon as they catch up with the rest of the group he is forced to acknowledge that, nourished by imaginary tales found in travel narratives rather than by actual experiences with the Nambikwara, his fears were groundless. It is, in fact, fear that induces the anthropologist to relinquish his actual experience of the other culture in favor of a projection drawn from his own cultural imaginary. Continuing the expedition, the Indians lose their way, fail to provide food, and generate widespread discontent with the chief, whom they hold responsible for complying with the anthropologist's request. Moreover, at the appointed meeting place, it becomes evident to Lévi-Strauss that the chief had coerced the Tarundé to come against their will.

Aware of the adventurous situation,[7] Lévi-Strauss proposes the very gift exchange that generates the writing lesson. For this purpose, he had brought pencils and writing pads as gifts. Knowing that the Nambikwara had not developed alphabetic writing technologies, he chooses as his first gift to the tribe a stack of paper and pencils, encouraging the people to write. At first they did not use the items, but one day, to his delight, he sees them fill their pages with minute wavy lines, careful imitations, if not abstractions, of the linear sequence of signs they knew from the anthropologist's own notations. In retrospect, Lévi-Strauss reads this event as the "advent of writing" among the oral tribe. In a sense, he inscribes the "prehistory" of writing within a teleological model of progress when he sets out to play this trick with his indigenous objects of study. It is, after all, designed to demonstrate his superior authority as an owner of what for the tribe is a new technology, namely alphabetic writing.

The actual writing lesson culminates in Lévi-Strauss's transactions with the Utiarity chief. In the process of the gift exchange, the chief asks the anthropologist for a writing pad and uses it dramatically to change his role as prime native informant. Henceforth whenever Lévi-Strauss asks him for information, the chief, in response, takes his writing pad and begins to *write*. With a polite smile, he then hands Lévi-Strauss a sheet of paper filled with carefully drawn and perfectly regular wavy lines. Lévi-Strauss interprets this exchange as the effect of a hierarchical distribution of the power derived from the possession of writing. The chief, he argues, understands this power and uses it to gain authority over his tribe:

> No doubt he [the chief] was the only one who had grasped the purpose
> of writing. So he asked me for a writing pad, and when we both had one,

and were working together, if I asked for information on a given point, he did not supply it verbally but drew wavy lines on his paper and presented them to me, as if I could read his reply. He was half taken in by his own make-believe; each time he completed a line, he examined it anxiously as if expecting the meaning to leap from the page, and the same look of disappointment came over his face. But he never admitted this, and there was a tacit understanding between us to the effect that his unintelligible scribbling had a meaning which I pretended to decipher; his verbal commentary followed almost at once, relieving me of the need to ask for explanations.

As soon as he had got the company together, he took from a basket a piece of paper covered with wavy lines and made a show of reading it, pretending to hesitate as he checked on it the list of objects I was to give in exchange of the presents offered me.[8]

Lévi-Strauss reads the chief's simulation of writing as an attempt to gain authority only with respect to his own tribe. He assumes that the chief recognizes writing as an instrument of power and leads his people to believe he shares the anthropologist's secret knowledge of writing. Lévi-Strauss sees himself, in turn, establishing a secret complicity with the chief. In front of the tribe, he openly affirms the latter's writing competence, while, in fact, both of them tacitly acknowledge to each other the chief's mere pretense. Lévi-Strauss further assumes that, in this hierarchical distribution of writing competence, he himself gains power over the chief. The latter's successful performance in front of his tribe depends, after all, upon the "unspoken agreement": the anthropologist's willingness to play along in the game and refrain from outing the chief as an imposter.

I would like to challenge some of Lévi-Strauss's assumptions about the emergence of writing. My own reading foregrounds the problem of the aesthetic and its creative use as a mode of communication that relies on indirections, detours, performative speech acts, and irony. It is the aesthetic dimension of the chief's performative speech act, I argue, that allows him to make a political intervention that unhinges the smooth operation of the cultural imaginary in the encounter between the Old World and the New World. As I mentioned earlier, Lévi-Strauss introduces the aesthetic signification of the Nambikwara's writing practice in relation to the word they use for the act of writing, *iekariukedjutu, a word that means "drawing lines."*[9] Lévi-Strauss infers from this word choice that writing for the Nambikwara has a predominately aesthetic signification. Derrida, in turn, takes issue with this assumption, insisting rightly that the aesthetic quality is intrinsic to writing and not extrinsic, as Lévi-Strauss seems to assume. Thus taking the aesthetic value of writing as a given, Derrida mentions the aesthetic aspect of the chief's speech act only in passing, without according it much importance. However, in order to draw out the political implications of the chief's performative speech act we need to closely scrutinize a particularly imaginative use of the aesthetic as it relates to cultural practices of the exchange of gifts and information.

In the context of the chief's exchange with the anthropologist, the aesthetic unfolds mainly in the performative dimension of the transaction, that is, in the chief's simulation of knowledge and tacit agreement with the anthropologist to conceal the simulation. I consider this performative simulation to play a crucial role in understanding what Derrida calls the aesthetic category.[10] It is the bilateral effect of the encounter's performativity that both Lévi-Strauss and Derrida miss in the "writing lesson." While Lévi-Strauss's observation that the chief plays a trick on his tribe doubtlessly obtains, he remains oblivious of an entirely different trick being played by the chief with the anthropologist as his target. The chief's mock simulation of writing is a performative action that operates differently for his double audience. For his tribe he may well pretend that he exchanges written information with the anthropologist, but to the anthropologist he also makes a metastatement about the intercultural exchange that is taking place right in front of everybody's eyes. Taken at face value, the chief's act of writing performs a highly ironic mimicry. At a more indirect level, however, it can also be read as a comment about the gift exchange, and particularly the "gift of writing" to members of an oral culture. Thus the metacommunication is carried out within the framework of a highly artful and performative play involving both the tribe and the anthropologist.

It is on the basis of this very metacommunication—not addressed by Lévi-Strauss or by Derrida—that the chief carries out a crucial element of colonial politics. As Lévi-Strauss notices, the chief mimes the practice of writing as an instrument of power. At the same time, however, he indirectly uses that very power against the anthropologist, thus subverting the latter's claim to superiority. His act of offering information to Lévi-Strauss in (undecipherable) writing plays with the very fact that the anthropologist's gift of writing has given the chief the power to offer information while at the same time withholding it. The very irony implied in this exchange challenges the anthropologist's assumed claim to superiority.

Moreover, since he stages the simulation of writing as a performance for a double audience, one could argue that, rather than marking the "advent of writing," the "writing lesson" constitutes an act of performative communication that uses familiar aesthetic devices such as irony, pastiche, and metaphoric indirection. The aesthetic is thus displayed in the form of a rudimentary artistic, if not literary, function in the chief's text. While the latter is, strictly speaking, not a literary text, we must agree with Derrida that the chief's scribbles undoubtedly constitute a use of *writing* in which the aesthetic is intrinsic. We thus witness the chief as the master of a highly playful performance that uses metaphor, pastiche, and irony to direct an artful ruse against the anthropologist, who tacitly assumes that the sheer imbalance between written and oral cultures puts him in a superior position of power.

Lévi-Strauss's view that the "writing lesson" demonstrates the "advent of writing" among the Indian tribe falls, as Derrida has rightly pointed out, within a history of ethnocentric classification that relegates the Nambikwara to a prehistoric culture. Yet if we read the episode against the grain of Lévi-Strauss's evaluation, we may learn a very different lesson that highlights the ruses of an adaptive mind capable of using "writing" as a tool of imaginary inscriptions into the cultural unconscious. Curiously, Derrida, in his critique of Lévi-Strauss, did not pay attention to a highly conspicuous detail that gives the whole episode an ironic turn, namely, the prime role of the gift exchange, which provides the context for the "writing lesson." If we recall that Lévi-Strauss had urged the chief to immediately proceed to the gift exchange in order to ease a tense situation, the chief's performative irony in his simulation of writing can hardly be overlooked. Lévi-Strauss, after all, opens the exchange by presenting the "gift of writing" to the tribe's alleged oral culture. In exchange, he expects the chief to serve as his native informant. But what does the chief give him in exchange? He returns the anthropologist's *gift*, albeit in the form of an *undecipherable* simulation of writing that could be seen, at the same time, as a simulation of the anthropologist's gift. He returns an equivalent of what he received in the sense that the anthropologist's distribution of paper and pencils was, of course, not really a "gift of writing" but a ruse that allowed him to use the tribe for an anthropological experiment. In this sense, the gift could be considered as unusable, if not as given in bad faith. In response, the chief performs an exchange in which his simulation of writing dissimulates what, knowingly or unknowingly, appears as a travesty of the anthropologist's offer. Given that an anthropologist's "gift of writing" to an oral culture operates within the framework of anthropology as a colonial practice, one could indeed read the chief's simulation of writing as a prime instance of a mode of indirection or "mimicry"[11] through which the "colonial subject speaks."[12]

In "Of Mimicry and Man," Homi Bhabha reminds us that colonialism "repeatedly exercises its authority through the figures of farce," thus producing a "text rich in the traditions of *trompe l'oeil*, irony, mimicry and repetition."[13] Mimicry, for Bhabha, represents an ironic compromise constructed around ambivalence. As the sign of a double articulation, mimicry is "at once resemblance and menace."[14] The chief seems to appropriate the very features that mark colonial discourse more generally, thus unsettling the distribution of power that is supposed to determine the hierarchy between anthropologist and native informant. Lévi-Strauss clearly experiences the chief's scribbling as a farce, albeit one in which he must become complicit lest he lose his native informant. Moreover, he is threatened by the chief's *mimicry* because in the very act of simulating the exchange of information, the chief in fact withholds it. If we look more closely at this transfer, we realize that the chief operates with a complex bifurcation between the exchange of gifts and the exchange of information. While, in seeming compliance, he returns the "gift of writing" in the form of the sheets of paper filled with scribbled lines, he tacitly defies the anthropologist by withholding the desired information, thus negating his role as native informant. However, even this very act of negation still mimics writing as an unusable gift, since after all the anthropologist presented the tribe not with written information but with a merely symbolical gift of writing in the form of material writing tools. The chief's answer to the anthropologist in the mode of *writing* thus constitutes a highly complex transaction that enables him formally to *comply* with the anthropologist's request, participating in the gift exchange and serving as native informant, while at the same time playing at *withholding* the desired information. The fact that the chief later readily supplies the desired information orally further suggests that the act of withholding and the message indirectly conveyed through this act are more important in this speech act than the withholding of information as such. In this very respect, the chief's play with the anthropologist in fact resonates nicely with the intended ambiguous pun in the French version of Lévi-Strauss's title "Leçon d'écriture" in which the writing lesson emerges from the "sound" (*son*) of writing. The chief thus performs his role as native informant in a language game that offers *his* information about the rules and modalities of gift exchange and cultural translation in a mode of metacommunicative indirection. I would argue that the chief's creative and artful shaping of the space that disconnects writing from referential information relies on his use of writing's intrinsic aesthetic dimension and the ingenious irony with which he supplements the (useless) advent of writing with (useful) oral information.

In "The Naming Game and the Writing Lesson," Marcel Fiorini looks back at the exchange between Lévi-Strauss and Derrida from the perspective of several years of his more recent fieldwork among the Nambikwara. He argues that the use of silence, secrecy, and erasure played out in the performative use of *writing under erasure* marks the language games of Amazonian indigenous tribes, including the Nambikwara, more generally:

> The performativity of holding the name or one's own knowledge of events in secrecy, of keeping them out of circulation, both emphasizes the persona of the name bearer and entreats people at the receiving end of this speech act to "read," or respond to this withholding in the same way. Here silence itself can be seen as a dialogical utterance, for it subsumes a text contingent on the presence of a potential reader. It is as though the Manairisu played the *fort-da* game in reverse.[15]

In this larger context, one could argue that only those able to read through or between the wavy horizontal lines would be able to decipher the information given by the chief in a mode of withholding. One must see these lines as writing under erasure in order to fully understand the double nature of the "exchange of secrets" between the anthropologist and the chief. After all, both participants in the exchange are aware of their respective games. The chief's indirect information comes in the form of a performative enactment rather than an indirect speech act in the narrow sense of the word. If the gift of the chief's particular information about the gift exchange had been given directly, it might well have offended the anthropologist. It contained, after all, a barely disguised critique of the first gift: you have given us something we cannot understand or use, and in addition you have used your gift to play a trick on us. Fiorini insists that, with his act of mimicking the anthropologist in the gift exchange, the chief was not only acting in lieu of the foreigner but also reflecting upon his own and his people's alienated position as a vehicle and instrument of this foreigner.[16] I would add here, however, that the chief's performance not only *reflects upon* the alienation of his people and his own role but also *counteracts* this very alienation by recapturing an agency that allows him to invert the conditions of the anthropologist's power play. Most important, the tools of this reversal of power lie in the performative and artistic use of writing as a tool that engages the imaginary underpinnings of the transaction and thus intervenes in the cultural imaginary. Interestingly, the "signs" used in this "language game" straddle the boundaries between pictograph and writing, art and literature.

Fiorini points out that the paper the chief feigned to read could be perceived as a mere prop in a performance, or as a sign that the chief carried out a tacit agreement between him and the foreigner.[17] One could, however, also argue that the chief uses writing as a pictograph of sorts—understood here in the minimal sense of using geometrical signs in order to communicate via indirection, play, and artifice. The chief would then have used writing as a medium of indirect communication that transcends literal meaning, using irony and pastiche as a source of pleasurable refinement. We might also consider the "wavy horizontal lines" as literary in Roland Barthes' sense of a discourse in which the word or the form leads the idea.[18] The knowledge the chief conveys in a quasi-literary or aesthetic mode, however, is accessible only to someone willing to enter the chief's language game and able to understand it in its function as the performative enactment of a different kind of information. We could transcribe the latter's effect of "talking back" as follows: "No, I will not comply. This is *your* medium of power, and I will not let you use it to assert your superiority but turn it against you." Lévi-Strauss misses such a reading because he assumes that the chief utilizes writing only as the object of a mimetic staging of roles, performing a pure simulation of signs. Therefore he fails to perceive the chief's particular use of writing, its irony and its role in a performative language game the meaning of which is conveyed via indirection and resides in its metacommunicative effect.

If we thus read the chief's simulation of writing as a performative enactment, the hierarchical distribution of power indeed takes a different turn from the one emphasized by Lévi-Strauss. Using the paper as a space of mimetic play, the chief turns the cultural self-representation that he is expected to perform as a native informant into a performance about cultural otherness and contact, as well as about intercultural communication. He thus performs a language game that contains a lesson that is less about the "advent of writing" in the oral culture of the Nambikwara than about the "advent of literature"[19] in the sense of a performative use of graphs as a mode of communication via indirections and detours. Moreover, his intervention engages the imaginary ground on which the performative interaction takes place. One could thus argue that the chief performs a literary speech act at least in a very rudimentary sense. It is a speech act based on the performative and nonreferential use of a sign for the purpose of a communication via indirection in which the form of the utterance takes priority over content. In fact, the utterance is all there is, since the content consists in illegible wavy lines. This speech act, moreover, constitutes a means of intercultural communication, one that relies specifically on the performative use of a pictographic aesthetic. More important perhaps, the advent of literature would in this case precede the advent of alphabetic writing. We may even read the episode allegorically as highlighting that in human psychobiology the natural proclivity to create literature/art[20] may well precede the proclivity to create an alphabetic written language as a tool of storing and exchanging information.

Given the broad notion of writing, literature, and the imaginary on which the above reading relies, a further elaboration of the use of these terms seems in order. If we look more closely at the exchange between the chief and the anthropologist, we notice that the chief performs much more than a simple imitation of writing. Ultimately at stake is that Lévi-Strauss and the chief display radically different notions of simulation or, more to the point, mimesis. For Lévi-Strauss, mimesis is the imitation of an action—a relatively narrow notion that is already centered in a rather reductive definition of writing. For the chief, mimesis is performative and dynamic, engaging in a complex cultural exchange that produces difference rather than similarity. He thus foregrounds the gaps of knowledge between the players, as well as the attempt to engage the imaginary in order to bridge them. Moreover, the chief's metacommunication involves a precise, albeit indirect and playful, statement concerning intercultural gift exchange. The chief's metacommunication addresses the very role of writing in the cultural contact with indigenous peoples, thus exhibiting the more general problem of the translatability of cultures. He even plays with the role of writing as the anthropologist's "gift" to an oral culture, alluding to, if not inverting, the hierarchy that Lévi-Strauss perceives in this particular gift exchange.

The chief's ironical metacommunication addresses the asymmetrical roles the anthropologist seems to take for granted in his gift exchange with the indigenous people. According to Lévi-Strauss, he himself owns the supreme instrument of power, while the tribe allegedly dwells in a state of innocence before the advent of writing. But the chief's intervention turns this asymmetry around, exhibiting that Lévi-Strauss faces problems in deciphering or translating information from a foreign culture that are ultimately not so different from the ones the tribe faces when Lévi-Strauss offers them the gift of writing.

The chief's act thus also conveys a crucial insight into the difference between knowledge and information. Doesn't the chief's language game suggest that ethnographic knowledge, and perhaps intercultural communication more generally, requires a more encompassing understanding than one based on pure information? Addressing the signification of the whole exchange rather than merely answering the anthropologist's queries with the desired information, the chief playfully inverts the relations of power. He demonstrates his power to withhold information by cloaking it in an undecipherable coding, and one that is, quite shrewdly, used as a pastiche, if not a caricature, of the anthropologist's own writing. The chief's response is thus a true act of colonial mimicry in Bhabha's sense of an ironic compromise that feigns compliance while it practices subversion. The chief demonstrates his power—and skill— to play the anthropologist's game while undermining its rules from within. In other words, he plays the anthropologist's game of withholding better than the anthropologist himself.

Read as a *"fort-da* game in reverse" (Fiorini) that operates as a metacommunication about imaginary substitutions and cultural transference, the episode reveals a dimension of power that escapes Lévi-Strauss, despite his preoccupation with power. As Derrida has shown in detail, Lévi-Strauss's narrative in the scenes that frame the "writing lesson" exhibits a tone that borders on paranoia. As I have argued earlier, this paranoia emerges when the anthropologist "reads" the tribe's actions on the basis of his own cultural imaginary, namely colonial travel narratives. In fact, these scenes of fear and paranoia reveal that he is not free from a certain projective hostility toward the very tribe that he otherwise describes in such nostalgic terms as innocent and good.

Lévi-Strauss's composition of his story about the writing lesson further demonstrates the dynamics of cultural transference that I emphasized in my reading of the gift exchange. He arranges his narrative in distinct sequences, each exhibiting a different phase in the cultural transference that colors the events. Immediately after writing about the chief's playful performance as a withholding native informant, Lévi-Strauss relates how the chief continues with his performance during the gift exchange with the tribe. Lévi-Strauss evaluates this scene with a rather tentative conjecture: "This farce went on for two hours. Was he perhaps hoping to delude himself? More probably he wanted to astonish his companions, to convince them that he was acting as an intermediary agent for the exchange of the goods, that he was in alliance with the white man and shared his secrets."[21] The sharing of gifts has expanded to include a sharing of secrets. However, the sharing of secrets is not as mutual as it might look on the surface. As Lévi-Strauss would have it, the chief pretends that he shares the anthropologist's secret of writing. To those lacking the competence of alphabetic writing, the letters on the page appear as hieroglyphs that bear a secret. The secret allegedly shared between Lévi-Strauss and the chief, however, is the latter's ignorance of the secret of writing. Could it be that the chief also shares a secret with the tribe? Could they simply play along in the chief's scheme in the same way as Lévi-Strauss does, fully aware of the fact that the chief plays a game of "giving by withholding" and perhaps even pretending that they are able to understand the meaning of the hieroglyphs that escaped the anthropologist? In that case, they too would share a tacit knowledge with the chief, who, in turn, would skillfully be playing a double game of cultural negotiation. The very possibility of such a complex cultural negotiation never occurs to Lévi-Strauss—or, for that matter, to Derrida.

In *Marvelous Possessions*,[22] Stephen Greenblatt explores the rhetoric of the marvelous that sustains the narratives of European encounters with the New World. Interestingly, Lévi-Strauss casts himself as the one who brings marvels to this world, and the marvels he brings are precisely the marvels of writing. "We were eager to be off," he says in yet another abrupt narrative turn, "since the most dangerous point would obviously be reached when all the marvels I had brought had been transferred to native hands. So I did not try to explore the matter further."[23] In Lévi-Strauss's narrative, the "transfer of marvels," however, opens upon a transfer of a different kind: a complex cultural transference. In this transference, the "marvels" function as a veritable allegory of the colonial imaginary and its exoticization of the Other. The latter's rhetoric symptomatically displays the phantasmatic overdetermination of the anthropologist's intercultural negotiations as well as his interpretations. The "transference of marvels" works simultaneously at the material level of an exchange of goods and at the ideological level of a cultural imaginary that exoticizes those goods and fetishizes them as marvels. Writing itself, as a "marvelous possession," clearly operates for Lévi-Strauss at both levels. Lévi-Strauss's very use of the term "marvel" must therefore be seen as overdetermined, signaling that the operations of the cultural imaginary imbue the real transfer (the gift exchange) with a phantasmatic transference that falls within the legacy of colonial fantasies. What turns writing into a "marvel" is not only the power it conveys by transmitting information but also the different power it gains by withholding, circumventing, or substituting information. In its refusal of mere referentialism, writing becomes a space in which indeterminacies and ambiguities reign supreme. Such a space becomes a fertile ground and container for imaginary projections and inscriptions that bear the traces of the cultural unconscious. We may stretch this point further by arguing that the chief's performative politics relies precisely on a cultural exchange in which the anthropologist tries to acquire or gain access to the "marvels" of the New World with the help of the marvels of writing. The chief's scribbles would then simply highlight the place of the marvelous in performance, mimicry, and inversion as they are played out in encounters between the Old World and the New World.

The writing lesson, in other words, opens upon a lesson on the cultural imaginary. "The abortive meeting and the piece of humbug of which I had unwittingly been the cause had created an atmosphere of irritation; to make matters worse, my mule had ulcers in its mouth,"[24] Lévi-Strauss continues. (Why "unwittingly," we may ask? What effect had Lévi-Strauss expected when he distributed the paper and pencils in the first place?) From then on, events precipitate one another in a slapstick mode. The ulcers cause the mule to rush ahead and then come to a sudden stop, whereupon Lévi-Strauss falls off its back and finds himself left behind in the bush, unarmed in a "hostile zone." Enter the imaginary travel narratives again, which advise the anthropologist to fire a shot in order to attract attention. He fires three shots, with the sole result that they frighten the mule and cause it to trot off. After hiding his weapons and photographic equipment, Lévi-Strauss runs after the mule. The mule lets him come close, but jumps each time he tries to seize the reins, leading him further and further astray. Finally, in despair, Lévi-Strauss takes a leap and hangs on to the mule's tail until he is able to mount him again, only to discover that he has lost his equipment. At this point, paranoia reigns supreme: "The sun was sinking towards the horizon, I had lost my weapons and at any moment I expected to be pierced by a shower of arrows."[25] Just as he plans to start a bush fire, his Utiarity companions return, free of any hostile intention. After finding his equipment, which was "child's play" for them, they lead him back to the encampment.

This ending of the episode leads to another rupture in the narrative, which now shifts to Lévi-Strauss's evaluation of the "writing lesson." During the sleepless hours of the night, he reaches his conclusions concerning the relationship of writing and power. Looking at Lévi-Strauss's own contextualization of the writing scene, we note that his reflections on the power of writing, and on his power over the chief, come at the heels of the very episode in which he felt utterly powerless. Ironically, in both incidents related in this episode, he becomes the dupe of his own imaginary projections. The framing of the *writing lesson* with a highly humorous account of his failures in correctly read-ing the Nambikwara turns into a *reading lesson* for Lévi-Strauss's audience. The anthropologist's storytelling exposes both his fear and a related tendency toward paranoid projections of hostility onto the Indians, and it displays the retrospective use of writing to restore dignity by converting fear into humor. But it also suggests that, because of a lingering fear of the Indians, the *writ-ing lesson* itself is most likely colored by the affective tensions under which the "experiment" of writing is conducted. Moreover, we might assume that the anthropologist's rhetoric of submission, displayed in his self-portrayal as a powerless dupe of his own fears, also serves to alleviate some of his guilt about the Western anthropological project. This assumption gains plausibility when we consider the fact that throughout *Tristes tropiques* Lévi-Strauss nostalgi-cally mourns the natural state of the indigenous people, which is threatened by the very importation of writing he describes in "A Writing Lesson." For the reader of Lévi-Strauss's text, the writing lesson thus also becomes a lesson demonstrating the pervasiveness of the cultural imaginary and the complexity of intercultural transference in both actual encounters and their retrospective narration.

Intercultural transference therefore provides an apt framework for reading "A Writing Lesson" differently. In their indeterminacy and overdetermination, the wavy horizontal lines on the white sheet of paper operate as empty graphs that invite imaginary inscriptions. Beyond their surface appearance as an at-tempted imitation of writing, these graphs reveal the complex power dynamic of a fully fledged colonial mimicry. They form an artful metacommunica-tion about writing, gift exchange, power games, and the ruses of the cultural imaginary. On the level of simulation, the scribbles appear as a metaphor of an unusable gift, while, on the level of metacommunication, they convey a message about intercultural exchange and transference. In using *writing* in a mode of performative indirection, the chief performs a cultural contact that produces an event precisely at the site where ethnographic knowledge is withheld. In this respect, the chief's use of writing resembles an artistic or poetic, rather than a merely informative, mode of communication. The "writing lesson" thus also turns into a lesson for the reader. We learn more and different things about a culture once we expand our cultural knowledge beyond ethnographic information proper and include the effects of cultural transference. Apart from serving as props in the chief's performative enact-ment, the "empty" graphs function not only like Lacanian "empty signifiers" (or what Lévi-Strauss calls floating signifiers) but also like a projective "empty screen" that invites imaginary inscriptions. We witness a negotiation that demonstrates how the deciphering of cultures and their texts is informed and permeated by the fantasies of the people who inhabit, produce, or read them. Concrete information is embedded in a performative politics and aesthetics of cultural contact that we must learn to read before we can begin to decipher the information.

In sharpening our vision for such a different mode of deciphering, the aesthetics intrinsic in writing plays a major yet often tacit role in shaping the modalities of cultural contact. By drawing the abstract lines across the sheet of paper, the chief performed a cultural intervention that resonated with the complex exchange of emotions that took place when Lévi-Strauss performed his ethnographic experiment with the tribe. The "writing lesson" the chief taught to the anthropologist occurred within a cultural transference in which the exchange of gifts and information was revealed as part and parcel of a hierarchical colonial politics. Above all else it was this very lesson that the chief offered as his "gift" to the anthropologist. Yet it was a lesson in writing that the addressee was unable to receive because he read the wavy lines as an imitation instead of a performative speech act. More important perhaps, he could not receive this lesson because he operated on the tacit assumption that the chief's agency and power in this particular cultural exchange were limited to his tribe. Agency in cultural contact and negotiation, however, may slide from a passively adapting subject to a subject whose imaginative and adaptive mind, in turn, shapes the cultural negotiation. Lévi-Strauss perceived the chief as merely imitating the shapes of writing in order to adapt to, and use to his own advantage, the allegedly superior technology provided by the ethnographer. In my reading, the chief, in contrast, assumes agency in a situation designed to make him a mere agent in another's game. He forcefully demonstrates that cultural adaptation or even appropriation need not be passive or merely reflective but can be imaginative, playful, and performative. This claim on agency in cultural contact has profound political and psychological implications. A performative speech act or language game that remains sensitive to the vicissitudes of projections and transference, and mindful of operations of power that threaten the integrity of cultural boundaries, also facilitates a psychic processing and integration of cultural contact for those able to comprehend its implications.

In "Style, Grace, and Information in Primitive Art," Gregory Bateson argues that the problem of art is fundamentally a problem of psychic integration of the conscious and unconscious parts of the mind.[26] I see a similar process of psychic and cultural integration at work in the chief's action. Rather than submitting to the rules of the game set by the anthropologist, he adapts them to his own cultural rules. His handling of the gift exchange integrates the foreign gift of writing without compromising the integrity of flexible cultural boundaries, precisely because he addresses both the conscious and the unconscious and unspoken dimensions of the gift exchange. The chief's "graphs" then are intimately linked to his tribe's own cultural aesthetics or "internal idiom."[27] They operate as agents that engage both his tribe's cultural imaginary and the intercultural transference with the anthropologist. The graphs serve, in other words, as vehicles for the internal processing of culture. Since their larger meaning unfolds subliminally, they straddle the boundaries between the two cultures and their unconscious, thus assuming both cultural and psychic valence.

We can finally draw a more general conclusion from these observations. My reading of "A Writing Lesson" suggests that, in order to understand intercultural encounters and modalities of cultural contact, we need a theoretical model able to account for the complex performances of intercultural transference that enter any exchange or translation between cultures. Cultural negotiations inevitably draw on the cultural imaginary and the cultural unconscious. In order to understand this interplay we need cultural politics and psychology as well as cultural rhetorics and poetics. Poetic, artistic, or performative exchanges establish a tacit meta- or subtext that not only reveals imaginary or unconscious investments in the other culture but also plays across the boundaries of the official rules and codes of the exchange, often counteracting its presupposed hierarchies.

Let me conclude by invoking another, more contemporary writing lesson also based on the use of wavy lines. In her piece *Written Language (line drawings) #V and #VI* (2008), Swedish artist Sophie Tottie uses ink on paper to produce two sheets of wavy lines. The works consist of line and only line. Tottie explains that each drawing "starts with a handdrawn line. Materials are a dip pen, pigmented ink, and paper. Every successive line is attempting to incorporate each previous line's deviation. In this way the drawing proceeds by way of the first barely visible, then more and more extreme shifts produced by the previous line."[28]

As a result of this technique, the wavy lines become horizontal as well as vertical, producing a sense of dynamic flow within the composition's visual static. What appears at the surface as visual white noise or as an enigmatic signifier assumes, as Tottie points out, a "tension between the signifying and nonsignifying line."[29] Very much like the chief's wavy lines, meaning emerges from metastatements that accrue to the evocative accumulation of nonsignifying lines. In a complex play of transference with the viewer, they begin to elicit memories of not only contemporary modes of information such as bar codes or a flickering late-night screen of television but also of the subtle weave of spiderwebs or transparent woven cloth playing in the wind. They thus convey one of the most basic rules of writing, just as true in today's world of technological reproduction as it was in the "pretechnological" world of the Nambikwara chief's first pencil strokes on paper: a hand-drawn line is never just a line.

2 Traveling Literature, Traveling Theory
Imaginary Encounters Between East and West

The Great Khan owns an atlas whose drawings depict the terrestrial
globe all at once and continent by continent, the borders of the most
distant realms, the ships' routes, the coastlines, the maps of the most
illustrious metropolises and the most opulent ports. . . . The atlas depicts
cities which neither Marco nor the geographers know exist or where they
are . . . cities that do not yet have a form or a name. . . . In the last pages
of the atlas there is an outpouring of networks without beginning or end,
cities in the shape of Los Angeles, in the shape of Kyoto-Osaka, without
shape.[1]
—Italo Calvino, *Invisible Cities*

The encounter between Kublai Khan and Marco Polo is one of the most
remarkable stories about the origin of globalization and the role of literature as a medium of cultural contact. As the founder of the Mongol dynasty in
thirteenth-century China and unparalleled patron of Chinese literature and
culture, Kublai Khan was also one of the first and most powerful imperial
minds. His colonial interests led him into many disastrous foreign expeditions
beyond the sea, adventures that generated a hitherto unknown oppression in
his home country. He chose foreigners from Turkistan, Persia, Armenia, and
Byzantium as ministers, generals, governors, envoys, astronomers, or physicians and invited Marco Polo, traveling adventurer from Italy, to pass many
years in his service.

It was Marco Polo who became his foreign agent, creating his illustrious
fame in the Western world with his travel memoirs, *Il milione*,[2] which were to
become a first classic of Western Orientalism. His tales abound in phantasms
of Oriental exoticism replete with picturesque imaginary creatures lifted from

well-known fairy tales—humans with dog heads, evil spirits, and bizarre monsters. At the same time, Marco Polo became an ethnographer of sorts, recording foreign customs and listing cultural objects found in the Khan's empire ranging from exotic spices and precious stones to paper money.

Il milione demonstrates the efficacy of literature as a medium of cultural contact in unparalleled ways. This late thirteenth century document was to become a model and prime intertext for colonial travel narratives during the so-called discovery of the New World, shaping the Western cultural imaginary with its Orientalist phantasms and its fascination with the marvels of foreign worlds. The impact of *Il milione* was so profound and lasting that it is still visible in fifteenth-century geographical, ethnological, and cosmographic conceptions. Columbus carried a carefully annotated copy of the manuscript with him on his journeys. Ignoring the boundaries between the factual and the imagined, between observation and fabulation, history and fairy tale, the memoirs may well be considered a founding text of the genre of imaginary ethnographies. Today, *Il milione* is also widely acclaimed as an early piece of Italian national literature.

Il milione is a testimony to the fact that, at least at the time, literature shaped not only the cultural imaginary but also the social imagination at large, including history, politics, and the sciences, as well as the multiple practices derived from them. The quote I use to open my reflections revisits Marco Polo's travels to foreign shores from a distance of seven hundred years. It is lifted from Italo Calvino's *Invisible Cities*, a highly experimental literary meditation on the encounter between Kublai Khan and Marco Polo that uses *Il milione* as an intertext. In postmodern fashion, *Invisible Cities* embeds its retelling of Marco Polo's story within an extended philosophical reflection on the relationship between map and territory. In Calvino's cartography, the map precedes the territory, revealing "the form of cities that do not yet have a form or a name." The maps Calvino envisions are the effects of a social imagination rooted in an imaginary cathexis of projected spaces. These maps, in fact, resemble Rheinberger's "experimental systems" in the sense that they explore, shape, and generate territory in a process of continual emergence and anticipate forms of becoming that are hitherto unknown. They are maps that encode a vision of the future.

"I think you recognize cities better on the atlas than when you visit them in person,"[3] Calvino has the emperor say to Marco Polo. Inverting the traditional notion that maps are merely abstract representations of territories, Calvino casts them instead as imaginary grounds on which territories are born: "Until

every shape has found its city, new cities will continue to be born."⁴ This is
the trajectory Calvino maps from ancient Beijing to postmodern Los Angeles,
where, he suggests, "the end of cities begins."⁵ Calvino's postmodern reflection on Marco Polo's narrative thus designs a futuristic archaeology of sorts,
that is, a paradoxical imaginary map that projects the effects of early colonial
encounters onto the present. The last pages of the Khan's atlas are said to
contain future cities that announce the end of cities. These cities of the future are today's cities, Los Angeles among them, envisioned as a rhizomatic
outpouring of networks without beginning or end—without shape. The city as
we have known it comes to an end, a city modeled on ancient European cities
organized around a center, a polis. The outpouring of Los Angeles into the
urban sprawl of edge cities also marks the end of a geographical imaginary in
which cities function as a locus for developing and trading ideas and relationships in a public sphere.

Today, it is the mass media that disseminate a global urban imaginary of
metropolitan spaces across the planet and into the last corners of the world.
Foreigners who travel to these spaces come with their own internal maps,
composed as idiosyncratic assemblages of a *Baedeker* or *National Geographic*
imaginary of globally disseminated images and of a diverse and idiosyncratic
array of travel narratives and literary figurations. Unlike Marco Polo, we already carry the images of cities we visit in the imaginary baggage we bring
along on our travels. These images color our travels to foreign countries per-
ceptually as well as affectively. Let me illustrate this with a few concrete examples of the "California imaginary" I brought with me when I moved from Germany to California—now my home—as a visiting professor in 1983. During
my early visits to Los Angeles, for example, it was a piece of this city's cultural
imaginary that facilitated my first profound experience of connection. Ironically, it was the memory of a TV show that aired nightly on German television
when I was a teenager that created the first of many experiences of excitement
in this city with its decentered spaces and diasporic local cultures that cultural critic David Rieff once called the capital of the Third World.⁶ Driving
through Hollywood, I inadvertently came across Sunset Boulevard and identified it, in a flash, as a street I knew from *77 Sunset Strip*, one of my favorite
detective series from childhood, featuring a character called Kookie as a private eye. Suddenly I felt at home; but "home" was an imaginary homeland
created by the cultural objects of my youth that had become part of my inner
world. I had a related experience during my first visit to Chinatown, which I
couldn't but see through the eyes of Roman Polanski's *Chinatown*, which was

a cult film among intellectuals in Germany when I was in my twenties. Such instances in which the actual encounter is filtered through an imaginary one are emblematic of contemporary experiences of cultural contact. When, in today's world, we travel to new places, we typically bring with us a whole body of imaginary ethnographic information composed of images and stories from films, books, journals, photography, and videos, as well as advertisements on television and freeway billboards. Such imaginary "knowledge"— in some cases no more than stereotypes, prejudices, or pieces of globalized exoticism—marks people profoundly, coloring the ways in which they process experiences of traveling across the world. It is almost as if we must practice a willful exercise of forgetting if we want to experience a new place or country on its own terms or with fresh eyes. Such a practice resembles psychoanalyst Wilfred Bion's ideal of listening or seeing without memory or desire, but it is important to realize that it is not a receptive attitude that comes naturally. It depends rather on a willful suspension of our available arsenal of cultural imaginaries.

Another example may illustrate this imaginary formation of cultural experience in more detail. Trying to recall my own literary socialization in post–World War II Germany, a few years ago I began to reread some of the most memorable texts of my childhood and teenage years. In this process, I became aware how much these readings have contributed to forming the structures of my internal world and to some extent even the direction of my life. It is no coincidence that most books I could get a hold of in postwar Germany were translations of foreign texts, mostly canonical works of popular American and, much less prominently, French and Russian literature. The selection of books in bookstores and libraries was deeply shaped by the Americanization of postwar Germany that was prominent even in the south, despite the fact that most areas in southern Germany were under French occupation. The literature German adolescents read at the time featured authors such as Ernest Hemingway, John Steinbeck, and perhaps most popular of all, Pearl S. Buck. We also devoured classics such as *Uncle Tom's Cabin* and *Gone with the Wind*, especially after the film version was screened in German movie theaters, when I was eleven years old. I vividly remember my age because in Germany the film was restricted to viewers twelve years and older, and it was my grandmother who smuggled me in. The screening was my most memorable film experience of all time.

Some of my favorite novels, foremost among them Steinbeck's *The Grapes of Wrath* and *East of Eden*, created a powerful California imaginary. *The*

Grapes of Wrath generated unforgettable images of workers in large orange groves that I would find again during my first years in Orange County, where I could still handpick oranges with my then six-year-old son. We came just in time because most of the groves have vanished under the rampant development. *East of Eden*, with its powerful depictions of the Salinas Valley, turned this part of California forever into Steinbeck country for me. *East of Eden* also created a primal scene of transgressive reading for me. I read the book when I was about eleven or twelve years old. That was the time when our local priest introduced us to the Index Librorum Prohibitorum, the Catholic Church's list of prohibited books, commonly referred to as the Index. Anyone reading a book in the Index will be doomed, he threatened. It was when I came to the chapter in which the mother is identified as a prostitute that it suddenly dawned on me that *East of Eden* must be in the Index. Faithful girl that I was at the time, I consulted the priest during confession about the issue. "If you even suspect that the book could be on the Index," he admonished me, "then it is a book you shouldn't read in the first place." My resolution to put the book aside lasted until three in the morning on the following day. When I couldn't stand it any longer, I turned on the light and continued reading. Curiosity had taken over when the suspense became unbearable. I finished the book in a few days and then went to confession to obtain absolution for my sin.

There was another novel, extremely popular among high school students. It was Gwen Bristow's *Jubilee Trail*, a trashy Western romance about which, apart from the love story, I remember not much more than the attacks by local indigenous people on a group of settlers on their way to California. The German title was *Kalifornische Sinfonie*, and this romantic title as well as the story remained ingrained in my memory as early pieces of my "imaginary California" that I brought with me when I permanently moved here in 1983. There was one problem with the plot for German kids in high school, though: the Indians were bad guys, which didn't fit into the romanticized Indian imaginary we had inherited from Karl May's popular novels about the Apaches and Winnetou,[7] their noble and brave chief. So a few of us got together to rewrite the story, turning the Indians into braves who saved the white woman from a group of white criminals and took her to live with their tribe. We hadn't even heard of the popular captivity narratives before we invented our own! But it was thanks to Gwen Bristow that Indians figured prominently in our California imaginary.

In order to fully understand the prominence of American literature in the literary socialization of postwar German children, one has to place it in the context of Germany's military occupation. Due to the educational politics implemented and enforced by the occupying forces, the education and literary socialization of postwar German children during the most formative years was transcultural. The military forces' reeducation program was the most significant force, which shaped virtually the entire educational system and range of available cultural experiences at the time. In most cases, the reception of these translated foreign texts took place around the time when German children of that generation first learned about the concentration camps and the genocide of the Jews. One may therefore safely assume that the two spheres — the childhood readings and the processing of historical knowledge — became psychically linked. Whether these readings explicitly dealt with the Holocaust or not, the childhood readings of the time inevitably served as a background for the first attempts to process the traumatic knowledge of the German atrocities and the recognition of belonging to a nation and culture of perpetrators.

One particular example makes this enmeshment strikingly obvious, namely my childhood reading of Pearl S. Buck's *Peony*.[8] The story of this reading illustrates the psychic linking of particular readings with traumatic historical knowledge as well as the fact that such linkages operate unconsciously. Buck's *Peony* was one of my favorite novels in my early teens. Rereading this novel decades later, I discovered a surprising instance of unconscious transference that I am only now, after all this time, able to link to the processing of the traumatic knowledge of the atrocities of the Jewish Holocaust. Unaware of its implications at the time, I now think that, while it may seem coincidental and even spectacular, this unconscious transference reveals in fact a paradigmatic dimension of the reading process. Set in late eighteenth century China, *Peony* deals with the tragic love of a young Chinese bondswoman for the son of a rich foreign merchant. As a child, I reread this novel many times, identifying with the main character, Peony, and her tragic love for the foreigner. Only when I reread *Peony* as an adult did I discover what I had perhaps never even consciously registered: the foreigner whom Peony loves is the son of a prosperous Jewish merchant who lived in Kaifeng in one of the old Jewish Diaspora communities. I now believe *Peony* gained its deep significance for me because it served as a medium of transference that helped indirectly to process issues of racism and the persecution of Jews. At a time when a direct confrontation with the war atrocities was silenced by a whole generation of parents and teachers, literature functioned as an indispensable medium to indirectly process what continues to operate as a transgenerational haunting.[9]

Even though such a processing operated on a comparatively minimal scale, it nonetheless contributed its share in disrupting the legacy of silence.

In the process of reading *Peony*, the veiled confrontation with traumatic history functioned, like in a dream or a daydream, according to a psychic logic of displacement, inversion, or reaction formation. There was no persecution of Jews in eighteenth century China; they lived rather as wealthy and respected merchants in a Jewish quarter in Kaifeng. The basis for a psychic linkage was provided by a kind of reaction formation prominent among German postwar children, namely the development of philosemitic "family romances" (in the Freudian sense) between Germans and Jews. With its story of Peony's interracial love affair with a Jewish man, Pearl S. Buck's novel provided the narrative framework for a "family romance" with which German postwar children could tacitly identify.

One can of course see that the transference facilitated by this novel could not escape the racist dynamic that continued to mark the cultural imaginary, albeit inversely. *Peony* could easily be used to nourish an emerging exoticizing philosemitism among the postwar generation, designed to displace and ease the profound sense of guilt. And yet, even though the exoticization of the Jewish Diaspora community in *Peony* by the German postwar generation must still be seen as an effect of racist Nazi politics, it is also a first attempt of dealing with and reacting against racism. This irreducible ambivalence must be seen for what it is: a transgenerational legacy in which the choice of children to idealize and identify with the victims of the parental generation still bears the marks of precisely the racist dynamic these children try to escape.

Perhaps the identification with the victim, while still part of the racist legacy, is a phase in reacting against this legacy that necessarily precedes a more mature antiracist politics. In fact, I understand cultural fantasies in which children of perpetrators identify with the victims of genocidal assaults as a highly complex and ambivalent mode of negotiating a traumatic legacy. While such fantasies undoubtedly evolve within and still belong to a history of racism, it is not enough to understand them merely as *inverse racism*, as some may contend. The dynamic of an indirect processing of transgenerational trauma requires a perspective that is sensitive to change, ambivalence, and the pitfalls of what Alexander and Margarete Mitscherlich call the "incapacity of mourning."[10] Of course, the transmission and processing of historical trauma across generations operates differently depending on whether one belongs to the culture of the victims or that of the perpetrators. Frantz Fanon's work is exemplary in outlining the psychic dynamics involved in processes of de-colonization.[11] Similar dynamics, particularly the unconscious identification with the aggressor, also operate in attempts to overcome a history of racism. I consider the identification with the victim, found among many descendants of cultures of perpetrators, to be a possible first phase in trying to overcome the legacy of racism, violence, and genocide. Even if this phantasmatic identi-fication still operates within racist parameters, it grows out of a willful attempt at rejecting racism, thus performing an inversion of values similar to the ones described by Fanon in his analysis of the psychic dynamic of decolonization in which the identification with the aggressor is subsequently inverted into a rejection of everything associated with the colonizer's values. Both inversions are based on a rejection of one's ascribed role within the cultural division of perpetrators and victims.

Within this general dynamic the unconscious transference in my child-hood reading of *Peony* may appear in sharper profile. Unable to trace all its complicated ramifications here, I focus on a few aspects that illustrate the affective coloring and unconscious underpinnings of the reading process. A brief outline of plot and historical setting may serve to highlight the suitability of the textual material for the mobile affective cathexis that my reading of the novel requires. *Peony* is set in the last decade of the eighteenth century and the turn of the nineteenth century, when many Jewish families in Kaifeng had already become sinicized culturally. The knowledge of Hebrew and the scriptures as well as the observance of Jewish holidays and religious customs had dramatically declined, and the last rabbi was getting old without having found an appropriate heir. Many passages in the novel deal with cultural and religious tolerance in China, invoking by contrast the persecution of Jews out-side China. Significantly, the Jews had not been persecuted among the excep-tionally tolerant Chinese people and government. The novel therefore deals instead with problems of cultural contact and assimilation as well as with the concomitant loss of traditional religious and cultural values.

In addition to dealing with issues of racial, cultural, and religious discrimi-nation, adaptation, and transculturation, *Peony* portrays the devastating effects of patriarchal laws and rigid class hierarchies on the lives and social status of women. Still more important, all the major female characters, including Peony, are strong women, unbroken in spirit yet crushed and ultimately de-stroyed by conventions that relegate women to submissive roles in society. The novel's emphasis on Jews and women, religious and racial tolerance, gen-erational conflict and the subordination of individual bonds to economic and sociocultural interests served as a ground for an intense transference that must have translated into my long-lasting cathexis of the novel during my childhood and beyond. Presumably, a great deal of this cathexis operated tacitly if not unconsciously. This explains why, of the many books by Pearl S. Buck, I singled out *Peony* as the one I read over and over. Obviously this transference worked despite the fact that I was only peripherally aware of the most important historical detail, namely the novel's setting in the Jewish Diaspora and its treatment of cultural, racial, and religious intolerance. Decades later, the discovery of how deeply my reading of *Peony* was overdetermined by the confrontation with the central issues that marked Germany's past and its transgenerational legacy came as a shock. With all my detailed memories of the novel, I had repressed precisely that element that must at the time have given it its deepest personal meaning.

The lesson I draw from this reading of *Peony* concerns the crucial role highly personal projection plays subliminally in the reading process. Trying to address the vicissitudes of transference and projection in ordinary reading experiences of children and young adolescents, I am deliberately eclipsing critical readings here. Adolescents commonly link literature to their rich fantasy life and often bend texts to suit their own desires or needs. Obviously, the *meaning* of *Peony* in this childhood reading reaches beyond the information conveyed by the story in its historical and literary contexts. In general terms, the affective cathexis of literature functions largely on the basis of a reader's transference, but in order to engage in such a transference, the reader must find a productive and generative literary space for such an engagement. Even though the projections that enter into processes of transference are as a rule intensely personal and idiosyncratic, they are not arbitrary, nor are they merely an *affective fallacy*. Whereas this critical term was coined in order to suggest that affective responses are better ignored in critical readings, I argue that instead they should be counted among the most prominent cultural and psychological functions of literature.

The example of my own particular cathexis of *Peony* in my early adolescence emphasizes the crucial role that both the personal circumstances and the historical, cultural, and political contexts in which a book is read play in the process of reception. Among other things, this is an effect of the dissemination of readings across cultural, national, and linguistic spaces. As books travel across boundaries, they adapt hermeneutically to new places, contexts, and knowledges, changing their meanings in the process. What Edward Said noted about "traveling theory"[12] is also true for "traveling literature": both are affected by the ambiguities of a dislocation from the original context when they are relocated in a new, often entirely different, cultural space. This does not imply that under the conditions of such displacements *meaning* becomes irrevocably distorted and compromised as projections reign supreme; it means only that transference and projection are central to such primary reading experiences. I am addressing here, in other words, not critical readings of literature. Rather, I am trying to trace some concrete examples of the inevitable, indeed necessary, distortions that happen in ordinary readings of literatures as they travel across an increasingly globalized world with its own particular economies of publication and distribution.

Indeed, it may in fact be one of the tasks of critical readings not only to reflect on but also to work through such culturally inflected transferences, to analyze them as cultural symptoms, and to work toward a fuller understanding and experience of texts on their own terms. Inevitably, literature and theory change under the impact of cultural contact just as people do, and such changes will always carry the traces of projections and transferences. But what happens if the Orientalist imaginary itself travels across national and cultural boundaries and is thus put under the pressures of cultural contact? The long history of the West's fascination with China persists to this day and is of course inevitably bound up with the legacy of Orientalism. In *Johanna d'Arc of Mongolia*, German filmmaker Ulrike Ottinger presents a satirical fairy tale that engages this legacy and plays with what happens when Orientalism travels back to the countries that nourished it in the first place. In this context, she specifically explores Mongolia as one of China's indigenous Others.

The film opens with a scene featuring a group of travelers on the Trans-Siberian Railroad who display the entire range of stereotypical Orientalist attitudes in baroque exaggeration. Lady Windermere, a nineteenth-century amateur ethnographer with a passion for all things Mongolian, embodies the Victorian colonist of the British Empire enamored with Mongolian nomadism. She offers her services to the other travelers by assuming the role of the anthropologist as nonnative informant. By contrast, Frau Müller-Vohwinkel, a caricature of a German high school teacher, filters her perceptions through the *Baedecker*, forever worried about the sanitary conditions of nomadic life. Ethnic music has a prominent role in the film's ethnographic imaginary: A three-woman entertainment group called the Kalinka Sisters (a Yiddish version of the Andrews Sisters), as well as Fanny Ziegfield, a late-1930s music star of the great music halls, and Mickey Katz, a Yiddish tenor, provide musical entertainment of different ethnic origins. Giovanna, the title character and most contemporary of the women, by contrast, wears jeans, sports a backpack, and listens to a different kind of music on a Walkman.

From its outset the film exhibits an exuberant baroque artificiality that partly emerges from its dense network of intermedial references to other films, texts, music, and popular culture, both East and West: a polytemporal setting mixes historical periods and styles from the nineteenth century to the present. Characters and scenes are cast as echoes of cultural artifacts ranging from road movies starring Bob Hope and Bing Crosby and old Westerns with train holdups and kidnappings to traditional Oriental tales and spectacular nature documentaries featuring vast desert landscapes and exotic mountain ranges. Linking the different times, genres, and narratives is a pervasive Orientalist imaginary. It finally unfolds in the kidnapping of the travelers by a group of Mongolian nomad women on camels and horses who take the prisoners across the Gobi Desert to their colorful and exotic yurts. True to Ottinger's signature, this artificial imaginary setting indulges in extravagant excesses while at the same time displaying a thoroughly humorous, playful, and self-ironical gaze on the complex misunderstandings of cross-cultural encounters. Even potential cultural clashes are deflected and turned into benign adventures to be remembered and traded as stories.

Johanna d'Arc of Mongolia is a tour de force of ethnographic surrealism if not an outright romance with a fanciful ethnographic imagination that borrows freely from ancient history, folklore, myth, and religion, as well as an entire history of Orientalist fantasies from travel narratives, novels, films, and music. What disrupts the familiar Orientalist imagination in Ottinger's film, however, is the fact that, in the context of this encounter between East and West, exoticizing the Other becomes a two-way street. It is the contemporary Mongolian princess, for example, who pursues and takes Giovanna, the exotic stranger from Paris, as a lover. And it is a group of nomad women who curiously peek at the foreign travelers through an opening in their yurt.

However, while the film indulges in a syncretistic mix of times and cultures, it all but eclipses the contemporary imaginary of China. Originally Ottinger had planned to shoot her film in the Chinese part of Mongolia until she was told that she could travel there only with an official entourage. Consequently, she moved the setting to the Republic of Mongolia, which is independent of China. This is why the film focuses on the encounter of the travelers with Mongolia and the Mongolian imaginary. If viewers were not given a polytemporal framework that includes the present time, the scenes displaying nomadic Mongolian culture could initially easily be mistaken as a remnant of precolonial times. However, this possible illusion is disrupted when the princess uses her camel to tow the motorcycle of a family of nomads who have run out of gas.[13] At this point, Ottinger openly stages the encounter between Europeans in period costumes and Mongolian nomads in newly designed traditional dresses as a performance in which the polytemporal framework is extended to the nomadic Mongolian tribes as well. If the Mongolian dresses resemble the lavish costumes of nostalgic Orientalist movies that recast ancient times, this effect is fully calculated and consistent with the artificial blending of ethnographic realism and surrealism, origin stories and fairy tales, past and present.

If we see such reworkings of the cultural imaginary as central to literature and the arts more generally, we may ask how to assess these aesthetic practices and techniques as a form of *writing culture*. If we resist the temptation to view ethnographic writing as simply a form of literature or, conversely, literature as a form of ethnographic writing, we can see that cultural fantasies as well as transference in cross-cultural encounters more generally have an entirely different status in anthropological ethnographies than they do in imaginary ethnographies. To be sure, the boundaries between the two will always remain fluid since no cross-cultural encounter can be free of transference. But in ethnographies proper, such transference is a form of interference that must be worked through and reduced as far as possible, while imaginary ethnographies enjoy the aesthetic freedom to use fantasy and transference as central creative impulses. Literature displays an entire range of incorporating cultural fantasies and projections from generating new fantasies to self-reflexively exposing or inverting the arsenal of available ones by using irony, satire, pastiche, intertextual play, or other forms of medial self-reflection.

In other words, the leveling stance, popular in certain trends in postmodern anthropology and rhetorical literary studies, loses sight of the particular cultural function of each discourse by conflating formal, aesthetic, and generic distinctions. The literary forms, discursive strategies, rhetorical devices, styles, and modes of composition literature uses in order to transmit cultural knowledge, for example, generate entirely different modes of reception, particularly in shifting the emphasis from cultural reflection, information, and analysis to a more encompassing experience that foregrounds affective, emotional, and unconscious responses. Again, the boundaries remain fluid, because some of the best anthropological ethnographies use literary strategies to draw readers in affectively and aesthetically. However, they do not have the same freedom of invention because, like autobiographies, they enter a contract with readers based on certain truth claims, however tenuous they may be.

Using literary forms of *writing culture* has, I argue, a different function than the use of other discursive or scholarly forms. Moreover, generic differences within literature, such as modernist experimentalism, new realism, the new documentary novel, or traditional ethnographic fiction each convey cultural knowledge in distinctly different ways and thereby create a wide range of different effects. The larger issue here is not only the mediation but also the translation and translatability of cultural knowledge into different forms of discourse and expression. The rhetorical turn in anthropology[14] as well as in literary and critical theory firmly established notions of *culture as text* and notions of *culture as translation*. Regarding the vexed issue of the "translatability of cultures,"[15] and the limits of translatability, some of the most challenging questions continue to generate heated debates: What are the epistemological and political implications of perceiving culture as a text? How can one account for what some see as the irreducible violence of language in representations of cultural otherness? What are the rhetorical choices and ethical obligations in speaking about and "translating" the Other? Posing such questions in relation to literature requires, I insist, theories that reach beyond an exclusive focus on conscious processes or modes of reading and reception.

This is also true for theories and models of cultural translation. In cross-cultural encounters we not only mutually *translate* the other culture but we also engage in a complex affective *transfer* ranging from conscious emotions to subliminal, if not unconscious, moods. Affective investments include not only positive responses but also negative ones such as resistance, rejection, paranoia, and even hostility. In all of them, projection and transference play a seminal role. Highly personal processes of fantasizing and projecting are among the most basic and perhaps most crucial aspects of reading experiences, shaping the very cultural function of literature. The particularities of literary form reflect a writer's processing of the world in such a way that it becomes meaningful for a large readership in a cultural, psychological, and aesthetic sense. This is precisely why readers can use literary texts as evocative and transformational objects to internally process their own experiences. Literature's deep engagement with the continual exchange between cultural and psychological experiences provides the basis for what I call *literary transference*.

Such transference operates in a mode of transitionality. D. W. Winnicott argues that we experience cultural objects such as literary and art objects in a transitional space reserved for negotiating the boundaries between the self and the outside world. In "The Location of Cultural Experience,"[16] one of the most seminal short texts dealing with the relationship between culture and psychic life, Winnicott asserts that the place where culture is negotiated is precisely the transitional space between self and other, in which the first personal object and henceforth all cultural objects are created and exchanged. In my own work, I have developed the psychological and cultural implications of such transitionality for a theory of reading, arguing that reading affects the boundaries of subjectivity as well as the negotiation of boundaries between cultures.

Winnicott's theory of the transitional space of cultural objects has gained new relevance for both postcolonial and global studies. Drawing on Winnicott, Homi Bhabha in *The Location of Culture*[17] develops a model of transitionality that posits a "third space," in which the cultural negotiation of literary texts takes place. For Bhabha, the transitionality that generates this third space enables a dynamic, if conflicted, negotiation between two cultures that come into conflict. In *The Mirror and the Killer-Queen*, I argue that literature and reading are strongly engaged in shaping the ways in which subjects relate to cultures and negotiate the transitional spaces of cultural contact. Literature always involves the translation of a cultural space into a psychological or interior space and vice versa. If literature conveys cultural knowledge, it is generally a highly subjective rendition of cultural images or culturally inflected imaginary worlds. We should not think of this exchange in terms of a one-directional translation but rather in terms of an exchange where inner and outer space are continually translated back into each other, thereby changing in the process. In this sense, literature has always been engaged with subjects, subjectivity, subjection, subject positions, and the relation of subjects to language and culture.

Among other things, this may explain why literature plays a crucial role not only in the figuration but also in the processing of violent histories and cultural or political conflict, including the processing of transgenerational trauma.[18] In order to disrupt the silences that cover violent histories, there is a need for voices capable of breaking through the affective barriers that prevent such confrontation, let alone the processing of violence, including the mass-mediated violence we receive on a daily basis as abstract and muted documentation and information.

My opening examples invoke the early history of colonialism and globalization through Marco Polo's travel narratives. Calvino's intertextual play with

Il milione introduces a polytemporality that insists on the incorporation of past and future in a fluid yet also striated presence. The traces and effects of colonialism and other violent histories in its wake are still with us. So is an anticipated future Calvino envisions in global forms of change and destruction that lead to the point where "the end of cities begins." If literary texts function indeed not only as diagnostic vehicles for assessing an anticipated future but also, in a much stronger claim, as experimental systems that generate what Rheinberger calls machines for producing the future,[19] then they must also become vehicles of intervention. This hopeful claim is grounded in an attempt to at least sketch in a brief glimpse the outer of literature's far-reaching cultural, material, and psychological effects. As Marco Polo's *Il milione* demonstrates, literature may influence a culture's beliefs and desires, its geographical, ethnological, and cosmographic conceptions, its relationship to itself and to others. This is not an innocent power. The cultural functions and effects of literature are highly ambivalent. While certain texts feed into ideologies, colonial greed, Orientalism, or even racism, others challenge them and open up or preserve an invaluable space of cultural critique.

Moreover, as my reading of Pearl S. Buck's *Peony* was meant to illustrate, literature also affects its readers in very personal and often idiosyncratic ways, helping them to internally process cultural experiences. In its deepest reaches, literature may help one indirectly confront and work through certain traumatic or haunting experiences. Literature's cultural and psychological effects unfold as a continual process that changes the boundaries of cultures as well as subjects, thus contributing to weaving the very fabric of cultures and lives. This is why we need to fight for its survival as a valued cultural object in our late capitalist global, corporate, and mass-mediated world.

Let me end with a small anecdote that traces my personal reception of *Peony* to the present and illustrates how traveling literatures and theories may on occasion produce surprisingly material effects. My anecdote loops back to the opening remarks on the imaginary maps we carry with us when we travel to foreign cities. Some years ago, my reading of *Peony* took a new turn when I included it in a series of lectures I presented at various universities in Beijing. After one of the lectures, a colleague spontaneously invited me to present my analysis of Pearl S. Buck's novel at Kaifeng University. Utterly excited about this unique chance to visit the city that figured so prominently in Buck's novel, I happily accepted the invitation. After my lecture at Kaifeng University, my generous hosts arranged for a translator to accompany me to Kaifeng's old Jewish quarter. There I was, guided solely by the imaginary map of a decades old childhood reading and a young woman who helped me bridge the gap of languages. It is hard to describe how moved I was to stand there in the back alleys of a Kaifeng that had, over the centuries, decayed and lost its splendor as a worldly center for commerce and trade. But the Jewish quarter was still there with the old synagogue and even a few people who remembered the Jewish community. What excited and moved me beyond the actual visit to this old neighborhood I had "known" as a child through one of my favorite novels was the fact that it seemed as if this very moment epitomized a singular passion of my adolescent world, namely the desire to blur the boundaries between the real and the imaginary and to bring my readings alive. As I interviewed the old people in the streets, and my translator helped us communicate with each other, we found out that the only remaining observant Jew was a very old woman who also tended the synagogue. The other descendants of the Jewish Diaspora community had become entirely assimilated into the dominant culture and were sinicized both racially and culturally. Will anyone take over once the old woman passes away? What, if anything, was she able to pass on to another generation? In *Peony*, Buck describes the beginnings of the struggle to maintain the Jewish heritage in Kaifeng's Diaspora community. Historically, at some point the knowledge of Hebrew seems to have gotten lost, and in response the practicing rabbi at the time brought in teachers of Hebrew from the Jewish Diaspora community in Shanghai to Kaifeng to restore the ability to read and speak Hebrew to the younger generation. At the time of my visit, the people no longer spoke Hebrew. The Jewish Diaspora community, however, lives on in memory. All the people we interviewed knew the history of Kaifeng's Jews and were happy to volunteer their stories. None of them knew Pearl S. Buck's novel, but they all were proud, and also somewhat amused, to hear from this foreign scholar about an American author and novel that was set not just in Kaifeng but in the old Jewish quarter, the very place where they lived as the descendants of the Jewish Diaspora community that inspired the foreign novel. Suddenly their familiar home environment seemed to become endowed with a sense of an almost exotic history, albeit one that they could nonetheless relate to as their own because of the old stories that had been handed down to them orally. This anecdote illustrates that literary transference does not end with the act of reading. The effects of certain books may extend throughout a lifetime, shaping our interior narratives and on occasion concrete actions that in turn might, like the wings of a butterfly, generate a surprising turn of events.

3 Restriction and Mobility

Desire, Transference, and

the Cultural Imaginary

There are areas of experience which can be investigated in one speech
code but not in another.[1]
—Mary Douglas, *Natural Symbols*

Ever since the anthropological turn in literary studies in the eighties, literary studies have raised the fundamental question of literature's cultural
function and value from the perspective of a repoliticized notion of text and
reading in an increasingly diverse global world. The vicissitudes of encounters
with otherness and the role of fantasies, projection, and cross-cultural transference in these encounters have further developed debates about the modalities and forms of *writing culture*. In *The Predicament of Culture* James Clifford
writes, "Ethnographies are both like and unlike novels. But in an important
general way the two experiences enact the process of fictional self-fashioning
in relative systems of culture and language that I call ethnographic."[2] Although
Clifford here emphasizes the affinity between literature and ethnography, he
simultaneously highlights the distinct, if problematic, boundaries between
the two. Despite the widespread agreement about the fictional and subjective aspects of any ethnographic discourse, these boundaries reassert themselves again and again—if only because fiction and subjectivity have a different function in literature than they do in ethnography. The anthropologist's
fictional self-fashioning or active fabrication of another culture emerges only
if one reads the ethnographic discourse against the grain, or if one performs
a rhetorical reading that foregrounds the effects of textuality in the writing of
culture. This is true despite critical reflections on the imaginary underpin-
ning of fieldwork and ethnography. One could even argue that fictional self-
fashioning and rhetorical fabrication belong to the "political unconscious"

of ethnographies, while in literature they may be used as a chosen mode of figuration. While literary texts enjoy a greater freedom of invention in the writing of culture, they may also self-reflexively foreground and thereby challenge and intervene in the overdetermination or transcoding of a culture under observation—one's own or a foreign culture—with preconceptions, stereotypes, projections, and fantasies. Because of a specific admixture of the cultural and the subjective proper to the literary, literature may use the space of the imaginary to play with or across the boundaries between cultures or between culture and subjectivity. Regulated by a certain dynamic of restriction and mobility, this play facilitates cultural negotiation in complex processes of exchange and translation between the cultural and the psychological.

The dynamics of such negotiation are reflected in Franz Kafka's "The Wish to Be a Red Indian"—a short prose piece that chooses restriction and mobility as central themes in the figuration of cultural desire:

> If only one were an Indian, ever alert, and, leaning into the wind on a speeding horse, always jerkily quivering over the quivering ground, until one dropped one's spurs, for there would be no spurs, until one hurled away one's reins, for there would be no reins, and one barely saw the countryside before one as a smoothly mown heath, but now without the horse's neck and horse's head.

> [Wenn man doch ein Indianer wäre, gleich bereit, und auf dem rennenden Pferde, schief in der Luft, immer wieder kurz erzitterte über dem zitternden Boden, bis man die Sporen ließ, denn es gab keine Sporen, bis man die Zügel wegwarf, denn es gab keine Zügel, und kaum das Land vor sich als glatt gemähte Heide sah, schon ohne Pferdehals und Pferdekopf.][3]

At first glance, it seems obvious that Kafka's short piece engages a prominent cultural fantasy that marked the Western imaginary since the invasion or so-called discovery of the New World. Ever since, the imaginary Indian has been a cultural icon, incorporating the attributes of the *brute savage* or its inverse the *noble savage*. The moment, however, we read Kafka's text according to possible cultural or ethnographic implications, exploring the "cultural contact" it performs within the medium of literary language, we seem to embark on a "forbidden reading." "The Wish to Be a Red Indian," literary critics commonly argue, cannot be read as an "imaginary ethnography" because the fable's self-referentiality supposedly undermines any cultural critique. According to such a perspective, one may perceive cultural contact within literature only as textual contact, thus reducing a literary text's cultural semiotics to a phenomenon of intertextuality. This critical approach privileges readings that emphasize the structural coupling of Kafka's piece with Kleist's "Fable without Moral" (Die Fabel ohne Moral) or with Kafka's own intertext "Reflections for Gentlemen-Jockeys" (Zum Nachdenken für Herrenreiter). By contrast, a reading that sees in Kafka's text also a literary staging of a prominent cultural fantasy—namely the wish to become an Indian[4]—would be considered obsolete, suspect of falling back on a naïve literalism.

Admittedly, as Reinhold Görling's reading of Kafka's text shows, Kafka's literary language makes its referential function disappear behind its materiality.[5] At the same time, however, the very "reference" that the text's self-referential staging is supposed to leave behind is a tremendously pervasive and powerful cultural fantasy. The popular figure of the Indian as noble savage has haunted the European cultural imaginary ever since the colonization of the New World, and it has even experienced a renaissance with the global appropriation and commodification of indigenous cultural objects and values during recent decades. Despite the fact that Kafka dissolves this fantasy in the process of its restaging within a literary language game, the fantasy as such continues to function as a horizon that enables multiple readings—a horizon comparable to a Freudian remainder, a day residue, or Tagesrest. One could further argue that, in the process of rendering the fantasy self-referential, Kafka displaces it to the text's cultural unconscious. An exchange has taken place that has transformed a cultural "outside" into a textual "inside." At the same time, this exchange also transforms the cultural outside into a "subjective" inside— a space for the enactment of subjectivity. While the textual performance transforms the wish to become an Indian, it nonetheless retains its tie to what it transforms. Moreover, the textual appropriation itself is mediated culturally. Since such processes of appropriation, transformation, and exchange are typical for the "appropriation" of culture through the medium of literature, Kafka's piece may serve here to highlight a more general dynamic of cultural transference.

The very fantasy of "becoming an Indian" places Kafka's piece in relation to the primitivist movement that marks modernist literature and the arts. Using the popular figure of the Indian, Kafka quotes a cultural phantasm of unrestrained desire that already served as a romantic version of the noble savage in the surrealist "Poetics of the Apache."[6] Desire for unrestrained movement, desire *as* movement—all these elements merge in Kafka's short piece. In the larger context of Kafka's work, the Indian is also cast as a counterfigure to the figure of the repressed office clerk, representative of a particular office culture, an *Angestelltenkultur*. Both the Indian and the office clerk figure as cultural ciphers of a desire or its repression, symbolizing free movement or its restraint in order to mark cultural boundaries. According to Stephen Greenblatt, the notion of culture always refers to an opposition between *restriction* and *mobility* that, in turn, is formative in the internal dynamic that regulates the boundaries of culture and the circulation of social energies.[7] One could argue that, as a vehicle for the mediation of culture, literature absorbs this opposition in order to interfere with its dynamics, thus affecting cultural boundaries and the flow of social energies within and across them. Greenblatt's notion of culture allows one to read Kafka's piece also as a self-reflection on literature's relationship to culture. From this perspective, the text uses the figure of the Indian in order to performatively enact a wish for cultural mobility, showing at the same time that literature is the very medium that works toward realizing such a wish. The textual performance evokes a visual hallucination of the desire for a breathtaking speed that leaves behind all restrictions: "For there would be no spurs . . . for there would be no reins."

Kafka's imaginary worlds generally exhibit an absolute arbitrariness of cultural restrictions that forcibly stifle internal movement. Instead of unfolding into free movement, mobility figures as an unwanted disturbance in the system, a derailment of its law, and a noise in its representational regimes. Mobility emerges when a "fantastic fissure"[8] disrupts the balance of a predetermined course of action. Balance in Kafka's imagined "systems" is always precarious, precisely because their "symbolic order" is aimed at a prohibition of flexibility and movement. In Kafka's imaginary culture of office clerks, mobility threatens the closed system of absolute control and therefore needs to be eliminated. In "The Metamorphosis," for example, the shattered control of balance is restored only when Gregor Samsa, the agent who stands, however involuntarily, for movement, is reconfigured as a sacrificial victim. By contrast, in "The Wish to Be a Red Indian," Kafka invokes the fantasy of free movement in a counterculture in which Indian and horse form a systemic unit. In the process of textual performance, Kafka links the transformation of the Indian with cultural transformation. Just as the Indian becomes the very movement and speed of the horse, culture itself (spurs and reins) is transformed into nature ("for there would be no reins"). This transformational process is conveyed through the highly eroticized unrestricted movement of the Indian "quivering jerkily over the quivering ground."[9] We witness expenditure instead of repression, exteriorization instead of sublimation, and deterritorialization instead of rootedness.

Significantly, however, Kafka's text presents a performative enactment of the wish to become an Indian not as a romantic return to nature but as a wish for an alternative culture. After all, it was the Spanish colonizers who introduced the horse along with its reins and spurs as cultural objects to the native population. And even though the indigenous people resisted adopting reins and spurs as instruments of domestication into their own culture, Kafka quotes them in a mode of negation, thus affirming the cultural remainder of restriction within the fantasy of unrestricted movement. This highlighting of the cultural is enforced by the image of a smoothly cut meadow that appears either as a projection of the landscape at home onto the foreign territory, or as an importation of Indian culture to the homeland. It thus offsets and makes strange the popular fantasy of Plains Indians riding over the wild prairie.

This hybrid image exposes the desire that nourishes the cultural imaginary—in Kafka's case the primitivism that inspires the wish to become an Indian. Kafka's text figures this desire as unanswerable: "If only one *were* an Indian." While the unattainable wish to become an Indian indicates the boundaries of one's own culture, its textual mutation follows the logic of a hallucinatory transgression of these boundaries. Spurs and reins, as well as the smoothly cut meadow, become ciphers of a cultural unconscious, reminding one that mnemonic traces of the constraints imposed by the symbolic order inscribe themselves even into the fantasy of unrestricted desire. Furthermore, if one reads the piece in the context of Kafka's "Reflections for Gentlemen-Jockeys" (1910), one realizes how pointedly Kafka juxtaposes the two pieces in a mutual, ironically inflected intertextual mirroring. This juxtaposition, in turn, bears upon Kafka's reflection on restriction and mobility as the forces that determine the dynamics of cultural self-fashioning. "Reflections for Gentlemen-Jockeys" exposes the familiar horse races in Kafka's own culture as paradoxically lacking the very mobility that motivates the wish to become an Indian. Their clearly defined rules locate these races within a rigid system of cultural restriction, enforced by the "envy of your opponents."[10] Instead of flying over the open field, the "gentlemen-jockeys" are forced to traverse a narrow enclosure, exposed to the mockery of the ladies, who merely ridicule the winner of a horse race. And instead of "quivering jerkily over the quivering ground," the winner must succumb to the restrictions of trivial conventional gestures: "the never-ending handshaking, saluting, bowing, and waving."[11]

Compared to this victory, the wish to become an Indian appears indeed as a utopian liberation. However, rather than evoking a romantic other, the text's performative enactment of this wish exposes instead the very cultural dynamic that produces this Other as a counterimage of one's own culture.

How, then, can we read the oft-quoted ending of Kafka's piece, opening onto a landscape "now without the horse's neck and horse's head"? This merging of rider and horse has been interpreted as a metamorphosis of the figure of the Indian: the wish to become an Indian is seen as transforming into another wish to fuse with the horse, the object of unrestrained motion. The agent of the wish is not only "becoming Indian" but also "becoming horse." From an ethnographic perspective, one may also think of this metamorphosis as a shamanic transformation. The Indian as "shape-shifter" transforms into the horse. In conjunction with the wish to become an Indian, "becoming horse"—in the sense of Deleuze and Guattari's "becoming animal"[12]—also partakes in a larger politics of deterritorialization. Envisioning unrestricted movement and the free flow of energies, Kafka's piece also bespeaks a wish to transcend culture with its boundaries and confinement to territories by becoming a nomad like some indigenous Americans before their colonization and confinement to reservations. It makes sense, then, that Deleuze and Guattari should write a book about Kafka in which they read him as the initiator of a "minor literature" (une littérature mineure). Mineure connotes "minor," "minority," and "minoritarian" at once.[13] But in Kafka's work "minor" or "minoritarian" always generates a radical deterritorialization rather than supporting the identity politics of certain minority literatures. At least in the cultural imaginary, cultural identity with its restrictions is superseded by the wish for mobility and traversal of territorial boundaries, and the desire not for conquest but for becoming other.

In performing the basic opposition between restriction and mobility, Kafka's prose piece appears as a form of cultural contact facilitated by a speech performance that uses cultural memories and the phantasms of the cultural unconscious as its props. In doing so, it mobilizes culture, thus altering the dynamic of restriction and mobility. Kafka's vision of unrestrained motion is thus part of a politics of deterritorialization that aims at escaping the identical through continual transmutations: just as the agent of the wish wants to transform into an Indian, the Indian transforms into a horse, and the horse dissolves into language. Such a politics of deterritorialization also bears upon the art-culture system that informs the cultural politics and public culture within which Kafka's work operates. In The Predicament of Culture, James

Clifford develops a schematic model for the classical binary conception of an art-culture system in Western anthropology in which art and culture are strategically deployed along different cultural territories. In this classificatory scheme, culture is conceived as traditional and collective, while art is measured according to standards of originality and singularity. This classification generates a history of reception in which the cultural products of indigenous cultures are defined exclusively as cultural objects, while Western cultural products are afforded the privileged category of art objects.

Modernism constitutes one of the first art movements eroding the binary opposition that assigned the categories of art and culture to Western and non-Western cultures, respectively. This challenge to the binary art-culture system occurred in part because modernism and surrealism insisted upon the *artistic* value of primitive forms, appropriating and incorporating them into their own experimental styles. Yet there is a deep ambivalence in this acknowledgment. Not only do many perceive the appropriation of indigenous art forms as a spiritual theft; appropriating indigenous forms and styles also goes hand in hand with the lucrative commodification of so-called primitive art. Created in a cultural climate where such primitivist desire pervades all spheres of public culture, Kafka's piece must be understood in this context of artistic primitivism. However, Kafka's choice of the conditional tense already exposes the primitivist appropriation of the Other as a fleeting phantasm. Colored with icons of Western acculturation, the iconic figure of the noble Indian is hybridized, if not contaminated, by mnemonic traces of the culture at home.

My reading of Kafka's piece in the context of modernist primitivism in literature and the arts is meant to prepare the ground for a more encompassing engagement of the debates that necessarily ensued after the anthropological turn in literary studies. We have, I contend, never fully overcome the effects of the binary art-culture system that Clifford exposes. Its classificatory scheme continues to condition our reception of both canonical Western texts, such as Kafka's, and the emergent literatures[14] from indigenous and Third World traditions. Critics who reduce Kafka's work to self-referential textuality still operate within the classical divide, thus positioning it exclusively within an art system at the expense of its intervention in the circulation of cultural icons. By corollary, equally confining standards are commonly applied to so-called ethnic or Third World literatures. Critics tend to interpret them primarily within the culture system, thereby ignoring their artistic import or treating it as merely ornamental. I maintain, in other words, that the very categorical separation of art and culture is detrimental to the reception of literature, regardless whether it is relegated to the art or to the culture system. As long as our critical apparatus works within this divide, it cuts literature off from either artistic validation or from cultural impact.

The effects of this art-culture system are astoundingly tenacious, continuing to mark theoretical debates with the stigma of an internalized colonial gaze. In a highly controversial article, Fredric Jameson, for example, labels Third World literatures as "national allegories," arguing that they lack the distinction between individuality and collectivity that is constitutive of their Western counterparts.[15] We recall that it was precisely the distinction between individuality and collectivity that, according to Clifford, generated the distinction between art (individual) and culture (collective). Aijaz Ahmad rejects Jameson's reduction of Third World literatures to allegories of national cultures, countering that, under the conditions of global capitalism, these literatures are subjected to the same processes of circulation, classification, and reception as those in the Western tradition.[16] Whereas Ahmad's critique emphasizes the institutional and economic changes in the circulation of indigenous, ethnic, and Third World literatures, we also need to emphasize the tenacity of the exclusive association of ethnic or Third World literatures with culture as a historical legacy of an art-culture system that continues to overdetermine literary classification despite these changes. It is a legacy that has even been smoothly incorporated into the global commodification of indigenous and Third World literatures.

Moreover, the distinction between individuality and collectivity Jameson invokes bears heavily on the relationship of literature to subjectivity. Homi Bhabha criticizes Jameson for denying Third World literatures their capacity to fashion an independent postcolonial subjectivity.[17] Bhabha defines Third-World literature as the site of construction of a postcolonial subject that is no longer reducible to political-economic processes or national interests but emerges from the various discourses that belong to a heterogeneous and hybrid cultural memory. Both Ahmad's and Bhabha's critiques can be assuaged only by a theory that bridges the divide between art and culture, acknowledging not only that they are irrefutably intertwined but also that literary or artistic evaluation cannot afford to eclipse the cultural and vice versa.

It is worth noting here, however, that I am not arguing for a simple obliteration of the boundaries between art and culture. I would even position myself against critics who argue that the conventional art-culture distinction has become obsolete in the wake of a global consumer culture in which both art and culture are subject to the dictates of popular markets. Against this leveling trend, I am, in fact, proposing that we assess both the cultural and the aesthetic functions of *all* arts and literatures in terms of their intervention in local and global cultures and their aesthetic practices. This assessment must also include the role of literatures and art in critically engaging other discourses and forms, including those of the mass media. It must also include their role in the emergence of new knowledges, including indigenous knowledges, new patterns of thought and emotion, and new forms and notions of subjectivity and community. Such an assessment can be made only on the basis of their functioning as literary or art objects and their choice of specific literary or artistic devices. The latter is, of course, impacted by the condition of their production and distribution, as well as by the available modes of information, communication, and experience. But this impact is never completely determined by cultural restrictions, just as the relationship between art and culture is never merely representational. Moving beyond thinking about this relationship in referential or self-referential terms allows one to shift critical attention to the role of literary and art objects in processes of cultural transference and in the emergence of new subjectivities, socialities, and relationalities, as well as new forms and patterns of thought, perception, and language.

Once again, Kafka's short piece may serve as an example to illustrate the larger implications of such a shift. If one insists that writing literature always also enfolds a writing culture, Kafka's very self-referentiality may be seen as working through the vicissitudes of culture and cultural knowledge. Do certain overly restrictive textualist critics not remain suspicious of culturalist readings precisely because, in reconnecting art with culture, these culturalist readings seem to establish a forbidden "reference," thus resisting the restrictive code of a binary opposition between art and culture? We need to understand that not every connection between literature and culture operates in referential terms. If one takes the anthropological turn in literary studies seriously, such simple epistemological literalism must appear at least as obsolete as the old art-culture binarism. Edward Said's notion of "contrapuntal readings,"[18] for example, insists that textual devices are never merely self-referential rhetorical play, and that we therefore need to scrutinize their own cultural implications. The "play of the text" is capable of reinterpreting cultural archives, thus working toward a *transformation* of cultural memory and the cultural unconscious. Literary and artistic forms play a crucial role in such reinterpretation, demonstrating that aesthetic practices must be seen as cultural utterances that carry cultural knowledge and facilitate the emergence of new cultural forms. If readings demonstrate the transcoding of culture, aesthetics, and cultural politics in *all* art objects, thus emphasizing the cultural function of artistic forms and devises, the vexed notion of aesthetics may finally be disconnected from its restrictive reduction to a bourgeois notion of the autonomous work of art that has overshadowed more productive debates for too long. Literary anthropology allows one to view the sphere of aesthetic production and experience in the context of other forms of production and reception within public culture. As a form of writing culture, literature is then placed alongside anthropological ethnography, historical narrative, or the discourses of sociology. All these forms of writing culture generate cultural knowledge, albeit in different ways. The type of knowledge they produce therefore needs to be addressed in its specificity. Rather than the mere transmission of cultural knowledge, literature, I argue, fulfills its most far-reaching function in facilitating the emergence of new cultural forms, experiences, and subjectivities.[19]

A perspective that focuses on the *generation* of cultural experience deeply affects the readings of specific literary texts because it situates them in both cultural and textual/aesthetic environments. Such contextualization is not necessarily bound to the historical context in which a text is written since some literature moves easily through cultures and historical time shifts. This mobility is precisely what makes literature interesting from an anthropological perspective. Yet no matter what cultural or historical contextualization a reader may choose, Kafka's "The Wish to Be a Red Indian"—to come back to our example—will appear as a cultural object that distinguishes itself by its aesthetic and literary devices. The same is true, however, not only for modernist experimental literatures such as Kafka's but also for indigenous and Third World literatures. As an example let us consider a story such as "Yellow Woman,"[20] by Laguna author Leslie Marmon Silko—a text that explores from within the indigenous oral tradition the fascination with and political use of an exotic encounter with an Other. Silko provides a good counterpart to Kafka because, like Kafka, she also recalls, and ironically quotes, Western primitivism. "Yellow Woman" tells the story of a Laguna Pueblo woman's mysterious encounter with a stranger in the desert. Posing as a ka'tsina spirit, the stranger manages to seduce her by using the very Yellow Woman stories about ka'tsinas that also define the cultural memory of her own community. Silko's text plays with the multiple coding of action and speech and the respective openness and ambiguity of possible references. The stranger's ambiguous double coding as a traditional ka'tsina and a Navajo horse thief who impersonates a ka'tsina plays out a complicated tension between traditionalism and modernism in contemporary indigenous cultures. The stranger's role as a "story thief" also introduces a textual self-reflexivity, exposing the dynamic of desire and seduction in the cultural appropriation of stories. Using his cultural knowledge of Laguna Pueblo stories, the Navajo stranger ironically impersonates the traditional ka'tsina who seduces Yellow Woman. He is aware that the woman can enter the play of seduction only if it is enacted within the traditional frame of the familiar seduction stories. A tacit knowledge about the stealing of stories thus allows both protagonists to engage in an illicit cross-cultural romance. The Navajo horse thief, we could argue, uses the traditional stories to prepare a ground on which the Laguna woman can meet him and enter his scheme of seduction. Fully aware of his scheme, the Laguna woman in turn plays along, thus allowing the satisfaction of her own desire for a sexual encounter with the stranger.

Upon her return to her own community, she needs to decide on her own story. Wavering between two readings of the Yellow Woman stories—one that follows the traditional story and one that partakes in the threatening modern disenchantment of her communal world— the woman opts for telling the modern version, guarding her tacit knowledge of the other story she enacted with the stranger as a secret. "I decided to tell them that some Navajo kidnapped me, but I was sorry that Old Grandpa wasn't alive to hear my story because it was the Yellow Woman stories he liked to tell best."[21]

Like Kafka, Silko thus confronts her readers with a story that works with a prominent figure of the cultural imaginary. The "story within the story"—that is, the traditional Yellow Woman story within its ironic modern appropriation—adds a self-reflexive dimension to the text that highlights the cultural function of storytelling, its ambiguities, and its possible modes of appropriation. Like Kafka, Silko uses an image of unrestrained motion in order to stage an imaginary encounter across cultures. The story begins with a fragment from the cultural archive of the Yellow Woman stories:

WHAT WHIRLWIND MAN TOLD KOCHININAKO, YELLOW WOMAN

I myself belong to the wind
and so it is we will travel swiftly
this whole world
with dust and with windstorms.[22]

If we recall the vision of unrestrained movement in Kafka's text we can detect a resonance with this fragment from Silko's "Yellow Woman" insofar as it also envisions a natural movement unrestrained by territorial boundaries or cultural regulation. Kafka and Silko thus both use a process of deterritorialization and mobilization of culture in featuring their imaginary cultural encounters. From this perspective, their stories may appear as "imaginary ethnographies" that mediate cultural knowledge through a fantasized, if not phantasmatic, desire for the Other.

Literary language or "literariness" as the aesthetic medium through which this knowledge is transmitted is, of course, itself embedded in diverse collective practices of storytelling and writing. At the same time, it bears the distinct signature of an individual storyteller or author. In the conventional art-culture system, Kafka's text would have been received as a modernist work of art, whereas Silko's text would have been allegorized as emblematic of Native American cultures of storytelling. Authors such as Silko, Gerald Vizenor, Maxine Hong Kingston, and others rightly oppose such a reductive classification of indigenous or ethnic literatures. Without denying their cultural affiliation, these authors insist that they simultaneously participate in a global context of inter- and transcultural literary production. Reducing ethnic or Third World literatures to their cultural intervention amounts to their imprisonment in an identity politics that many of the authors vehemently resist.[23] Ironically, such classification operates within the cultural legacy of the very primitivism that both Kafka and Silko expose as a mode of cultural appropriation and translation.

Another feature links the two texts in their figuration of cross-cultural encounters: the operation of transference and desire. At stake in both Kafka and Silko are not only the "translatability of cultures" but also the desire for the Other, that is, the dynamic of cultural transference. Cultural translation is, in fact, often profoundly shaped, if not marred, by the operation of desire. But a desire projected onto a cultural Other can, as Kafka's piece demonstrates, also operate as a tacit critique of one's own culture, or, inversely, the stories that figure such desire can be, as Silko's "Yellow Woman" shows, used to transfer it to and enact it in contemporary contexts. What then is the role of desire in the literary translation of and encounter between cultures? And what is the status of translation and the translatability of cultures in literary texts as compared with that in anthropological ethnographies? As Talal Asad reminds us, in anthropology the concept of cultural translation emerged only in the 1950s.[24] In literary studies, by contrast, the "translatability of cultures" has been a central concern ever since, in "The Task of the Translator,"[25] Walter Benjamin insisted on the writer's role as a translator of culture. Vincent Crapanzano points to a crucial distinction between the different tasks of the translator and the ethnographer: "Like translation, ethnography is also a somewhat provisional way of coming to terms with the foreignness of languages — of cultures and societies. The ethnographer does not, however, translate texts the way the translator does. He must first produce them."[26] Like anthropologists, literary authors too need to produce the texts that one can, metaphorically, consider as translations of culture. It seems, however, that a different notion of translation of culture is at stake in the case of a writer and an ethnographer proper. The difference lies, as I have been trying to show with the examples of the two short texts by Kafka and Silko, in the status and the use of the imaginary and of cultural transference.

Mediated by literary texts, cultural contact is always already subjectively overdetermined, which implies that in literary "translation" of cultural knowledge and experience, transference plays a fundamental role. I deliberately use this term in the psychoanalytic sense because literature is concerned not only with the materiality of culture, or with culture as a social and economic formation, but also, and often predominately, with the fantasies and phantasms that aggregate around cultures and form the cultural unconscious. Literature thus not only foregrounds the figuration of cultural transference but also functions itself as a medium that facilitates such transference. While the fact that cultural contact pervaded by transference presents itself as a dilemma, if not an embarrassment, for ethnography, literature often uses cultural projection and transference in order to perform the very role that Said's notion of "contrapuntal readings" highlights, namely to reinterpret the cultural archive and memory. I would add that literary transference also transforms the cultural unconscious. The shift from perceiving the relationship between art and culture in representational or referential terms to casting it in terms of emergence and cultural transference thus also expands the scope of art's cultural function beyond a concept of information and knowledge.

As N. Katherine Hayles has shown, Gregory Bateson, in his move away from a realist epistemology, argues that "the internal world of subjective experience is a metaphor of the external world."[27] Literature, one could say, fulfills one of its cultural functions in creating or transforming internal worlds by facilitating such metaphors. If literature has traditionally mediated what we used to call inner experience, contemporary literatures operating in a global literary context and marked by inter-, cross-, and transcultural reflections also mediate the highly subjective experiences of cultures and cultural contact. Such literatures not only engage but also intervene in the vicissitudes of cultural transference. If anthropologists must attempt to account for the dilemma of transference, trying to reduce it to a minimum, cultural transference thus assumes a quite different function in literature. The latter may indeed focus on highlighting the cultural "baggage" we import when we encounter a foreign culture. Walter Abish, for example, writes imaginary ethnographies about countries that he claims he never visited and therefore knows only through the discursive mediation of modern media. His novel *How German Is It?*[28] is set in an imaginary German town, constructed with images and stereotypes about Germany Abish picked up from American popular culture, history books, newspapers, and films. As a purely imaginary tourist who traverses only texts and cultural objects, Abish also suggests that in today's global world it is impossible to approach a culture without bringing along an abundance of prefabricated images. Seen in this way, a paradoxical requirement for a less-imaginary cultural contact would be an exercise in forgetting: we need to learn how to forget our imaginary Germany, Spain, America, or Africa in order to be able to see these foreign cultures both on their own terms and in their foreignness. Such "forgetting" would indeed be similar to a process of transference that uses projections in order to loosen their anchorage in the unconscious—a process that can be seen as an "unlearning." Certain self-reflexive literary texts may facilitate such a practice of "forgetting" either by exposing, like Abish, familiar stereotypes or by choosing a literary form that, like Kafka's, foregrounds their own otherness. Abish's *Alphabetical Africa*,[29] moreover, plays with the idea of the arbitrariness of the referential systems used to approach a foreign culture. The alphabet as a frame for both selective orientation and aesthetic constraint seems not more or less arbitrary than, for example, an atlas, a history book, or an ethnographic narrative. We always approach a culture with certain restrictions, Abish seems to suggest, and the more conscious we are in our choice of restrictions, the higher the mobility we gain in encountering a foreign culture. Paradoxically, literature may use formal restrictions to address the ambiguities of desire and repression commonly encountered in dealing with other cultures.

The dynamic of restriction and mobility thus marks not only the formation of cultural boundaries but also the modalities of cultural contact. Literature may assume a crucial role in the complex processes of cultural negotiation in which boundaries are continually traversed, abolished, and redrawn in new ways. Literature opens up a "transitional space"[30] whose function consists in simulating cultural contact in an imaginary mode and in thus intervening in the politics of representation and self-representation of cultures and their experience of an Other. Homi Bhabha, for example, argues that a Third World literature cannot be grasped exclusively from either the perspective of the representatives of these literatures or from that of Western literatures.[31] A "space between" or a "third language" is needed, Bhabha insists, for a fuller understanding and mediation of the contact and conflict between the two traditionally separate literatures. According to Bhabha, it is in this "space between" that new positions and traversals of the boundaries of culture occur. As Lévi-Strauss argues in "Race and Culture,"[32] cultures cannot exist without boundaries and restrictions. If the latter, however, stifle cultural mobility, they lead to monadic enclosures, cultural indifference, or hegemonic assertion of boundaries, thus fostering respective regimes of exclusion and inclusion. Cultures therefore need to provide special spaces for the negotiation of boundaries necessary to maintain vital cultural mobility. Literature and the arts can fulfill their most urgent function in providing such a space within the larger sphere of public culture.

If I insist that literature plays such a crucial role as a mediator of cultural contact, it is because, among other reasons, in the transitional cultural space of literature the imaginary comes into play with all its phantasms, projections, and transferences. In order to account for these rather idiosyncratic processes, the paradigms of "culture as text" and "culture as translation" must be expanded to include a paradigm of "culture as transference." It is not only reading and translation that are at stake in the encounter between cultures but also a working through of unconscious transference. Such a working through may develop in the transitional space of literature or the arts. In this space we can encounter and transform fantasies or phantasms such as the wish to become an Indian as well as their inverse — the colonial paranoia that figures the Indian as a "savage brute" that Melville worked through in "The Metaphysics of Indian-Hating."[33]

Cultural transference always presupposes a double movement: on the one hand, the translation and transference that occurs in the space between one's own and another culture, and, on the other, the translation of cultural experience into inner experience. Culture and cultural contact are in this respect irreducibly intertwined with subjectivity because the subject marks its boundaries toward the outside as well as the inside. Both the concrete cultural encounter and its translation into "inner experience" are, of course, culturally coded and mediated by the discursive systems, regimes, and codes of the symbolic order. The cultural imaginary informs not only encounters and translations between cultures but also the ambivalences, risks, and vicissitudes of a cross-cultural traffic of desire. Increasing movements of globalization and migration have made cross-, trans-, and intercultural negotiations a matter of daily intercultural encounters. This alone is a reason why forms and institutions of mediation such as literature and the arts retain their relevance—if only because they often reflect and thereby transform the subliminal, often unconscious, processes of cultural transference. In this process, literature contributes in a significant way to cultural mobility, facilitating the emergence of new flows of energy, new ways of being in the world, or new forms of language, subjectivity, and life.

Part II

Cannibals, Children, and Aliens

4 The Melancholic Cannibal
Juan José Saer's *The Witness* and
Marianne Wiggins's *John Dollar*

We never know when we might be born; the idea that we are born when
we are delivered from our mothers is pure convention. Many die without
ever being born; some are born, but only just, others badly, like aborted
babies.[1]
—Juan José Saer, *The Witness*

"My Story Can Mean Many Things":
Juan José Saer's Ontology of Cannibalism

In his uncompromising turn against Enlightenment notions of civilization,
self and other, rationality and desire, Freud returned to us the darkest icon of
the Enlightenment imaginary: the cannibal. Cannibalism serves in Freud's
metapsychology as a core trope that organizes the dynamic between self and
other, the vicissitudes of love, and the failures of mourning. Moreover, in *Totem and Taboo*, Freud suggests that eating the father is the founding act that
initiates the civilizing process. In Freud's imaginary archaic organization of
kinship, a horde of brothers becomes envious of the father's primary claim
on the available women. They band together, kill the father, devour him in a
ritual feast, and set out to enjoy his mates. Soon, however, they are overcome
by guilt and mourning. Forsaking the prize of patricide, they renounce their
claim on the father's women and invent the incest taboo in order to alleviate their guilt. The father, Freud concludes, thus becomes more powerful in
death than he could ever have been in life, because the sons now enact his
internalized prohibition as the primary law that marks their culture.

While Freud tells his myth of origins in a strikingly literal fashion, its
effects on the cultural imaginary operate metaphorically in providing a

narrative that facilitates a pervasive rhetorical transcoding of the cultural and the psychological. The myth combines not only the very raw materials but also the building blocks that, for Freud, underlie the construction of cultures and psyches alike. The myth of the horde of brothers tells of the vicissitudes of power, the intricacies of law, the entanglements of desire and prohibition, and, most prominently, the phantasm of cannibalistic incorporation. While in Freud's myth the cultural and the psychological are not yet differentiated, we can already see that the basic dynamic identified here, as well as its structures and operations, will persist through a later differentiation of culture and psyche.

It is this transcoding of the cultural and the psychological in the dynamic of incorporation that I want to explore further. Anchoring my reflections on mortality, melancholia, and incorporation in the figure of the cannibal is no arbitrary choice. I agree with Freud, and more recently Derrida,[2] that issues of cannibalism pertain to the very core of any conceivable ethics of otherness. Both culturally and psychologically, the cannibal operates as the phantasm of incorporation par excellence. Its prominence in the early travel narratives that celebrate the discovery of the New World resonates not only with the fear of being devoured but also with the insatiable desire for incorporation that fed the voracious energies of the colonial enterprise. It is important to understand that this highly ambivalent obsession with incorporation functions prior to, and ultimately regardless of, the vexed question of the historical reality of cannibalism. Concomitantly, the prominence of phantasms of incorporation in children's fairy tales and fantasies testifies to its psychological power, especially during an early oral phase in which the infant's mother is experienced primarily as a nourishing breast, and its entire small world is taken in and tasted. We could even say that *reality tasting* precedes *reality testing*,[3] just as incorporation precedes differentiation proper.

These opening remarks indicate that I am less concerned with historical cannibalism than with refigurations of the cannibal in the cultural imaginary. Approximately from the late nineteenth century on, the figure of the cannibal appears as a trope of psychic incorporation. In order to unfold the cultural implications of this rhetorical use of the figure of the cannibal, I trace the notion of psychic cannibalism from its emergence in the colonial imaginary to its recent return in postcolonial literature and theory. "What has the cannibal to say to us now?" asks Frank Lestringant in *Cannibals*.[4] I address this question by looking at how the figure of the cannibal shapes the cultural imaginary, and the stories we tell to organize and comprehend psychic life. "For the

Cannibals did really exist, and have never ceased to speak to us,"[5] Lestringant argues, challenging the facile reductionism of those who simply deny cultural anthropophagy. The very modes in which the cannibal speaks to us requires, I suggest with Derrida, a radical rethinking of our ethics of otherness.

I anchor my reflections in two literary texts, Juan José Saer's *The Witness* and Marianne Wiggins's *John Dollar*. Revisiting the figure of the cannibal in the colonial imaginary, both texts foreground melancholia as a cultural and psychic symptom based on a particular failure of mourning—a disturbance that results in the incorporation and encryptment of a lost object. Finally, both texts unfold these issues by tracing at the heart of narratives and discourses on cannibalism a pervasive transcoding of the cultural and the psychological. In highlighting cannibalism's intimate tie to melancholia, Saer and Wiggins also introduce a particular cultural relationship to separation, loss, and mortality.

Arguing that literature functions as a "speculative anthropology," Saer unfolds his philosophical reflections on cannibalism in the form of a fictional text. Published in 1983, *The Witness* returns to the figure of the cannibal at a time that, as Laura García-Moreno has pointed out, "coincides with the end of what many consider as the most brutal episode in modern Argentine history."[6] It is the time of disappearances, a time in which an innumerable amount of people are kidnapped and disappear without a trace. It is a time in which the mourning of lost ones is foreclosed because they have disappeared without leaving a trace. How does one mourn a disavowed history of loss? How does one write such a history? These are political questions that inform Saer's text without ever being posed explicitly.

Saer's text is a deeply melancholic philosophical meditation. He chooses a narrator who, after having lived for ten years among cannibals—the *colastiné*, an imaginary Indian tribe from the Amazonian rain forest—returns to his own civilization and, without intending to, becomes complicit in the tribe's genocide. After a long period of depression, he tries to fulfill the role the *colastiné* had assigned to him, namely to bear witness to their culture. Trying to write their imagined ontology, he becomes an ethnographer of sorts, albeit one who not only testifies to the customs of an indigenous tribe but also questions the accuracy of his account and exposes his inability to distinguish between reality and speculation, memory, and fantasy. His account thus also reveals the intricate links of anthropological narratives and, more specifically, cannibal tales to the colonial imaginary. The reader then encounters the indigenous cannibalistic culture through the multiply refracted lens of an outsider's fictional testimony.

The Indians' desire, if not need, for differentiation forms the core of the narrator's imagined ontology. Differentiation, the text seems to suggest, is the precondition of psychological birth. As Saer states in the passage I chose as an epigraph to this chapter, "Many die without ever being born; some are born, but only just, others badly, like aborted babies." In order to be fully born, the text suggests, we must not only be able to distinguish between self and other but also develop an ethics of otherness that regulates the boundaries between the two. This seems to be true for individuals as well as cultures. Saer casts cannibalism as a transitional practice of a culture caught up in the vicissitudes of differentiation. The *colastiné* use cannibalism as a practice that enables them to transform the outside into an inside (incorporation) and, vice versa, the inside into an outside (subsequent elimination). This process, however, can at best create only a fragile ontological security, because it requires a renewal whenever the boundaries between inside and outside threaten to become rigid. Without a more stable differentiation, on the other hand, there can be neither a sense of culture nor one of self. Cultures and selves need to acquire a certain externality, an outside perspective, but such externality comes with the imperative of an ethics of otherness. In the *colastiné*'s culture, the sense of externality and otherness is mediated through cannibalism. As long as they had no sense of an outside, the narrator speculates, they simply ate one another. Only when they invented a taboo that prohibited them from eating one another could they form a sense of an outside. The narrator leaves open the question of what might have generated the need to create the taboo. Once it was established, however, the world became divided into insiders who could not be eaten and outsiders who could be eaten. This taboo, in other words, operates with a displacement of cannibalistic desire from insiders to outsiders. The narrator then speculates that with this division between inside and outside, another need emerged, namely the need to be mirrored from outside: "Their principal problem was the outer world. They could not, as they might have wished, see themselves from the outside. On the other hand, the impression they made on me, a stranger from the far horizon, was precisely their externality."[7] Only those mirrored from outside are able to gain the differentiation necessary for the formation of a sense of culture. In an almost Lacanian move, Saer postulates the need for a cultural mirror phase.[8] The *colastiné* thus faced the dilemma that those outsiders who were eaten could not fulfill the function of mirroring them. This is why they needed to keep one of their captives alive as a witness.

Initially, the narrator defines the human through the possession of self-consciousness and the constitution of an outer world. He arrived in the New World as a fifteen-year-old orphan, hired on a ship, bound to conquer new territories. He was part of the colonial enterprise, part of what turned out to be a genocidal mission. When the *colastiné* attack, kill, and devour his comrades in an orgiastic feast, they select him to be kept alive as a witness. They adopt him into their tribe until they send him back ten years later, all the time anxious to maintain his status as a stranger who perceives their life and culture from the outside. After the *colastiné* put him on a boat and send him back to the "civilized world," he arrives at a colonial settlement in the island's vicinity. When he tells his story, the narrator betrays the Indians' geographical location, whereupon the soldiers set out to exterminate the tribe. In his old age, the narrator begins to write his reflections on the life and the ontology of the *colastiné*. By then his vision of the human condition has changed:

> For me the Indians were the only men on this earth, and . . . since the day they had sent me back, with the exception of Father Quesada I had met only strange, problematic beings whom only custom or convention dignified with the name of "man."[9]

We may easily trace in the narrator's reflections the legacy of visions of the noble savage. Indeed, Saer freely draws on philosophical intertexts ranging from Herodotus, Montaigne, Jean de Léry, Voltaire, and Rousseau to Freud, Lacan, and Lévi-Strauss, as well as on literary intertexts ranging from Cervantes to Defoe and Borges. In this vein, he casts his novel as a speculative anthropology that rethinks the human condition against a pervasive philosophical and literary legacy. If Saer puts cannibalism at the core of this exploration, it is because the figure of the cannibal, more radically than any other figure in the cultural imaginary, embodies the dynamic of a differentiation of inside and outside, self and other. A transitional figure, the cannibal inhabits the boundary of externality and the space where an outside world is constructed.

In "Des cannibales," Montaigne reminds his readers of the Greek use of the word "barbarian" for all foreigners, including those of the Western world. After the discovery of the New World, however, the term becomes restricted to the New World's indigenous peoples.[10] Among the "barbarians," it is the cannibal who, in travel literature and chronicles, most incites a vision of the foreign as wild and uncivilized. Challenging such reports, Montaigne's essay becomes the foil for Saer's postcolonial response. The very figure of the narrator is cast after the "witness" whom Montaigne mentions at the beginning of his essay: "I had with me for a long time a man who had lived for ten or twelve years in that other world which has been discovered in our century."[11] Like Montaigne's witness, the narrator appears as simple and uneducated when the tribe chooses him as a witness—an ideal condition, according to Montaigne, for the ability to convey a genuine, that is, undistorted and unembellished testimony. Like Montaigne himself, the narrator comes to invert Western norms of distinguishing civilization from barbarism, with the added irony that, belonging to Western civilization, it takes him decades to grasp the sophistication of the *colastiné*'s indigenous ontology. Montaigne's polemical notion of barbarism as an effect of deviance from the laws of nature prepares the ground for his revaluation of cultural values and his distinction of natural culture and alienated civilization:

> Those people are wild, just as we call wild the fruits that Nature has produced by herself and in her normal course; whereas really it is those that we have changed artificially and led astray from the common order, that we should rather call wild.[12]

Montaigne of course uses the figure of the cannibal in order to advance his own political agenda. Pointedly, he contrasts the cannibal warriors' dispassionate ritualistic cannibalism with the cruelty of Europe's religious wars and colonial conquests that devour entire countries and cultures. The troping of colonialism as cultural cannibalism retains its central role in the cultural imaginary because the metaphor of "eating the other" is replete with cultural, political, ethical, and psychological determinations. As many critics have pointed out, even discourses that allegedly deal with historical manifestations of cannibalism as a socially significant act cannot avoid being inflected by the highly overdetermined cultural rhetoric of cannibalism.

Saer's *The Witness* uses the narrator's imagined ontology of cannibalism to merge history, culture, ethics, and psychology in a synthetic vision. The timeless oceanic infinity the crew confronts before arriving on the island induces in them a delirium that gradually dissolves the names and meanings of things. When the cannibals attack and slaughter his comrades, the narrator—then a young boy—perceives the events as a dream that happened to someone else. The "horde of naked dark-skinned men," and the heap made of the corpses of his comrades, seem to pertain to a different world. With the death of the crew, he says, "all certainty of a common experience was gone and I was left alone in the world."[13]

This isolation at the center of the world will mark him as an "eternal outsider"[14] among the *colastiné*, the one they have chosen to keep alive as their witness. They call him *def-ghi*—a primordial name, or *urwort*, with a whole sequence of metonymical meanings that designate things foreign, unfamiliar, or other:

> *Def-ghi* was what they called people absent or asleep, or people who were tactless, or visitors who outstayed their welcome; and *def-ghi* was the name they gave to a bird with a black beak and green and yellow plumage that they would sometimes tame and which made them laugh because it repeated certain words they taught it, as if it really had the gift of speech. *Def-ghi* was also the name given to certain objects the Indians put in the place of someone absent and which they used to represent the person at meetings. . . . *Def-ghi* was what they used for things reflected in the water; something that lasted a long time was *def-ghi*.[15]

The narrator speculates that they want him to "share some common essence with everything else that was *def-ghi*":[16]

> They wanted me to reflect like water the image they gave of themselves, to repeat their gestures and words, to represent them in their absence, and, when they returned me to my fellow creatures, they wanted me to be like the spy or scout who witnesses something that the rest of the tribe has not yet seen and retraces his steps and recounts it, meticulously.[17]

This desire of the Indians for a witness appears almost like an inversion of the *curiositas*[18] that propelled the institution of anthropology as an Enlightenment discipline. Unlike the colonial travelers, the *colastiné* seem to be aware that they need the stranger to supplement a lack caused by their inability to see themselves from the outside. The narrator's vision of the *colastiné* indeed suggests that, in order to realize itself, a culture needs to be mirrored in an outside. The Indians use him in this fashion as a *def-ghi*, who, like a bird that imitates a language without understanding it, mirrors them, helping them to differentiate between an inside and an outside and thus protecting them from sinking into the contingency of the material. It is through the mediation by his outside perspective that they are able to perceive their own rituals as meaningful.

Attributing to the Indians an ontological insecurity as their basic mode of existence around which they organize their entire culture, the narrator's vision could not contrast more sharply with the romantic primitivism that has marked anthropological constructions of indigenous cultures since the Enlightenment. According to the latter, indigenous tribes lead an Arcadian existence in primordial undifferentiation from their natural environment. The *colastiné*'s alternative ontology contrasts sharply with this primitivist myth of a harmonious and undifferentiated unity of human and nature. Lacking a sense of primordial belonging and duration, the *colastiné* in fact face the utter unreliability of their world. Even the permanence of things appears as foreign to them. "Things that last" are called by the same name as the stranger: *defghi*. Yet if the only things that are potentially reliable already appear as Other, there can be no ontological security.

If, as Jean-Jacques Simard[19] and others have argued, spontaneity, naturalness, timelessness, and primordiality are the most pervasive attributions Euro-Americans use to characterize Indians, then Saer's text strikes at the core of the colonial imaginary. The narrator describes the *colastiné*'s everyday life as so meticulously regulated that even the games of children lack spontaneity. The dreary daily routine is, in fact, broken only during the rare times when they practice their cannibalistic rituals. Yet whenever they follow their instincts without restraint, as in their cannibalistic and sexual orgies, they lose themselves completely, falling prey to morose acts of self-destruction that endanger their very lives. Timelessness fails to describe them because their very ontology reflects the transitory nature of things. This lack of duration marks their sense of the world so profoundly that they see the moon's eclipse as the ultimate proof of a merely transitory universe.

Even their cannibalism defies the notion of primordial undifferentiation. If there ever was a sense of primordial undifferentiation, it was not marked by blissful unity with nature but by a sense of "old, confused, rudimentary . . . nothingness."[20] According to the narrator, the Indians use their cannibalistic rituals to "return to an ancient experience beyond memory"[21] from a time when they "used to eat each other."[22] As an ancient experience beyond memory, the act of eating each other has left a mnemonic trace that marks the *colastiné*'s cultural unconscious. The creation myth that the narrator constructs around this assumption of a primordial cannibalism reads like a legend of the fall that separates the tribal community from the world. Renouncing eating one another becomes the primal act of differentiation: "They knew no other way of separating themselves from the world."[23] Yet the taboo placed on eating their own kin leaves them with an insatiable desire to return to an experience that lingers as an unthought collective knowledge,[24] a desire they try to satisfy in a cannibalism turned outward toward strangers they encounter on their voyages.

Saer bases the *colastiné's* imagined ontology on the assumption of an unconscious cultural knowledge that organizes cultural life with its desires and anxieties, its visions of the world, and its ethics of otherness. Clearly indebted to psychoanalytic theory, this ontology presupposes a dynamic concept of the unconscious that includes some of the major tenets of Freud's metapsychology such as repression, the return of the repressed, and repetition compulsion:

> Above all, their old, confused, rudimentary sense of nothingness which they brought with them from the past became their way of being. If it is true, as some people say, that we always try to repeat our early experiences and in some way succeed in so doing, the anxiety the Indians felt must have had its origins deep in the past, in the bitter aftertaste their desire still left them with even though the object of that desire had changed.[25]

The primary impulse that underlies their desire, however, is not to incorporate the foreign Other but "the more ancient, more deeply rooted desire to eat one another."[26] Saer's ontology thus presents an alternative creation myth to the one developed by Freud in *Totem and Taboo* and in *Civilization and Its Discontents*.[27] Like Freud, Saer presupposes that the cultural unconscious leaves deep imprints on cultures. An unthought knowledge motivates cultural achievements, nourishing them with the affective energies that ground desire while at the same time regulating it. But whereas Freud places at the center of this cultural unconscious a cannibalistic devouring of the father and a culture that tries to cope with this archaic crime, Saer foregrounds the creation of an outer world and an Other as the very condition of culture. This turn, in fact, presents an equivalent in cultural theory to the post-Freudian turn in psychoanalysis toward a focus on the pre-Oedipal early phases in infant development that deals with the differentiation of self and other—a phase that Margaret Mahler and others have identified as the infant's psychological birth.[28]

In Saer's text, tropes of psychological birth, in fact, mark the differentiation of outside and inside from the narrator's perspective:

We never know when we might be born; the idea that we are born when we are delivered from our mothers is pure convention. Many die without ever being born; some are born, but only just, others badly, like aborted babies. Some pass from one life to another through a succession of births and, if death did not come to interrupt them, would be capable, through endless rebirths, of running the gamut of all possible worlds, as if possessed by an inexhaustible talent for innocence and abandon.[29]

If psychological birth presupposes the creation of an outside and the differentiation of self and other, it also requires a mirroring that affirms one's boundaries. The narrator, an adolescent at the time, experiences his psychological birth among the Indians because his isolation as a stranger among them mirrors the existential loneliness of his childhood as an orphan. In imagining the *colastiné*'s ontology, the narrator assumes an isomorphism of sorts between psychological and cultural birth. Because cultures, like humans, have to be born through the creation of an outside, the *colastiné* need a stranger to mirror the boundaries of their own culture. This is why, in each of their cannibal raids, they spare one whom they keep as an internal stranger to witness their culture for a determinate period of time. Their behavior in front of this witness is highly performative, even playful. It is a staged form of cultural contact in which they invent themselves for a stranger, thus endowing their existence with a self-conscious, albeit imaginary, permanence and duration to counter their ever-changing and uncertain world.

Historically, Western theories that establish an isomorphism between psychological and cultural development have relied on assumptions of primordialism.[30] Saer's narrative invokes the tropes of primordialism, yet only to undermine them in subtle ways, thus challenging the legacy of Enlightenment anthropology. Saer's most central attack on primordialism is that on the underlying politics of emotion. Primordialism presupposes an affective inner core of the subject, a carrier of archaic instincts that are assumed to be culturally ubiquitous. Accordingly, indigenous cultures are assumed to have a collective core of primitive cultural instincts manifested in ritual ecstasies.[31] At first glance, the narrator's detailed accounts of the Indians' cannibalistic rites and orgiastic excesses invoke all the clichés of primordialism. A close reading, however, reveals that he in fact inverts its very premises. Rather than developing in an archaic, instinctual fashion, the *colastiné*'s emotions are regulated by a scrupulously conceived cultural regime of discipline. This regime determines not only the norms of correct behavior; it inscribes itself into the expression of corporeality and leaves its imprint on the most intimate spheres of affective life. The narrator characterizes the latter in terms of a self-imposed "moroseness,"[32] an aridity of the heart that virtually bars the Indians from the experience of pleasure. While the hypothesis of primordialism presupposes that ecstatic rituals release an explosion of archaic instincts and affects, Saer's narrator describes the *colastiné*'s cannibalistic and sexual excesses rather as a secondary implosion that temporarily suspends their overly rigid symbolic order.

What the narrator calls moroseness in fact carries all the traits of a deep existential melancholia. Their orgiastic excesses leave the participants in a melancholic depression that lasts until the next outbreak. Even the cannibalistic feast itself appears as an act of driven voraciousness, ultimately depriving them of its supposed pleasures — "as if for them, guilt, disguised as desire, were the concomitant of sin. As they ate, the gaiety of the morning began to give way to a thoughtful silence, to a morose melancholy."[33] In fact, the Indians need to make their ritualistic excesses unconscious in order to guarantee the division of their two modes of being. Their violently promiscuous and incestuous sexual orgies verge on a psychosis from which they reemerge, as if from a severe illness, without a trace of memory. Their bodies, however, carry the mnemonic traces of their outbursts not only as scars but also as more subliminal corporeal memories. It is this unthought knowledge that, from time to time, is forced to rearticulate itself, as if under an existential compulsion. In making the narrator attend their ecstatic rituals, they also choose him as a witness to whom they tacitly convey the unconscious knowledge that governs their culture. Ultimately, they assign him the role of testifying to the mutual dependence of the two modes of being that for them must remain exclusive.

The intimate tie between cannibalism and melancholia in the *colastiné*'s ontology is enforced in the narrator's effort to commemorate their vision of the world. When after decades of melancholic silence, the narrator begins his account of the experience among the tribe, he is also engaging in a belated mourning. Saer thus operates with a complicated transcoding of discourses that oscillates between cannibalism as a socially significant practice and a psychic mode of incorporation. In both cases, he identifies melancholia as the psychic equivalent of cannibalism. Indeed, in the *colastiné*'s ontology, cannibalism appears as overdetermined with psychic valence. It is the ancient guilt, beyond memory, of eating one another, and the insatiable desire left from this unthinkable experience that link the *colastiné*'s cannibalistic rituals to melancholia. And it is another guilt and desire for incorporation that haunts the narrator's melancholic narrative.

A paradoxical failure haunts the narrator's testimony. While he exposes in his narrative his own sense of failure of memory and representation, we can also trace a failure of mourning at the affective level. It is as if the ontological insecurity he accords to the *colastiné* has been transferred onto him, causing him to doubt not only his writing about them but also the very functions of memory as such:

> Indeed everything I think I know about them comes from uncertain signs, blurred memories and hypothetical interpretations, so that in a sense my story, drawn as it is from so many questionable sources, can mean many things, without any one meaning necessarily being the right one.[34]

What does Saer's speculative anthropology then convey to its readers, given the narrator's own admission of failure? Considering Saer's recourse to the psychoanalytic construction of a tie between cannibalism and melancholia requires one to understand the narrator's melancholia as a sign of failed mourning. And indeed, isn't the core of the narrator's report an event that is mentioned only in passing, which barely gains importance in the orchestration of his narrative but which nonetheless determines every one of his utterances? I am referring to the extermination of the Indians as a consequence of his testimony to the colonial governors. While the *colastiné* had kept him alive as their witness in order to bestow some permanence onto their fleeting existence, it is paradoxically his very testimony that precipitates their genocide. The narrator's lack of hesitation to disclose the Indians' location to the colonial officers and missionaries is striking. When upon his disclosure the soldiers immediately set out on an expedition, he observes the events with a composure that borders on passivity. Registering the officer's colonial megalomania, he seems simply to take the genocidal expedition for granted. Even when the corpses of his former companions—men, women, elders, and children—are drifting by their ship, the narrator refrains from any indication of emotional response. He equally fails to address it in his later recording of their history, despite the fact that he has undoubtedly become complicit in the tribe's extermination. Instead, he confronts his readers with a sharp narrative cut, continuing with his return to Europe and his gradual remembrance of his mother tongue.

One can hardly overlook a profound denial at work here, both in the reaction to the immediate event and in the composition of the report decades
later. Initially, the failure of mourning can be attributed to a traumatic re-
alization of the loss of the tribe, not only the narrator's but also the world's.
While he has no certainty of their complete extermination, the evidence that
his testimony has caused their destruction lies already in the Indians' floating
corpses. To the extent that we become attentive to the traumatic silences at
the core of the narrative, we realize not only that it is about the *colastiné*'s profoundly melancholic vision of the world but also that the very act of writing
about the tribe becomes an enactment of melancholia. How then does this
deeply melancholic narrative render trauma and loss, mourning and incorporation? And why does it foreclose grief, replacing it with a dark melancholy
that marks narration, imagery, and rhythm alike?

The narrator does speak of the deep depression that overwhelms him after
his return, reducing him to vegetate in apathy and dejection. Father Quesada, who oversees the narrator's education after his return from the *colastiné*,
speaks of a suffering in which the world, even in its humblest manifestations,
seems a scorched and deserted place."[35] The loss of the Indians has emptied
his entire world, depriving him of speech as much as of a sense of self and
world. More than a mere social death, he experiences a death of the soul.
Even after he emerges from his catatonic state, this melancholy persists as the
core mood of his existence. Futile attempts to disperse it into an active life of
pretense leave him with a shameful sense that he has betrayed the Indians all
over again. Joining a theater group where he performs his captivity among
the Indians, he succumbs to utter cynicism, feeding an audience hungry for
primitivism with fake stories of cannibalism and sexual orgies, thus misleading
them with blandishments of their own cultural imaginary. It takes decades of
betrayal and self-prostitution before he turns away in disgust, finally ready to
assume his role as a witness.

At a deeper level, his narrative is an exercise in belated mourning, an attempt to give back to the outside what had been lost inside him in melancholic encryptment. Perhaps unbeknownst to the narrator, it is his very melancholy that resonates with the melancholy he perceives in the Indians. This
resonance creates an emotional attunement with the *colastiné* that marks his
written testimony throughout, overriding his self-doubt and lapses of memory.
As if he had enclosed them in the crypt of his soul,[36] they seem to create this
melancholic mood from within him. His very self is being rewritten by the
colastiné from inside. Unable to mourn them, he has incorporated them in

the long periods of depression in a sublimated form of cannibalism that has turned them into a part of himself and him into a part of them. This melancholic incorporation of a lost object remains severed from consciousness, language, and representation. We now better understand the silences in the narrator's text as well as its mode of indirection. His very testimony constitutes itself around the question of how one can represent what is merely incorporated. In order to fulfill this task, Saer develops a technique to present his readers with a discourse that conveys more than its narrator is aware of.

The narrator never overcomes his melancholic severance of words and world,[37] a severance that inscribes itself into his actual narrative as an ontological insecurity. Like his melancholia, his ontological insecurity mirrors the Indians' world. This is perhaps why the most faithful aspect of his testimony consists less in its historical or ethnographic information than in the melancholic mood that marks its affective coloration, and in the ontological insecurity manifested in self-reflexivity and epistemological skepticism. The narrative's discursive testimony is thus doubled by the tacit testimony of its structural unconscious. The narrator, in other words, bears witness because the most intimate spheres of the incorporated Indian culture become exteriorized in the structures of his thought, and in the moods that carry his narrative.

We are thus presented with a narrative that enfolds a carefully crafted discourse from the crypt. To begin with, the surface narrative, the story proper, undermines the assumptions of primordialism that have marked anthropology since the Enlightenment. In addition, the narrator consistently questions the reliability of his own story with self-reflexive insertions of epistemological doubt, thus undermining the very premises of a consistent anthropological narrative. The only aspect of the narrative that escapes this skeptical self-scrutiny is the intensity of its melancholic mood. He practices a kind of devouring of the signifier—a *Diskursfresserei* (Görling)—that affects his own linguistic system of difference. Beyond all difference in language and signification, the narrator has turned into the very expression of the incorporated world of the *colastiné*. His claim that the Indians' main problem was their inability to create an outside is now true for his discourse as well. Despite all the distance he maintained as the "eternal outsider" among them, they now no longer form an outside for him. Incorporated, they occupy his inside, thus inscribing themselves into the very semiotic structures of his discourse. In light of these structures, the testimony as signification remains secondary.

This perspective allows one further to characterize the strange emptiness and silence at the core of the narrator's discourse. If melancholic encryptment is an attempt to fill the emptiness left by a lost object, the discourse from the crypt is an attempt to externalize the emptiness, making it symbolically accessible in a paradoxical figuration. In the discourse's melancholy, this emptiness becomes the object of a double transference from the narrator to the text and from the text to the reader. To the extent that we are responsive to this melancholy, it will be passed onto us in the act of reading. If in this oral world of incorporation and elimination the "empty mouth" is the first memory trace of a lost object,[38] language may indeed serve to sublimate this emptiness. But sublimation can succeed only if words fill the emptiness by performing the work of mourning. If they merely exoticize or fetishize the lost object, they will fail.

The narrator dedicates the last years of his life to this struggle for words that transcend the mere fetishization of the Indians as an exotic lost object. His task as witness thus merges with a struggle for the translatability of cultures. "The cannibalistic fantasy of colonial discourse devours the space of language that would facilitate a metaphorical articulation of lack,"[39] writes Reinhold Görling in "Universal Cannibalism." The narrator attempts to articulate such lack in the confessions of self-doubt and failure that lace his report. At the same time, he searches for a transitional speech able to locate itself in the space between cultures. Instead of creating the illusion of merely describing a foreign culture, such a transitional speech takes the dynamic of cultural contact and cultural translation itself as its object. Rather than evoking the illusion that we witness the culture of the Indians, the narrator thus makes us witness their absence, their unstable inscription, in his memory and imagination.

If within this inscription we also find the traces of their unconscious encryptment, the translatability of cultures Saer explores is inevitably bound to transference. Saer thus frames his figuration of the *colastiné*'s culture with the traces of a narrator's transference. The reader's imaginary contact with the *colastiné* is then filtered by a double transference. While Saer chooses a narrator whose transference colors his perception of the foreign culture, we as readers will color the reception of the text and hence our sense of the *colastiné* with our own transference. One could say, then, that *The Witness* facilitates an imaginary mode of cultural contact, which, beyond the translation of cultural knowledge, reflects the processes of transference that constitute such knowledge in the first place.

The transcoding of the cultural and the psychic or, in this case, of cannibalism in both a literal and metaphorical sense is crucial to this process because the transitional space between the narrator's culture and the culture of the Indians manifests itself as a space between body and language. The melancholic discourse of the narrator bears the traces of the body in the empty mouth. This perspective may finally illuminate why Saer defines literature as a speculative anthropology. Perhaps we need an imaginary literary ethnography in order to foreground the dynamic processes of exchange, transference, overdetermination, and transcoding that mark the writing of culture. "True knowledge is recognizing that we know only that which condescends to reveal itself to us,"[40] says Saer's narrator toward the end of his narrative. Foreign cultures reveal themselves in multiple forms, performances, and masquerades. What we can know about them, however, always bears the traces of our own transference. To realize this may be at least a first step toward a less cannibalistic ethics of otherness.

The Island of Outlawed Dreams: Cannibalism, Mourning, and Memory in Marianne Wiggins's *John Dollar*

> A person without passion owns a different kind of fear: a fear of emptiness, a length, a sentence.[41]
> —Marianne Wiggins, *John Dollar*

During the Enlightenment, narratives of being stranded on an uninhabited island commonly functioned as historical allegories bound up with the concerns of an emergent capitalist and colonialist society. Daniel Defoe's *Robinson Crusoe*, for example, incorporates the cultural values of the new prototype of *homo economicus*. In a similar vein, Ballantyne's *The Coral Island* (1857) casts a group of shipwrecked schoolboys as prototypes of imperial manhood. Traditionally, these fantasies map out an exclusively male space, reducing women—if they appear at all—to remnants of an old and all-but-forgotten world. Desire is, at least at the surface, sacrificed to a keen survival instinct, sublimated by a will to power and a ruthless civilizing drive that threatens to lapse at any time into a rigid regime of self-castigation or terror. Throughout the eighteenth century, these narratives commonly featured an ambiguous "happy end": a rescue that virtually erases decades of isolation in the protagonist's painless reabsorption into the civilized world. Highly ambivalent allegories of survival, however, these texts' overt celebrations of the triumph of civilization can barely conceal their deeper appeal to an exotic primitivism replete with fantasies of savagery and cannibalism. In this context, the figure of the cannibal serves as a veritable cultural phantasm to rationalize the abjection of indigenous people in the colonial imaginary.

Despite the highly phantasmatic overdetermination of the cannibal in the Enlightenment imaginary, the firm belief, at the time, in the historical existence of cannibalism was experienced as a material threat to colonial adventurers. In the postcolonial imaginary, by contrast, the cannibal has become mainly an allegorical figure, a cultural icon of the past. Surprisingly, however, in recent decades we have witnessed a veritable revival and flourishing of postcolonial and postmodern cannibal narratives, including rewritings of colonial tales of cannibal encounters, such as Juan José Saer's *The Witness* and Marianne Wiggins's *John Dollar*. This revival indicates that the cannibal has reemerged in today's cultural imaginary under new premises. While they continue to focus predominantly on a male space, contemporary texts foreground the terrors rather than the skills of survival and the disintegration of civilization and community rather than the conquest of wilderness. William Golding's *Lord of the Flies* has become canonical in marking this inversion of a colonial imaginary.

In 1989, Marianne Wiggins published *John Dollar*, an award-winning novel that intervenes in the genre's long-standing gender politics by rewriting *Lord of the Flies*, featuring a group of British schoolgirls as protagonists. Set in 1917 in Burma during British rule, the novel tells of an ill-fated expedition during which a group of English colonists and their children set out toward an uninhabited island they intend to claim and offer to King George as a birthday present. The girls are on a special ship, supervised by Charlotte Lewes, their teacher, and her lover, John Dollar, a sailor. After a cannibal raid on the expedition and a tsunami that smashes the ships, the girls find themselves alone on a deserted island. Initially assuming they are the sole survivors, they have already begun to form a survivalist community when they find John Dollar, the only male protagonist, paralyzed below the waist and thus symbolically emasculated. The novel's plot culminates in two cannibalistic scenes: when John Dollar and the girls discover the British ship that is supposed to rescue them, they witness an attack by cannibals during which, before the eyes of the girls, their own fathers are devoured in a cannibalistic meal. The whole drama on the island unfolds as an effect of this trauma, illustrating one of the main philosophical presuppositions in Wiggins's text, namely "the failure of community that comes with grief."[42] The second climax unfolds as a repetition, a restaging of the trauma. Two of the girls, Menaka and Gaby, discover that their companions Nolly and Amanda are engaged in nightly cannibalistic rituals during which they take advantage of John Dollar's paralysis to consume the flesh of his thighs, thus causing his slow and abject dying. The novel ends with an ellipsis that conceals yet another trauma—a mysterious murder that is invoked by implication at the very beginning but is then never mentioned again until the very end. In fact, one needs to have read the end in order even to understand the elusive reference to the murder at the story's opening. To enforce the narrative eclipse of this climactic event, Wiggins repeats the structure of the ellipsis when she returns to it at the end of the novel. In order to understand the ending of the narrative, one therefore needs a memory of its beginning in order to infer the details about the murder. This is why, when the book ends, one has to go back to its beginning in order to see what Menaka, then a girl, had refused to see at the time, namely the killing of Nolly and Amanda and the burial that she now remembers as an old woman:

> She and Charlotte had killed them, not Monkey so much, although Monkey had beaten their heads with a stone, after their hands had stopped moving. Then Charlotte and she had dragged their two bodies down to the sea for the vultures and the sharks. Then Charlotte had said, "*I want you to bury him.*" Charlotte was crazy by then.[43]

What is the desired effect of this elliptical allusion to a murder that the reader can comprehend only in retrospect by bringing the beginning and the end of the novel together? Wiggins certainly performs more than a mere exercise in taxing her readers' textual memory. At the beginning, the reader is left in the dark about what actually happened, witnessing only the flashbacks of Menaka's fragmented memory many decades after the occurrence of the trauma. *John Dollar* begins with the very ending of a story that happened sixty years ago, thus guiding the reader through the traumatic remainders, rather than the actual facts, of a murder that remains unexplained until the novel's ending loops back to its beginning. Its elusive quality notwithstanding, this memory loop perfectly orchestrates the introduction of its main themes: death, burial rites, and the practices of mourning, cannibalism, colonialism, and murder, language, and the translation of cultures. The opening scene thus emphasizes trauma while withholding its actual content until the end. In the structure of this ellipsis that restages the trauma and effacement of actual memory, the core events that bring closure to the shipwreck narrative remain in the silence of an empty space suspended between end and beginning. As readers, we are thus drawn into the effects of trauma and amnesia since, in its orchestration of narrative time, the narrative mimics the effacement of conscious memory as well as its unconscious effects.

The novel opens with a burial scene, featuring Menaka, or, as everybody calls her, Monkey, with the dead body of her former teacher Charlotte. It is Charlotte's outlawed burial that anticipates, in inverted chronology, another outlawed burial, that of John Dollar, that happened earlier but is not yet revealed to the reader. Thus opening with the effects of a traumatic event that is not unraveled until the very end, Wiggins sets up the framework for the narration to come from the distance of an old memory. We witness the story through a memory that is silenced and a voice that is muted by the effects of trauma. At the beginning, we see how Menaka tends with great tenderness to Charlotte's body. Only later do we learn that she is actually performing the last rituals to prepare her corpse for burial. Wiggins thus introduces mourning via a perspective that figures the body as if it were still alive, including Menaka's corporeal gestures of grief.

The old Indian descended first, leading the donkey on a tether; Charlotte rode across the donkey's back. Charlotte's hair had gone from gold to white when she was rescued from the island years ago, and it fell around her now, wild and full and loose.[44]

The tenderness and care Menaka displays in her ritual of preparing Charlotte's body for the burial recall loving gestures of mourning. Such gestures often accompany the process of a beginning psychic introjection of a lost love object. Yet Menaka's thoughts almost involuntarily link images of corpses with images of eating and cannibalism, especially when she portrays the culture of the English colonizer in cannibalistic terms. As if following a desire to deny the loss and devour the lost object, Menaka's inner monologue invokes cannibalism and its intimate relation to death, mourning, and burial.

As I have argued earlier, from a psychoanalytic perspective, in acts of failed mourning, the lost Other is incorporated and henceforth lives inside the self like a cannibal ghost, eating up the survivor's life energies from the inside, crushing the vital interest in the outside world. In melancholic withdrawal from the world, the mourner and her lost beloved are fused into a deadly union. A death-in-life scenario is created in which the incorporated lost object virtually consumes the survivor. Menaka's inner monologue, however, goes beyond the dynamics of a melancholic psychic incorporation, highlighting also the historical linkages of cannibalism to colonialism and its violent forms of cultural incorporation. In a similar vein, critics of colonialism suggest intricate links between colonialism and melancholia. Colonialism manifests itself through diverse forms of violent cultural incorporation. Often the colonial powers devour the resources of other cultures, only to return later and form a melancholic attachment to the "vanishing race" or the disappearing culture. The photos of Edward Curtis that staged the indigenous peoples of North America in traditional Native American garments are perhaps the most famous example of a melancholic reaction to colonial destruction.[45] More generally, there is an abject oscillation between voracious incorporation and aggressive elimination marking the relationship between colonizer and colonized. Wiggins's indigenous Burmese protagonist Menaka invokes this dynamic in her thoughts after Charlotte's death:

> The english would never fill rivers with corpses, he hides them instead in the ground. He eats with sharp knives. He chews with a knife and a fork. He buries his dead so the other white castes will not cook and eat them. Worms and maggots are better than the teeth of one's enemies, that's why the white caste is always at the table. He eats and he eats. He eats mountains and ore. He eats diamonds and rubies, blue sky. He eats cities, chews names. He eats people.[46]

More than simply inverting colonial fantasies about the natives as cannibals, this passage ironically reflects on the translation of cultures, or, more specifically, on the double standards of their translatability. Even the very translation of Menaka's proper name into Monkey resembles a cannibalistic practice, eating up the native's cultural identity along with her name—a practice that brings to the surface the very violence that the seemingly innocent word "translation" effaces. Menaka, however, has learned the art of cultural mimicry.[47] Defying the colonial rule that Charlotte cannot have a Christian burial without a proper birth certificate, Menaka, in an act of resistance through appropriation, performs the funeral rites according to her own translation of the colonizers' practices:

> The Indian knew a translation, though, too. She translated his laws into liquid, into the likely suspicion of outlawry, floating face-up on her being,

pretending a surface, a sea: she could bury, *o yes*. She had buried before.
She could translate while smiling, bow down and back up.[48]

In her funeral rites for Charlotte, Menaka tries to repeat the words she
vaguely remembers Charlotte using at John Dollar's funeral decades ago. Her
involuntary distortion of these words appears at first glance like a mere parody
of cultural translation, but in fact there is a more profound cultural transference at work since, rather than being reduced to signifiers emptied of sense,
the distorted words retain the original rhythm and affect and thus transmit the
appropriate meaning in the highly cathected formal repetition of the mourning rite:

Say after me: *Earth to earth ashes to ashes.*
—Ashes. Two ashes, Monkey had said.
Dust to dust.
—A Dust. Two Dusts.
As it was in the beginning is now and ever shall be world without end.
'Without end,' Monkey said.[49]

Although this cultural translation has emptied the words as signifiers, their
performative function as a ritual expression of mourning remains intact for
Menaka, even after decades. Throughout the novel, Wiggins uses performative speech acts to mark the relationship of language to mourning. Under the
impact of traumatic loss, language too loses its meaning, falling into either
melancholic silence or a ritual performance of primordial functions. Inconsolable grief transforms words into carriers of memories that invoke a symbolic community with the dead.

These highly lyrical rhythms of the novel's opening attune the reader to
a narrative that evokes the horror and abjection of a remote past from the
melancholic distance of a permanent, inconsolable grief. While distancing
from the immediate impact of the traumatic events, this emotional coloring
of melancholic beauty conveys rather their long-term psychic effects—their
imprint on a vision of the world. Choosing Leonardo da Vinci's *Notebooks* as
John Dollar's most prominent intertext, Wiggins highlights the force of vision
and perspective on the interior modeling of worlds and the composition of
texts. She figures closeness and distance between the characters by highlighting both their visual and psychic valences. Wiggins also plays with repetition

and resonance in order to convey a sense of the imprint of earlier experiences on the specific processing of trauma. In the story, the actual attack of the cannibals is foreshadowed by a mass slaughter of female turtles that came to bury their eggs on the beach. Mute witnesses to their male peers' slaughter of the turtles, the girls will later return to the same scene to witness the slaughter of their fathers. This first traumatic scene remains as an unspeakable, tacit knowledge that colors the girls' later vision. Repetitions also convey the sense of a permanence of certain patterns, a psychic thickness of structures of condensed experience.

Betraying a deep ambivalence of affect, acts of witnessing and voyeurism link the two scenes. The onlookers stare at the first scene without interfering:

> No one tried to stop it. Matlock didn't, nor Fitzgibbon, nor did John or Charlotte. . . . Charlotte in her terror thought, So this is how it happens, and she kept the girls behind her and away from it. She stood and watched John watch it. *Stop them, why aren't you stopping them?* she wondered.[50]

Voyeurism betrays the complicity of those who watch the horror with irresistible fascination. In this case, the forgetting of trauma is then also an erasure of one's own complicity. Another scene enforces the doubling of witnessing and voyeurism, a collective *Urszene* during which the girls spy on Charlotte and John Dollar when they make love. Transfixed in fascination and horror, the girls misread the scene of the sexual act, "mistaking the sad echo of extreme joy for a noise of an ungodly agony."[51]

These two scenes are followed by a reflection borrowed from *The Notebooks of Leonardo da Vinci* on the relationship of the eyes and soul. "The soul is content to stay imprisoned in the human body because thanks to our eyes we can see these things; for through the eyes all the various things of nature are represented to the soul."[52] More radical than the familiar trope of the eyes as mirror of the soul, the eyes here function as agents of the soul's formation. "Representation to the soul" does not refer to a perception of the outer world that mirrors the soul but rather to a processing of the external world according to internal perception; whatever can be perceived bears the imprints (*Prägungen*) left from former visions. In witnessing the slaughter of the turtles, Charlotte also "sees" complicity in a destructive lust, and in witnessing the ecstatic fulfillment of the sexual act, the girls "see" its "godless agony." It is this linkage of eye and soul in the girls' acts of witnessing and voyeurism that mediates their experience of orality (cannibalism) and sexuality (aggression). As the two most elementary expressions of corporeality, orality and sexuality in this scene appear under the sign of a profound ambivalence that marks all raw forms of mute fascination.

As the cannibalistic scenes demonstrate, in the highly oral world of the girls, orality and sexuality are not yet quite differentiated from each other. Eating the other is fascinating because it recalls an illicit act of love that devours the other and takes him inside one's body. The scene of the devouring of the fathers is introduced with John's plea to forsake vision: "Don't watch, for godsake, close your eyes, don't watch, the two of you, don't watch, don't watch."[53] John's knowledge that certain forbidden visions do not mold but dissolve the soul is lost because a child's fascination with a taboo is stronger. Mediated through the metonymic connection of the three scenes, in which the girls watch the slaughtering of the turtles, the passionate act of love they mistake for violence, and finally the devouring of their fathers, violence and sexuality become inextricably intertwined in voyeuristic pleasure. "*Shut your eyes. They couldn't. What girl could shut her eyes against a dragon.*"[54] Hence the girls become witnesses to the devouring of their own fathers. Their vision, however, derealizes the event, placing it at a safe distance of a theatrical performance in which the cannibals appear as "children" at play. Oversized puppets, the fathers are roasted on the stake, props in a fairy world:

> They watched their fathers writhe and pop and as they watched, the wind brought an aroma to them on the hill. Their eyes watered but they watched because they couldn't stop their eyes from watching—they didn't mean to watch but once it was begun it was a thing they couldn't stop. They couldn't make themselves believe that what they saw was true and so they kept on watching, waiting for a proof, a final stroke, a termination in the horror, something, anything, a moment to arrive to signify that all hope, every hope, had ended.[55]

This scene provides a perfect illustration of how the real becomes psychically derealized as an effect of traumatic experience. That the girls cannot bring themselves to believe in the reality of perception is only the beginning of a dissociation that aims at the symbolic transformation of a traumatic event. The unspeakable trauma is enforced by the fact that the ending of horror coincides with the ending of hope. Compulsively returning to a trauma rendered unconscious, the girls eventually re-create it in symbolic transformation. They begin to perform oral gestures that precisely repeat the eating of the fathers. But in these mimetic gestures, the girls also try to transform the cannibalistic act they witnessed into something less threatening. They fill their mouths with sand and, gathering the leftovers of the cannibalistic meal—indeed their fathers' bones—they transform them into religiously guarded sacred relics. At the limits of symbolization, however, they succumb to unspeakable grief:

> As they mass the bones they start to see that reconstruction is impossible, no daughter can rebuild a man . . . no resurrection is at hand, the act is final, they're alone. They mass all that they can find and wait for something to arise. When nothing does, their grief is such that it transcends the physical, becomes sublime. When there is nothing left to do within one's understanding of the world one does what can't be understood. On the sand, all over, up and down the beach, wherever they had squatted when their feast had ended, the other children left defecations, there were mounds of them, like offerings. Amanda is the first to understand their meaning. Falling with a cry onto her knees, she smears her face with some, her neck, her chest, she eats it. Immediately, elsewhere, Nolly does the same.[56]

Where understanding fails, actions are guided by unconscious knowledge, almost as if there were an archaic script of corporeal symbols to convey what is unthinkable.

Eating the feces left over by those they perceive as "other" children, the cannibals, the girls literally incorporate the digested remains of their fathers— remains that function, in fact, very much like Lacanian "remainders" in their relation to the death drive. The very act of this symbolic "eating of the father," however, releases them from the roles of helpless, passive victims of a traumatic experience. Now it is they who, in a cannibalistic meal, devour their fathers, albeit in digested form. Thus they become the active agents of a traumatic ritual. Once their meal is over, they smear their hair and paint their limbs and faces with the feces, until their whole bodies are covered with the corporeal eliminations that *contain* the fathers. This is nothing other than a collective incorporation of the fathers in which the literal becomes one with the figurative. With the digested fathers as a "second skin,"[57] they feel renewed, able now to collect their fathers' bones as amulets. Whatever is left over from their ritualistic meals, the girls amass into a totem. A circle in the sand is formed around the totem to mark what henceforth will remain taboo:

> Without speaking they withdraw from it, understanding it is never to be spoken of, never to be touched, the bones, never to be broken, that perimeter, its ultimate offense, obscenity, its inviolability. They are different now. Even those whose fathers were not massacred are different. They are silent, changed, contaminated, beyond grief, ecstatic.[58]

Ecstasy here means not only the obscene sacrality of the sister horde's totemic meal[59] but also the ecstasy of *being beside oneself*—the *loss of the soul* as an effect of the girls' secret complicity in the cannibalistic devouring of their fathers. While their victimization by an unspeakable catastrophe remains indisputable, their complicity tragically resides in the fact that the most abject horror coincides with their most illicit dream. Borrowing a phrase from Marco Polo's diaries, Wiggins appropriately calls their isolated space the Island of Our Outlawed Dreams.[60] Like the brother horde in Freud's *Totem and Taboo*, this *sister horde* devours their fathers too. But rather than desiring to incorporate the fathers' power, the sisters' incorporation enacts their unspeakable grief. Wiggins presents us here with a literalized image of the crypt, that is, the psychic crypt that buries a lost object within the soul. In the girls' fantasies, their fathers—that is, their *lost objects*—continue to live forever in incorporated form. Wiggins creates, in other words, a story that literalizes the image of the conditions of deep melancholy. *John Dollar* thus exposes the connection between cannibalism and melancholia in a story that illustrates the *working through* of a great loss through the girls' symbolic incorporation of their fathers.

In *The Shell and the Kernel*, Abraham and Torok distinguish between introjection and incorporation as two qualitatively different responses to a loss. Incorporation is based on an unconscious fantasy that denies loss. In contrast, introjection is a process during which the emptiness left by the loss is filled by giving memories and emotions a figurative shape and taking them inside the self. Acts of creation and communication that figure the loss thus perform the important task of mourning. In this process, speech acts are used to make up for and transform the absence of the object. Incorporation, by contrast, operates as a fantasy that introduces a lost object (or parts of it) inside one's body. The boundaries between the literal and the figurative are ambiguous in this process, because something is implemented *literally*, which has only *figurative* meaning. Abraham and Torok speak of "de-metaphorization," because the melancholic who incorporates a lost object takes literally what is meant figuratively:

> Incorporation is the refusal to reclaim as our own the part of ourselves that we placed into what we lost; incorporation is the refusal to acknowledge the full impact of the loss, a loss that, if recognized as such, would effectively transform us. In fine, incorporation is the refusal to introject the loss.[61]

It is because of this refusal to mourn that the loss becomes unspeakable:

> The words that cannot be uttered, the scenes that cannot be recalled, the tears that cannot be shed—everything will be swallowed along with the trauma that led to the loss. . . . The crypt also includes the actual or supposed traumas that made introjection impracticable. A whole world of unconscious fantasy is created, one that leads its own separate and concealed existence.[62]

There are also "false incorporations,"[63] in which the very loss of an object is denied. Often such denial is enacted in the form of an imaginary meal:

> Such a meal is reminiscent of the wake, which must have a similar purpose, namely the communion of the survivors through the partaking of food. The communion here means: instead of the deceased we are absorbing our mutual presence in the form of digestible food. We will bury the deceased in the ground rather than in ourselves. Necrophagia, always a collective practice, is also distinct from incorporation. . . . Eating the corpse results in the exorcism of the survivors' potential tendency for psychic incorporation after a death.[64]

In *John Dollar*, the girls' totemic meal appears as an unconscious act of necrophagia. When they are eating the remainders of their dead fathers, the girls perform all the elements of a necrophagic ritual. Eating the remainders of the cannibalistic meal symbolizes the impossibility of introjecting the loss of the fathers. The trauma has been so severe and the girls are too young to face a loss that moreover signifies the end of their hope of being rescued.

"Eating the father" seems to have become such a pervasive and psychically overdetermined fantasy for the girls that we encounter it in a whole sequence of enactments. The most chilling of them occurs when Nolly and Amanda engage in a monstrous repetition of the cannibal act, using John Dollar as a Christ figure whose body they sacrifice and take in during a sacred meal. Witnessing the original cannibalism, Nolly merges it in her fantasy with the Holy Sacrament. Thus literalizing the cannibalistic trope of the Eucharist, Wiggins uses the New Testament as an intertext to highlight how cultural and psychological imprints condense into a single structure. Quoting the litany of the Holy Sacrament, Nolly had already symbolically transformed the cannibalistic devouring of the fathers into a Satanic rite: "Take, eat; this is my body. . . . Woe to the inhabitors of the earth and of the sea! For the devil is come down into you because he knoweth that he has but a short time."[65] Tragically, John Dollar had nourished Nolly's religious obsession of being Satan's chosen disciple with an anecdote that it was the devil who had bitten his leg and threatened to eat him up.[66] Priestess and devil's servant in one, Nolly condenses religious ceremonies and Satanic rites, choosing John Dollar, the impotent father figure, as the object of her ritualistic sacrifice. In their nightly holy meal, Nolly and Amanda devour John Dollar's living body, cutting pieces out of his paralyzed leg. This travesty of the Holy Sacrament repeats the symbolic devouring of a father figure. Moreover, it carries a necrophagic resonance, because the girls eat the very part of John Dollar that is already symbolically dead. That they also take advantage of John's paralysis to manipulate his sexual organ shows the Oedipal eroticization of their cannibalistic desire. When they ritually wash and adorn him before blessing and eating his flesh, he figures both as a lover whom they offer to the devil and as a savior whom they sacrifice for mankind.

These abject nightly rituals take place with the tacit knowledge of the other girls, who find themselves unable to interfere. Their passivity repeats their reticence to act during both the slaughter of the turtles and the devouring of the fathers. Here too we encounter complicity, bespeaking the uncanny fascination with unspeakable horror as much as the insurmountable fear of the abject. Paralyzed in the face of horror, Menaka and Gaby remain passive until they realize that Nolly and Amanda are literally eating John to death. But at this point it is too late. Tragically, their discovery coincides with another discovery that could have turned the events around if it had come earlier. Menaka finds their teacher, Charlotte, who has survived inside the forest, blinded by the accident. When she brings Charlotte back to the other girls,

John's life is gone. The only act that remains, equally unspeakable, is the one that links beginning and end, the act that Monkey refuses to see: "A child and a woman, making their way on the sand toward the smoke on the hill, and they walk, Monkey sees, refusing to see what happened next: they walk and they walk and they walk and they walk and they walk, she believes."[67]

With these words the novel ends. If we recall its beginning, however, we know that the actual scene ends with Charlotte and Monkey killing the two girls, leaving their bodies for the vultures. The story has come full circle, then, with the novel's ending, emphasizing a "refusal to see." With one character initially blinded by the catastrophe and the other refusing to see her complicity in this final, vengeful murder, the last image focuses on the blinding force of trauma. Melancholic grief turns the eyes away from the world, recalling Menaka's story about the indigenous mourners who must bury the dead with their eyes facing down into the earth. They walk and they walk, the child and the woman, Menaka recalls. It is only when the child is an adult herself and buries the woman who walked with her that she could finally face what really happened. Only then can she look back and comprehend the story that needs to be told, the story of an illicit act of cannibalism, a horrendous wrongful death, and an act of revenge in which the child and the woman killed the two girls who murdered the woman's lover.

Tracing the intimate link between cannibalism, grief, and melancholia, this reading of John Dollar highlights a pervasive "transcoding"[68] between historical and psychological discourses of cannibalism. Cannibalism is figured in John Dollar as more than a mere cultural practice of cannibals proper. Wiggins emphasizes not only its prominence as a phantasm in the colonial imaginary but also its sublimation into the psychic disposition of melancholia and incorporation. The link between historical and psychic cannibalism is a particular ethics of relating to the other through incorporation. This ethics of eating or not eating the other lies at the core of today's critical interest in, and fascination with, the figure of the cannibal.

John Dollar uses the transcoding of the cultural and the psychological in narratives and discourses of cannibalism to reveal processes of continual exchange and mutual transformation that shape the fluid boundaries between culture and psyche. In their cannibalistic performance of mourning, for example, the girls immediately translate and transfer the foreign cultural practice of cannibalism according to their own psychic disposition. Similarly, Nolly's religious mania is based on a perverted appropriation of the cannibalistic trope of the Eucharist. Fantasies are highly pliable and mobile. They can be transferred onto other people, objects, or even entire cultures. In colonial fantasies, psychic material and dispositions are projected onto an imaginary Other. Fantasies can also be remodeled according to internal psychic needs. When Nolly, for example, inverts the story of the Eucharist for her own dark purposes, she turns Christ into a satanic figure. At stake is a complex process of exchange between the cultural and the psychological. This exchange determines the psychological underpinnings of colonial encounters. Just as the children had already internalized the structures of colonialism before their arrival on the island, they externalize them in building their failing community on the island. It doesn't take long before the girls exclude Menaka, the only girl of indigenous heritage, from their inner circle. Even renaming her Monkey follows the logic of colonial renamings. The "failure of community" Wiggins depicts in her story certainly comes with grief, but the forms of enacting the failure are modeled on the destructive patterns of colonial encounters. Wiggins establishes a psychohistorical link between grief as a psychic disposition that leads to the failure of community and colonialism as a cultural condition that destroys the very basis of operative communities. Melancholia is the disposition that facilitates this link, and *John Dollar* exposes melancholia as both a psychic and a cultural malaise.

Wiggins also deploys melancholia to inform the narrative energies and moods that carry her novel. *John Dollar* is a deeply melancholic narrative, poetic in its rhythms and imagery. The text performs a poetic sublimation of the grief and horror it depicts in its narrative. After all, the girls' grief is not simply the grief that comes with unbearable loss. It is a grief that needs to be suspended, because the loss is too horrific and traumatic to be processed. It is not only the horror of the events that exceeds the scale of bearable grief; it is also that the events operate at the level of an uncanny familiarity, tapping into a secret fascination—a wish even—too horrific ever to acknowledge consciously. It is the illicit wish to eat their own fathers that causes the girls' mouths to water. It is an unspeakable horror, in other words, that doesn't lend itself easily to sublimation but requires rather a sublime transposition.

Cannibalism as a literary topic seems to lend itself ideally to an aesthetic of the sublime able to address the abject horror of a foreign yet uncannily familiar practice. Wiggins sublimates this horror in the novel's lyrical language, its imagery, and its rhythms. Derived mainly from the intertextual use of Leonardo da Vinci's diaries, *John Dollar*, in fact, invokes an aesthetic of the beautiful to supplement the aesthetic of the sublime. Rather than relying on a classical notion of harmony, however, the beautiful in Wiggins's text emerges like the sublime from a transitional space where culture and psyche merge. "Beauty lasts. Its memory lasts. Beauty, in its moment, fixes time, halts rationality, stops thought, transforms, amends the heart, reverses. Its power is despotic, but its kingdom is not absolute," we read in a passage directly lifted from Leonardo da Vinci and reiterated as if to assert the returning rhythms of a psychic space: "Beauty lasts, the memory of beauty stays, a memory of beauty lingers, the law of nature, of perspective, of proportion incline toward the symmetry among extremes of one's existence, toward a harmony among one's keepsakes and one's relics."[69]

Thus the aesthetics of beauty merges with the aesthetics of the sublime, leaving its inscription on Wiggins's politics of textual memory. Horror and trauma lend themselves to dissociation, repression, displacement, and forgetting. An aesthetic of the sublime therefore resembles an aesthetics of loss based on incorporation or sublimation of lost objects. The aesthetic of the beautiful, by contrast, cathects the objects found in the world, including language, in order to reshape them, in a process of exchange between outer and inner vision, as *cultural objects*. This process engages culture and psyche in one. Aesthetic categories, such as perspective, proportion, symmetry, and harmony, acquire both cultural and psychological properties. For example, Oopi, one of the girls, prepares her own death by surrounding herself with beautiful objects and treasures, transitional objects that help her exit from this world because they have already become part of her. Different from the crypt with its incorporated objects, these transitional objects create a connection between the outer and the inner world and are therefore cultural objects in the full sense of the word.

Incorporating the sublime in an aesthetic of the beautiful, Wiggins uses the transitional space of cultural objects in a unique fashion that contains an implicit statement about the function of literature. Literature, the aesthetics of *John Dollar* suggests, creates a space for the exchange between culture and psyche in which cultural objects are processed internally and psychic objects are refashioned as cultural objects. Wiggins's highly rhythmical and lyrical language, imagery, and tropes always already transcode inner and outer worlds. The beauty of her poetic language invokes and contains the horror of the real without diminishing it, or letting it be forgotten. Perhaps this is why we experience, as a mood of the text, the very mourning that its characters are incapable of living. Performing a work of mourning, the text passes it on to its readers as an emotion that returns them to a history of loss and shame in which "eating the other"—in colonial or psychic incorporation—was not yet challenged on ethical grounds. That in this work of mourning the sublime and the beautiful coincide may well be *John Dollar*'s unique contribution to a postcolonial aesthetic. It may also be an indispensable asset for an imaginary ethnography of cannibalism written from a perspective that revisits the colonial imaginary from within an ongoing and necessarily conflict-ridden postcolonizing process.

5 War Children in a Global World

Richard Powers's *Operation Wandering Soul*

The perennial losers . . . in the aggressive restaging of the new world order were certain categories of "superfluous" people, among them periph-
eral peasants, indigenous peoples, and poor children. The dependent
and "supernumerary" child of the poor and marginalized populations of
the world has emerged as one of late capitalism's residual categories — its
quintessential nonproductive, "parasitical," Other.[1]
—Nancy Scheper-Hughes and Carolyn Sargent

The figure of the child has always been pivotal in cultural attempts to
define the boundaries of the human. If, as Nancy Scheper-Hughes and
Carolyn Sargent argue, late capitalism casts the child as parasitical Other,
this signals a growing tendency to reduce the definition of the human to economic production and productivity. But as Sharon Stephens argues in *Children and the Politics of Culture*, in the structuring of modernity, children also
function as "symbols of the future."[2] The following reading of Richard Powers's *Operation Wandering Soul*[3] focuses on the figure of the child, including
the child as a symbolic marker of the future of the human.

Operation Wandering Soul was published in 1993. Beginning with Neil
Postman's *The Disappearance of Childhood*,[4] first published in 1982, the 1980s
and 1990s saw a flood of publications on the crisis, endangerment, and disappearance of childhood. Postman's study was followed by such books as *The Rise
and Fall of Childhood* (1982), *Children Without Childhood* (1984), *Innocent
Victims* (1988), *Stolen Childhood* (1989), *Broken Promise* (1989), and finally
Children in Danger (1992).[5] In 1989, the United Nations ratified its Declara-
tion on the Rights of the Child, and since the 1990s a variety of conferences

on "children at risk" and "war children" have supplemented the pervasive cultural concern with the vanishing of childhood. Symptomatic of a more encompassing species anxiety in the face of precarious planetary survival, this cultural imaginary of disappearing children provides the backdrop for Richard Powers's "imaginary ethnography" of childhood in *Operation Wandering Soul*.

Powers constructs his narrative with a layering of stories and textual materials dating back to the Middle Ages. The novel's contemporary setting is Los Angeles, featuring a group of destitute children at the pediatric ward of a Watts hospital. In charge of their care, surgical resident Richard Kraft and his lover, therapist Linda Espera, unfold before the children's eyes the world's bleak history of childhood with a myriad of stories of migrant and disappearing children, including *The Pied Piper* and *Peter Pan*, the medieval Children's Crusade, the transport of children to Auschwitz, and finally the evacuation of the children during the Blitz in London. Their stories portray the fate of war children who perish under the never-ending transgenerational legacies of violence. The novel's apocalyptic ending stages a hallucinatory rescue mission in which a delusional Kraft escapes with the children from the hospital in an exodus designed to prefigure the dystopian vision of the final "departure of children from planet Earth."[6]

Operation Wandering Soul maps out a comprehensive global history of war children, supplementing and juxtaposing the stories from the early colonization of eastern Europe and the history of European wars with the children's and finally Kraft's personal stories and memories of the wars in Vietnam and Cambodia. The children in the ward collect this syncretistic mix of stories, old legends, historical narratives, diaries, and their own journals in pursuit of their dream to perform a theater play modeled on *The Pied Piper*.

Linking older genres of legends, fairy tales, and myths to newer genres of journalism and journal, Powers explores storytelling as the material basis of ethnographic fieldwork, casting *Operation Wandering Soul* as an imaginary ethnography:

> Journalism and journal . . . These two late-day narrative styles round out the brief but comprehensive sampler, the trading-card sets of story that Joy and her accomplices have been busy collecting. . . . Now they have them. She can return, like an ethnographer at the end of her field trip year. "Dear Kitty: I grow hopeful now; finally, everything will turn out for the good. Really, good!"[7]

This quote asserts ethnography's inflection by stories, be they the official stories told by public media or the confessional stories revealed in private journals. As an imaginary witness to the Holocaust, Kitty, the addressee of the quoted *Diary of Anne Frank*, introduces the novel's thematic core: the disappearance and genocide of children. The invocation of Kitty, the "secret pen pal that the little Frank girl created,"[8] highlights the role of imaginary witnesses in violent histories. Anne Frank, whose diary provides the most intimate witness account of a child during the Nazi persecution of Jews, figures as the allegorical Holocaust child who stands for a collective destiny.

Anne Frank's diary highlights the problem of the child's agency. Her statement "I grow hopeful now; finally, everything will turn out for the good" establishes a mood of resilience and survival in the face of persecution and genocide.[9] Powers creates a resonance between Anne Frank's resilient tone of voice in the diary and the hopeful voices of children in *Operation Wandering Soul's* apocalyptic narrative. Like Anne Frank, the novel's child protagonists cling to hope against all evidence to the contrary. Since we know of Anne Frank's murder in the camps, however, the hope and resilience of children are exposed in their fundamental precariousness. If we read Powers's figuration of a millennial disappearance of children as "ethnography of the future,"[10] Anne Frank's destiny casts a dark shadow over the novel's open ending.

A novel about the disappearance of children faces the challenge that, in the politics of representation, the figure of the child is always at risk of sentimentalizing appropriation. Traditionally, the child has been figured as an "internal other," metonymically linked to the primitive, the subaltern, the victim, the one outside the law, and even the animal. Aesthetically as well as morally, the pathos of victimized, abandoned, and dying children is vulnerable to sensationalism and is immensely commodifiable. Powers tries to meet this challenge with a persistent self-reflexive exploration of storytelling. Stories trigger and mirror other stories so that the pathos of individual and local stories is reflected, and to a certain extent deflected, in an ever more dense historical and geopolitical web in which the individual stories become concrete manifestations of Robert Coles's dictum that "a nation's politics becomes a child's everyday psychology."[11]

Powers's technique of layering narratives in order to enfold different historical times into a polytemporal memory suggests that no matter where we are located in today's world, contemporary imaginary ethnographies can no longer be thought of as merely local, nor can they eclipse the many histories of violence from which today's cultures have emerged. Stories drawn from centuries of violent world histories evoke a global vision of childhood under conditions of war. This technique combines individual and collective, actual and historical, local and global perspectives in a condensed narrative whose different frames are highly permeable, provisional, and overdetermined.

It is as if Powers reconstructed for his readers a collective multidirectional and polytemporal memory of childhood that engages the present through memories and stories of the past while simultaneously using the figure of the disappearing child to invoke a cultural imaginary of the future. Powers links the ethical imperative of "thinking the future"[12] to issues of cultural reproduction. Cultures reproduce themselves through future generations and therefore have a moral responsibility to safeguard the future. Children become a prime target of genocidal politics precisely because they embody the future. Powers, however, also aligns stories of genocide with other stories in which cultures sacrifice their own children in wars, and with stories in which children are neglected to the point of annihilation—a form of cultural suicide, which, the narrative suggests, is based on the lack, inability, or egotistic refusal to "think the future," if not on a more sinister drive toward self-destruction that encompasses the entire human species. The stories Powers assembles engage a long history of peoples whose lack of a global ethics that encompasses the survival of future generations has led to the abandonment of children.

Moving across varying scales and textures of time and space, *Operation Wandering Soul* challenges the conceptual separation of local and global ethnographic knowledges. Powers's imaginary ethnography of South Central Los Angeles transcends the local by emphasizing the dislocations of global capital flows, the intertwinement of local politics with global forces, and the impact of global warfare on child migration. Migratory movements of people, capital, information, and cultural objects turn the city into an ever-changing, ever-contested space in which languages and cultures compete with one another, generating both new, hybrid formations and entrenched segregations. More than mere rhetorical play, David Rieff's term "capital of the Third World"[13] reminds one that the majority of people in Los Angeles speak a foreign language, are subjected to an economy oriented toward the Pacific Rim rather than Europe, and belong to one of the many "foreign" cultures that evolve in both its segregated and mixed neighborhoods. Invoking the long and diverse history of mass migrations while re-creating old homes in miniature simulacra, the names of the sprawled-out centers of Angel City in the novel still bespeak the nostalgia for lost homelands—Little Tokyo, Little Weimar, Little Oaxaca, Little Ho Chi Minh City. When twelve-year-old refugee Joy finds a classical Sukhothai pavilion a dozen blocks away from her L.A. apartment, this temple—which otherwise would have seemed "as distant as the epic's monkey kingdom"[14]—becomes "her one touchstone in a landscape as arbitrary as the language she must use to make her way through it."[15]

In this ever-changing world, the play of similarities and differences follows new rules. Countries and histories fold into one another through hitherto unnoticed mnemonic resonances. Memory work becomes crucial in accounting for the impact of interlaced histories on cultural imaginaries and personal experiences alike. The decentered space of this contemporary city, which has learned to perceive itself as a Pacific Rim metropolis rather than a replica of Old World capitals, seems like a gigantic hologram, containing the whole world in each of its diverse parts. While otherness may surprise its inhabitants from anywhere, the utterly strange is, paradoxically, also the most familiar. Arbitrariness and bewilderment displace structure and pattern. "Bewilderment is always bilateral,"[16] we are told, tongue in cheek, especially for those exposed, like Joy, to the "enlightened pedagogy" of the L.A. school system. In the face of this bewilderment, the fascination of children with the strange becomes perhaps the most sustainable mode of inhabiting this global city.

Language, too, is approached as a play of similarity and difference, an encounter with migratory words seemingly without history or origin. A new ecology of words emerges in this "city of a thousand languages, half of them invented here,"[17] as the narrator remarks, a linguistic ecology in which each word is potentially able to connect with multiple environments of imported foreign languages, assuming ever new meanings with each new mutation:

To every relocation camp its own transitory lingua franca, built up by the accidents of mass migration. . . . Words, she [Joy] has learned, in all manner of reeducation programs along her route, have no origin and no end. They are themselves the touring urgency they try to describe. *Barrio*, where she now lives, comes from Spanish, from Arabic, from the idea of the idea of open country. No word could be more English now, more *American*, although all the open country here has been closed for lifetimes.[18]

Operation Wandering Soul mimics this history of migration in the structure of its intersecting stories, which traverse centuries, countries and continents, folklores and legends, always looping back through multiple narrative crossings to medieval Europe. The heart of the text's ur-narrative is the *Rattenfän-*

ger von Hameln, or, in its Americanized version, *The Pied Piper*. While the cast of main characters—Kraft, Espera, and the children from their ward—provide a central narrative, the latter meanders through a labyrinth of mirror images drawn from perennial favorites of children's literature such as *Peter Pan, Winnie-the-Pooh, The Wizard of Oz, Alice in Wonderland, The Jungle Book, The Secret Garden, Raggedy Ann and Andy, Pinocchio*, and *The Diary of Anne Frank*. Three tales in particular—*The Pied Piper*, the medieval Children's Crusade, and Kraft's childhood story—replicate the main plot structure, figuring doubles of the protagonists from Carver's hospital in ever new embodiments of migrant stories.

As if to mimic in bitter irony the allegorical names of their migrant forebears—the Puritan pilgrims—the names of the child protagonists invoke their role in this infamous script of childhood history: Joy, renamed Joyless; a rapper nicknamed the Rapparition; a genetically deformed boy called No-Face; and a prematurely aging child suffering from Hutchinson-Gilford disease, referred to as the ancient child. Their current predicaments are prefigured by the age-old legends and stories that are now presented to them as "reading therapy." While Joy allegorizes the colonized body of the refugee child, her companion Nicolino, the "ancient child," is eternally deprived of childhood yet paradoxically condemned to remain a child: "Methuselah, a spirit older than entire generations who perversely refuses to detach himself from boyhood."[19] A child "dying of a parody of old age,"[20] Nicolino appears as the emblematic child of today, deprived both of childhood and a future. His prematurely aging body also carries the signature of the textual body's paradoxical time: condensing past, present, and future, Nicolino's facial features conjoin his impending death with the narrative's sense of an ending.

Among the other children is Chuck, the child "born with nothing from the eye sockets down to the anterior palate."[21] Chuck's allegorical name No-Face invokes the horrors of genetic mutation and de-faced humanity. Symbolically, this "de-facing" threatens to push Chuck beyond the boundaries of the human in the sense that a recognition of shared humanity is based, according to Levinas, on the response to another face.[22] Then there is the double amputee, Ben, one of L.A.'s daily freeway casualties, and Joleene Weeks, the schizo girl, who replaces her own speech with her fetish doll Chatty Cathy's ventriloquizations. Rapparition figures as the group's surrealist voice, a prophetic rapper and street performance poet who "has chosen speech over any of the deadlier assault weapons in aggression's arsenal."[23]

Rendered grotesque by deforming illnesses, genetic disorders, malnutrition, chronic neglect, and mutilations inflicted by urban violence or abuse, these children's bodies reflect "the breakthrough forced on an industrialized world by the arrival on the doorstep of a permanent surplus of maimed child veterans who, for the first time, survived their treatments in numbers beyond ignoring."[24] Apocalypse reveals its carnivalesque face when the children use these grotesque bodies as props to simulate performances of ancient, legendary childhood trials. In baroque exaggerations, Kraft's childhood patients replay the script of the *Pied Piper*, written as far back as the thirteenth century in the small rat-infested German town of Hameln (Hamelin)—a script that teaches them their fate as well as that of a world that mortgages the future of its children.

More than halfway through the novel, Powers retells the German fairy tale of *The Pied Piper*. This tale evolves into a center of gravity from which other stories emerge and to which they loop back in ever widening circles. Transposed into a contemporary setting and told in L.A. street lingo, Powers's story condenses the different historical times of medieval Germany and postmodern L.A., thus enforcing the sense that, under the impact of trauma and millennial fear, time breaks out of its monotonous chronology, forming a "still" that will be replayed over and over under new historical conditions. The retelling itself reenacts the trauma, but at the same time it also functions like a *pharmakon* or a homeopathic cure. As a kind of ur-text, *The Pied Piper* inspires not only the novel's main plot and cataclysmic ending but also a sequence of intertextual doublings. Powers uses the tale as a matrix for an ecological vision in which the roots of environmental destruction and corporate mismanagement are traced back to early Western history, and especially the colonization of Eastern Europe invoked in the *Pied Piper* narrative.

The Pied Piper also features medieval precursors of "the sickling trio"[25] from Carver's hospital cast: Nicolai, "wrinkled, sagging with a disease that made his parents turn him out without provision";[26] the blind boy prefiguring faceless Chuck; and Joy's double, "whose leg has been taken off above the knee by a crescent of Romanesque iron."[27] The Pied Piper himself is cast as an illegal immigrant advising Hamelin's citizens that their town needs "structural adjustment." Rhetorically superimposing Hamelin and L.A., Powers uses current political slogans in the response given by the mayor of Hamelin. While he bemoans the fact that they have already tried in vain, capital injections, tax incentives, urban development zones, belt tightening, and a "buy native" campaign, the Ratcatcher counters that, by borrowing increasingly more against principal, "the town is burning itself out, chasing its own decline."[28] This rhetoric casts the Ratcatcher as an ecocritic who blames the pending decline on the very destruction of an ecological balance that would have allowed the town to retain or increase its level of subsistence and self-sufficiency:

> Increase in disease; costs to health, education, and welfare. Loss to tourist income and investment from abroad. "None of the effects, taken separately, is disastrous. But taken together, they create a threshold effect, preventing the town from reaching economic takeoff."[29]

In superimposing medieval Hamelin—as well as other cities such as Jerusalem, Bangkok, or Beirut—on contemporary L.A., Powers extends his technique of historical doubling to the city itself as a quasi protagonist, thus teasing his readers into seeing all cities as prophetic mirrors of Angel City, remote prefigurations of its apocalyptic decline:

> Between negative balance of payments, debt servicing, capital depreciation, investment failure, population increase, water poisoning, field exhaustion and erosion, diminishing revenue returns, graft, tax evasion, currency softening, brain drain, corporate flight, disease, defense burden, and mushrooming social service costs, the town is clearly racing toward a condition of Infinite Sink.[30]

If these descriptions fit contemporary L.A. and the medieval German city of Hamelin in 1284 equally well, Powers's technique of interlocking different narratives, times, and places compels one to rethink the status of the novel's actual setting. While its opening sections invite immersion into the compulsive lane-change mentality of the local L.A. freeway culture, the interwoven stories open out into the astounding polytemporal and polyspacial actuality of ever new competing cultures or times.

In one of its narrative strands, *Operation Wandering Soul* draws on historical speculations that link the figure of the Pied Piper to the Children's Crusade, suggesting that he came to Hamelin as a military recruiter in order to form an army of children.[31] Using the story and surrounding history of *The Pied Piper of Hamelin*, Powers traces the roots of this assault back to the early history of inter-European colonialism, and specifically to the colonization of Eastern Europe, as well as to the religious wars and the Children's Crusade. Two of the most prominent hypotheses for the origin of the legend of the Pied

Piper establish links to both the Children's Crusade and the colonization of Eastern Europe. One hypothesis is that the children left Hamelin to be part of a pilgrimage, a military campaign, or a new Children's Crusade led by the Pied Piper. The original Children's Crusade happened in 1212 and is likely to have left its impact on the formation of the legend. The second hypothesis argues that, recruited by the Pied Piper, the children might have left Hamelin during the colonization of Eastern Europe. Several indices suggest that the children might have abandoned their hometown to become founders of their own villages. This hypothesis is supported by names of villages in the region that echo Hamelin, such as, for example, Querhameln. Modern scholars consider this emigration theory, in which the Pied Piper figures as a military recruiter that lured the young generation of Hamelin away to participate in the colonization of Eastern Europe,[32] to be the most likely source of the legend.

It is through the story of the Children's Crusade that Powers, in turn, invokes Jerusalem, the Holy City, as another double of Angel City (Los Angeles). In using contemporary inflections of voice to retell the fall of the Holy City when Jews and Muslims were slaughtered by the crusading Christians, Powers recalls another time governed by millennial visions, thus invoking a long history of violence to ground the apocalyptic fantasies that aggregate around today's global L.A.

Adapting the story of the crusade from a children's book, the narrator presents it to the children as a double of their own story. When in 1212 Stephen of Cloyes, an illiterate boy "on the threshold of his teens,"[33] is asked by a Pilgrim to bear the message of Saint John's vision of the end of the world to the king of France, he is soon followed by myriads of children, who decide that it is up to them to "recover the Holy Sepulcher, besiege the city of Jerusalem by love, doing what force of arms could not."[34] Ten-year-old Nicolas, medieval double of Nicolino, a medieval child soldier and leader of the crusade's German contingent, prefigures the fate of Los Angeles's abandoned children at the new millennium. "An estimated hundred thousand innocents are lost, sold, killed, betrayed, evacuated from this world by faith."[35] Leaping into the twentieth century, Kraft reads to the children a narrative from a schoolbook that features UPI wire photos displaying boy soldiers marching through the Lion's Gate while their enemies, other boy soldiers, flee through the back streets. Thus establishing connections between Jerusalem and Los Angeles by superimposing their imaginary geographies, the text alludes to the global orchestration of the current Middle East crisis. More generally, the layered stories of child migration link the displacement of children during the Children's Crusade and the colonization of Eastern Europe to the current displacement of children as an effect of worldwide poverty and wars in the wake of globalization, neoliberalism, the transition from state to global capitalism, free-trade organizations, and the new global warfare that have affected the social construction of childhood across the globe.

The novel's organization of narrative time through layered stories from different spatial and temporal locations relies on a nonlinear conception of time and history, suggesting this to be a more appropriate way of assessing present spatiotemporal configurations than linear historical or ethnographic narratives. Powers lets his fictional children migrate across the map of history as it is sketched out by myths, legends, and popular children's literature in recursive loops through self-similar sets of characters. All these nested stories of disappearing children "recapitulate and extend one another at different magnifications,"[36] thus generating a self-similar structure within which history emerges according to the principles of nonlinear dynamics.

Powers sees nonlinear dynamics as pertaining to a form of ecology that inspires his textual organization of *Operation Wandering Soul*. As he states in an interview, the nonlinear dynamics of cultural change, or "the discontinuity in gauges between the frames of local and global history,"[37] has been a central preoccupation in his work. What Powers says in an interview, quoting from one of his characters, also applies to the textual ecology of *Operation Wandering Soul*, including its concept of history and culture: "Ecology's every part— regardless of the magnification, however large the assembled spin-off or small the enzymatic trigger—carries in it some terraced, infinitely dense ecosystem, an inherited hint of the whole."[38]

Using child characters designed to convey a "hint of the whole" of global histories of disappearing children, Powers constructs a nonlinear spectral history in which past histories emerge as the enfolded order of the present and the future. From a psychological perspective, this enfolded order is also an encrypted order because the spectral history contains and "returns" the crypt of the disavowed losses of history, including the disavowed abandonment of children. Within this nonlinear historical configuration, the child characters become spectral embodiments of past histories. Joy, for example, a survivor of the boat people from Southeast Asia, figures as placeholder of myriad immigrant children devastated by the wars in Southeast Asia. Her oral report on American history implodes into a kaleidoscope of migrant stories that, according to the novel's logic of nonlinear polytemporalities, is a more appropriate writing of history than any bounded linear tale:

Her American history is a travelogue of mass migration's ten anxious ages: the world's disinherited, out wandering in search of colonies, falling across this convenient and violently arising land mass that overnight doubles the size of the known world. They slip into the mainland on riverboat and Conestoga, sow apple trees from burlap sacks, blast through rock, decimate forests with the assistance of a giant blue ox. They survive on hints of the Seven Cities, the City on the Hill, the New Jerusalem, scale architectural models of urban renewal, migration's end.[39]

Joy's syncretistic appropriation of her new culture makes no distinction between history and legend, that is, between the narrative of early colonial settlements and its translation into the legends of Paul Bunyan and Johnny Appleseed. Her personal history epitomizes age-old histories of child migration. Assimilating words as sounds and history as accumulated stories, Joy's present experiences are already contained in the anticipated future of the particular (yet in a sense universal) history of one of the world's masses of refugee children. In her own stories, myths, legends, and fairy tales are all recoded as autobiography. "Everything she relates she has already lived through," even the traces of early colonial history, which she reprocesses through the legends of Paul Bunyan and "joe-nee ap-al-seet."[40]

Orphaned or abandoned, homeless, stateless, permanently impaired or fatally ill, the children from Carver's hospital incorporate a grim millennial vision of this Pacific Rim metropolis. Anticipating its apocalyptic decay, their bodies carry visible inscriptions of urban as well as planetary violence. Global flows circulate this violence, export it from the empire to other places—Southeast Asia, the Middle East, Latin America, Africa—until it is brought back, reimported and recycled, so to speak, by the refugee and immigrant children who carry the often lethal marks of global wars, environmental destruction, and poverty.

To bring the ironies of history back full circle, the United States, as the very country from which much of this violence originates, later appears to many of the refugees as the last remaining safe haven, granting a sanctuary to those who are left with uninhabitable homelands and invariably transformed if not destroyed cultures. Los Angeles as "capital of the Third World" acquires yet another connotation here. It is the sheer mobility of "capital" that implodes the center. The flows of capital across the globe have folded back on themselves: its casualties are now returning, like Joy, as refugees or immigrants to Los Angeles as the very source that generated their economic and cultural decline. The multiplicity of cities figuring as L.A.'s historical doubles suggests that in today's global world, ethnographic accounts are always already mediated through an exceedingly diverse and ubiquitously disseminated arsenal of global cultural sites and knowledges that are connected through histories of violence. Interlaced transferential memories from different historical times and locations suggest that the new cultural literacy that is necessary to understand these interwoven nonlinear histories beneath today's global politics and warfare has become so complex that it can be grasped only with the mind of a transcultural bricoleur of stories.

Powers's technique of circulating stories is not restricted, however, to the figuration of a polytemporal imaginary ethnography. The technique also has a psychohistorical dimension linked to the fact that the childhood histories in question are traumatic histories that shape personal and collective memories. Trauma plays a crucial role in determining which stories can be told and which remain silenced. There is a central, silenced story at the heart of *Operation Wandering Soul*'s layered narratives: Kraft's childhood in Southeast Asia. Withheld until the very end, this story operates as a generative ellipsis. In refusing to reveal the very story that links all other narratives, and which we need to know in order to understand the intricate web of connections, *Operation Wandering Soul* maintains a marked silence as an invisible trace of trauma and repression. Powers uses various modes of indirection to point to a traumatic ellipsis in Kraft's narrative. The narrator disperses allusions to Kraft's childhood, whose meaning is established only retroactively. As a result, there is a fragmentation, splitting, and dispersion of partial stories over the entire text. Recurrences and repetitions lead to a cumulative determination and overdetermination of story lines without revealing the secret at their core. These techniques figure silence as one of the text's most signifying elements, thus echoing the silencing of Kraft's childhood story and re-creating the effects of erased traumatic memories in the reading process.

Emblematic of the history of the West's colonial wars and the ill-fated encounters with the East, Kraft's personal story unfolds in a story of mystical dimensions. During his stay at a Buddhist monastery, the young Ricky develops an inexplicable fascination with a ceramic statue of the Enlightened One that, among thousands of similar images, stands out for him in its utterly alien appearance. The abbot attributes the statue's strangeness to its being "under the spell of the West. Half Hindu, half Roman."[41] Ricky, however, is most attracted to its face, which is "all opposites . . . the face of a thousand-year-old boy."[42] Feeling a "summons from the childlike wrinkles of that face,"[43] Ricky reaches out to the statue and, with an involuntary spastic movement, knocks it down, causing it to break into a thousand pieces. In mournful withdrawal, Ricky plagues himself with an unanswerable question: "Had he wished to destroy the thing? Why?"[44]

After finding the largest shard of the broken statue placed on his doorstep, Ricky carves a minute replica that the abbot, in turn, declares to be "the voice box of the last child to leave the Wheel. . . . The place where the final farewell shout will appear."[45] The abbot's remark about "the last child," in turn foreshadows the disappearance of children in *Operation Wandering Soul* and their "final farewell shout" placed in "the voice box" of a spaceship: "Greetings from the children of Planet Earth."[46]

Kraft is reconnected with the story of the statue of the thousand-year-old boy and the abbot's mysterious apocalyptic prophesy when, decades later, the ancient boy appears as Nicolino in his hospital ward. It seems as if Nicolino's appearance is designed to propel him to fulfill an unknown destiny that first revealed itself through the old statue. In carving the broken shard, Ricky had discovered all that time ago "that his hands, alone of his willful body, would do what he told them."[47] Mending the broken shards of the statue of this ancient child was what eventually led Kraft to "Carver's hospital," where he carves up and stitches together the ancient child's contemporary offspring. The story of Kraft's hands, however, also prefigures the surgeon's later predicament. Ricky's sense that his hands would do what he told them was treacherous to begin with since it was their "uncontrollable spasm" that had destroyed the statue. The story's traumatic core thus prefigures Kraft's later "wrong move," namely the wrong surgical move that condemns Joy to die. Once again his hands assume a life of their own, playing God over life and death. As he works the appallingly sharp scissors, his hands detach from him. They carry on working, as discrete and sovereign as the Invisible Man's white gloves."[48]

While Kraft performs his surgery on Joy, flashes of fragmented memories, told in interior monologues, transport him back to his school years in Bangkok, where he had organized a group of children to build a schoolhouse in Nam Chai, an impoverished village in the mountains of Thailand near the Cambodian war zone. "Those fourteen days rise up out of the girl's cracked-open hip."[49] In another merging of L.A. and Southeast Asia, Joy becomes "indistinguishable from the Asian twelve-year-old from the other side of the river, the one his pilgrim party met on its tropical Christmas operation a half world ago."[50]

Joy thus becomes the catalyst for Kraft's recollection of his forgotten trauma. During the fateful surgery, the girl's body converts under Kraft's eyes into the injured colonized body, emblematic site of a violent intrusion that he sees himself repeating on the operating table. In this hallucinatory transference his surgical operation becomes overdetermined with the military operation that destroyed Joy's double during the Vietnam War. Remembering that the military assault on Vietnam was hypocritically staged as a charitable act, Kraft now undermines the charitable purpose of the surgery he performs on Joy with a wrong move of his hands. It is as if a fate beyond control compels him to repeat two earlier scenes of destruction: the wrong move that shattered the statue and the wrong move that killed the Vietnamese girl.

Kraft conveys this traumatic episode in an erratic and fragmented stream of consciousness that reveals an alarming inability to "screen out" overwhelming stimuli, increasingly precipitating psychic disintegration. Post-traumatic intrusions of toxic memories precipitate a mental breakdown, as if the old protective barrier in the self's ecology (Freud's *Reizschutz*), that is, the ability of the mind to screen out overwhelming experiences, has reached a breaking point and reverted to its opposite. Due to a failure of the protective barrier, Kraft, whose memory was formerly but an empty slate, is now inundated by intrusive memories and sensations. After decades of willful amnesia, Kraft succumbs to the opposite symptom, a relentless onslaught of unbearable recollections and associations. His incapacity to forget, even temporarily, and to relegate the media's dose of daily disasters to a manageable background level, plunges him into a mental mode of high anxiety in which every event aggregates around his trauma, thus assuming immediate urgency and presence.[51] At his breaking point, his lover, Linda, finds him in cataleptic calm, surrounded by hundreds of milk cartons featuring the familiar photos of missing children. Each of these children seems to hold a claim on him, tapping into the legacy of the one story that emerged when he opened Joy's hip.

Kraft's and Joy's traumatic childhood memories of the Vietnam War finally converge in the story of Operation Wandering Soul that inspired the novel's title: the Foreign Service's fighting wing used native collaborators on a helicopter mission and coerced them to imitate the spectral voices of their villagers' ancestors. Transmitted from helicopters, uncannily familiar voices—the most sinister of the text's many luring Pied Piper voices—call out through loudspeakers: "Our babies . . . Our offspring! Have you forgotten us."[52]

Disembodied chill semaphores, piped through megaphones at three A.M., a crude and bizarre attempt at demoralization howled down from haunted heaven into the animist jungle. A monsoon of invisible, amplified voices from out of an unreal parallel. . . . The whole project might have been pure theater, cinematic American weirdness in the jungle. But the account was too outrageously surreal for Kraft to be anything else than the recognizable exploits of the Foreign Service's fighting wing.[53]

This cynical exploitation of an indigenous belief in the communication with dead ancestors stages a haunting simulacrum. American soldiers on a helicopter mission turn the Vietnamese people's spectral history against them by cynically using it as a supernatural weapon. It is as if they had co-opted the people's very ancestors to fight against their own. This faking of spectral voices[54] and simulated haunting of the Vietnamese people is used for the most perverse psychological warfare. It creates a violent invasion and appropriation of the sacred and, indeed, a desacralization of the dead. As such it is a form of necropolitics in the full sense of the term. The Foreign Service's fighting wing performs the "work of death"[55] by enlisting the dead in a simulated haunting of their own people.

But now, after all these years, this spectral history returns with a vengeance to Kraft, the child of the Vietnamese people's former enemies. Its haunting legacy becomes materialized in the uncanny circulation and return of a fetish object that discloses the fateful karma that connects Kraft with Joy: a charm that Joy offers Kraft as a gift mysteriously turns out to be the very necklace he had given to his own father who, in turn, had lost it in the Vietnam War.

"It fell out of the sky,"[56] Joy had said, revealing that it was Kraft's father who had dropped the necklace during the fateful military Operation Wandering Soul. Falling from the sky like the bomb whose lethal metal festers in the girl's leg, this "charm" then follows the child refugee's trajectory back to the origin of destruction. Unknowingly, she returns the necklace to the son of the enemy who had bombed her village. This scene stages a sequence of haunting returns. For Kraft, the necklace is like a ghostly message from his dead father, delivered by the child who was wounded and maimed in his own father's military operation. As the father's necklace becomes a haunting presence, an emblem of shame returned to Kraft via Joy, so Joy herself now becomes a haunting presence for him, "returned" as a refugee to the very country that destroyed her world, waiting for the debts to be paid to the Pied Piper—the war debts to the ancestors mocked in Operation Wandering Soul. Yet Kraft, who does everything to save her, acts as if under a cruel spell to complete the father's mission and condemns her to death with an involuntary wrong movement on the operating table. Once again it is the children who inherit the transgenerational trauma of war and are called upon to pay their fathers' debts. Tragically, Kraft, who had chosen his profession in the pursuit of redress and reparation, only further compounds his father's guilt. The legacy of the Vietnam War is thus embodied in the complementary traumatic memories and entangled life histories of Joy and Kraft, two descendants of the war's victims and perpetrators, enjoined by cruel karma.

When readers finally get Kraft's entire story, it is disguised as yet another "fairy tale" about migrant children. Kraft tells this story in the form of a "spoken hologram,"[57] cipher of the condensed spatiotemporal world of a child who "had lived everywhere, belonged nowhere."[58] As a boy, Kraft participated in a school service club, "aiding at a state asylum where concrete cubicles swarmed with children—deformed, diseased, degeneratively crippled, industrially poisoned."[59] Under conditions not so different from those in L.A.'s children's hospital, little Ricky proposes the building of a school, a project christened Operation Santa Claus. In close proximity to the Cambodian war zone, tribal peoples from the hills surrounded the chosen site for the school. Operation Santa Claus is figured as another replica of the Children's Crusade. Joy's double, a "rice sack girl"[60] from the hill tribes, lures the children away from the school site, chanting "in some form of Ur-pali"[61]—"Come away!"—the very words issued from the abbot's statue the instant before Ricky smashed it. Refusing to recognize a bad omen, Ricky, who feels like the girl's infant (thus turning her into another ancient child), incites the children to follow her into the river current—like the rats following the Pied Piper. Hit by the dreadful recognition that the girl "had come to lead a unit of foreign imperialists into ambush,"[62] yet unable to break the spell, Ricky follows her into the water. The girl steps on a mine, setting off the gigantic explosion that kills her. It is this traumatic experience that motivated Kraft to become a medical surgeon: "When the obligatory three wishes came and ambushed him, he politely refused all but one. Just let me try to cure things."[63]

The "obligatory three wishes," of course, are the stuff of fairy tales. When trying to cure things seems impossible in L.A.'s zones of abandonment, if not urban war zones, Kraft resorts to fairy tales and stories as a healing force. *Operation Wandering Soul* explores storytelling as a resource of survival. Storytelling, poetry, and music are invoked as the most basic forms of cultural production shared across the globe. Storytelling as "the oldest recorded remedy"[64] is as vital in a pediatric ward today as it has been since time immemorial: "poetry, antique verse so strange and illegally alien in this place that it holds even hardened and dying children spellbound for the scope of a few stanzas."[65]

In its self-reflexive explorations, *Operation Wandering Soul* links storytelling to death and survival, remembrance and mourning. Powers asserts the human urge to tell stories and hurl them against disaster and destruction, even if there is nobody to listen, and they are sent into the void like the greetings of the children from planet Earth, waiting for an imaginary addressee in outer space. While storytelling translates our mortality into an endless productivity,[66] stories also bear witness to the destruction humans bring upon themselves and their planet. Powers pushes this activity one step further: today's stories need to bear testimony to the planet's precariousness and mortality, even if these stories can only be hurled into space, floating emptily and signifying nothing.

This is also the context of *Operation Wandering Soul*'s engagement with apocalyptic visions. This imaginary ethnography of the future engages history through affect. Its kaleidoscope of apocalyptic stories conveys an emotionally embedded "sense of an ending." But *Operation Wandering Soul* seems to contest Kermode's assumption that apocalyptic visions are concord fictions that make the end imaginable in order to provide imaginary closure.[67] The novel also seems to exceed the two temporal modes of the disjunctive and the linear Robbins describes as the hallmark of millenarian temporality.[68] Affectively, Powers's nonlinear polytemporality emerges from a spectral historiography that opens the crypt of the past and returns its ghosts. In this respect, it is part of a politics of mourning that includes mourning both the past and the future. Powers opens up a disquieting choice between different ways of mourning the future. What Freud says about mourning and melancholia holds for anticipations of future loss as well. Humans today may become melancholically devoured by the pending devastation of the Earth and its resources—the livable space they take away from future children. They may choose to remain blind and deny loss altogether, or they may mourn what is irretrievably lost and move to protect what is left.

Looking at a long Western history of mortgaged futures, *Operation Wandering Soul* calls for an ethics that includes the care for future generations. Such an ethics precludes a mourning of the future in apocalyptic gloom or nostalgic glorification of the past. Rather, such an ethics calls for a mourning that translates apocalyptic scenarios into an imperative for action. Accordingly, loss (past, present, or anticipated) in Powers's stories is repeatedly turned into an affirmation of life by those whose lives have been mortgaged—the children. They affirm life without nostalgia, continuing to do so simply as long as they still live. Another of the text's Pied Piper figures, Chriswick, a

London teacher who leads the evacuation of children during a World War II air raid on London,[69] witnesses how a group of children gathered in a church spontaneously conducted a musical service to counter fear and despair, and concludes that the future of children is perhaps the only thing worth saving: "This one thing alone of his race might be worth saving from the coming bombs, these soaring, high, head voices said what it was to be alive, to be anything at all."[70]

Voice and music function as the most viable unit of survival in Powers's tale—be it in the lure of the Pied Piper, the transcendent voices of the children's choir during the air raid, or the music of Kraft's Thai childhood tunes that bring back his memory. But there can also be manifestations of spectral voices that come to haunt the present. Like the ancestral voices of the Vietnamese hill tribes, they can be appropriated in the staged hauntings of warfare. Spectrality can become wedded to a cynical necropolitics that performs the work of death through a desacralization of the dead.

Powers's own tale of an ending becomes spectral in a different way, recalling like a musical invocation the haunting question young Ricky poses to himself after destroying the statue: "Had he wished to destroy the thing? Why?" This question comes back to haunt Kraft like a spectral voice of the past. In this respect spectral voices are speaking trauma, and one can even read Powers's text itself as a spectral voicing of the past inscribed by traumatic hauntings. In a similar vein, the questions left to readers at the end of *Operation Wandering Soul* pass on and transfer a haunting legacy: Had we wished to betray the ancient children? Had we wished to destroy the future for new generations of children? Why?

"Kraft alone is left to tie apocalypse to vanishing children,"[71] says the narrator toward the end of the novel. The sense of an ending that transpires from the final convergence of Powers's stories is not teleological or eschatological but cyclical: the cultures from which the novel's stories arise have continually reenacted apocalyptic scenarios, "mortgag[ing] the future"[72] of generations to come. Given this temporal ecology of an amputated future, how are we to read the novel's ending? Does Powers double the Pied Piper's lure, not of music but of a musical voice whose "soul-ravishing ripples"[73] push the ancient millennial question, "Whence evil?"[74] Does *Operation Wandering Soul* offer but a Pied Piper's "Apocalypse Aid,"[75] exposing the "proximity of ecstasy to horror?"[76] The novel ends with the children's exodus from Carver's hospital. Kraft is "becoming Pied Piper," embodying the role the children had assigned to him in their staging of the play. Traumatized by the mutilated bodies of child victims from a shootout at an elementary school, a delusional Kraft takes the play's destitute cast and escapes through the hospital roof, carrying, in shifts, the dying Joy and other wounded children in his arms. Trailing along Imperial Highway and sleeping in the open—another migrant group among L.A.'s homeless—the children ask their Pied Piper for stories to ward off their fears.

In this final delirium,[77] the text loses narrative gravity. The ending marks a finale that condenses space and time as the world's stories of disappearing children finally converge when Kraft takes his cast of children toward their apocalyptic exit. Flying into orbit like the children in *Peter Pan*, they look down upon the "terminally ill Angel City neighborhood,"[78] the Watts Towers, City Hall, the Observatory, the desert, and the world's other continents. The novel ends with the vision of a global exodus from Los Angeles's shantytowns as they extend in time and space:

> They are leaving now in all epochs, all regions, packing off by candle-light. Stories continue to pour in. Myth shades off into reportage, fact into invention. . . . So many are adrift, out of doors late tonight, too far from home, migrating, campaigning, colonizing, on pilgrimage, displaced, dispersed, tortured loose, running for their lives.[79]

In Kraft's final story, medieval Germany, contemporary L.A., and all other countries harboring stories of disappearing children merge in the alien vision of an interplanetary future:

> They study economics, they write long books, always lavishly illustrated. They fill walls with murals of overgrown, forgotten, impossible lands of Cockaigne. They formulate a history longer even than the hope of its imminence. They send a deep-space packet-boat probe straying in the muted vacuum for millennia, seeking, searching for a place it might finally touch down, carrying as interplanetary barter a parcel of stories, pictures, messages in threescore and ten globe-bound languages all unintelligible to any being the Voyager might one day come across, each reading, "Greetings from the children of Planet Earth."[80]

The strange, nostalgic beauty of this passage affirms life in death, against death. In this sense *Operation Wandering Soul* is about transcendence, nourished by millennial fears and the operational paranoia of one who looks back at his century's end through the lens of a thousand years of history. But we should not misread the transcendence in *Operation Wandering Soul* as following the legacy of American transcendentalism and its male fantasies of rebirth out of death.[81] If Powers resorts to transcendentalist imagination, it is to radically invert its premises and goals. There is no phoenix emerging from the ashes in Powers's text, and no redemptive consolation. His children's voices stray in a muted vacuum, and the message they carry will be unintelligible for the aliens they are addressing as their last witnesses. Having lost its colonizing impetus, transcendence has become homeward bound. Its scope is reduced to little more than a way of looking back at a "home [as] a way of leaving."[82]

Emerging at the end of Powers's novel, the aliens from outer space have not come to destroy planet Earth, but are called upon to witness the disappearance of its children, however undecipherable the message, as if these children needed an imaginary, alien ethnographer to write their history of destruction and indestructible hope. Mourning forms the core of this "millenarian feeling."[83] At stake is not only the mourning of what humans have destroyed or are about to destroy but also the inability to mourn what they have repressed or disavowed, or what they are unable to conceive. In a two-page-long epilogue, Powers finally reverts back to the story of the spacecraft carrying the "Greetings from the children of Planet Earth." This final coda, which reads as if Powers could not, just yet, come to terms with his apocalyptic ending, reframes the novel, declaring it to be a transposition of Powers's older brother's story. "My best intentions had failed to disperse the bleakness of the real,"[84] he confesses and proceeds to rewrite the ending. Fantasizing a new turn in Kraft and Linda's previously doomed love, Powers gives us the mock version of an imaginary happy ending: the story of a nuclear family. This story rewrites an earlier scene in which Linda has a vision of an imaginary child that will never be born:

> It will never happen now, the ending they were supposed to have. . . .
> They would have made the worst parents in any event. With their combined professional commitments, real children would have been impossible, except perhaps through some offspring time-sharing arrangement, two weeks out of the year, like a gulfside condominium.[85]

Here Joy, their substitute child, appears to Linda as a sacrificial victim, mutilated to undercut their own reproductive desire:

The marks he has made on this girl, the skilled, high-tech dismember-
ments, were all for this: to keep her soul from coming back, raiding the
world again in the form of their child, a child she has just glimpsed, but
who will never, now, return.[86]

But it is precisely this "soul" that Powers brings back in the epilogue's second
ending, inventing an imaginary child, figured as a ghost haunted by the return of Joy's soul. The "rewriting" is then not a "writing over" or effacement
of the earlier story but a displacement to another scene of writing. Within the
apocalyptic narrative, this imaginary child is a survivor so to speak, who becomes the last recipient of his mournful stories about disappearing children.
With the fantasy of a child that lives to hear the story of the departure of children from planet Earth, the novel thus undercuts the finality of its apocalyptic
narrative. The children's departure becomes just another story in the string of
apocalyptic narratives, deferring the ending into yet another future.

How then do the two endings relate to a mourning of the future? To the
extent that future loss can be predicted, Powers seems to suggest, one must be
able to mourn in the mode of an anticipated future. This imaginary mourning
depends, of course, on the projection of emotions into the future. Drawing
its emotional energies from the stories we tell about a threatened future, this
mourning differs from the mourning of a real loss but is nonetheless linked
to it. Fantasy facilitates transference. It is a mourning bound up in a call to
action. I see Powers's literary intervention in contemporary discourses on
the vanishing of childhood as related to this ethics of mourning the future.
The novel shares a pervasive critique of the exposure of children to neglect,
abandonment, violence, poverty, starvation, and war with recent theories of
childhood in global cultures. Sharon Stephens, for example, highlights the
neglect of the impact of globalization on children in political and economic
theories:

> Models of political and economic transformations leading to correspond-
> ing shifts in consciousness, subjective experience, and social relationships
> do not adequately account for increasingly widespread notions of the dis-
> appearance, contamination, invasion, and colonization of domains such
> as childhood, previously regarded as relatively noncommodified.[87]

Operation Wandering Soul traces the connections between economy, politics,
and the social construction of childhood in various historical settings. Just as

children did in the thirteenth century, children today flee poverty, famine, and social disenfranchisement, and many of the displaced Third World children end up as immigrants in the heart of metropolitan urban centers where they join and sometimes clash with the city's own disenfranchised urban youth. Powers's stories trace the ways in which early modern notions of childhood were predicated upon European colonialist experiences. In juxtaposing old and new stories, he suggests that the worldwide colonization of children and their uses for slave labor, sex work, or warfare continue under a new guise. Powers's child protagonists are carriers of a transgenerational trauma that reaches back to the Middle Ages and the early religious and colonial wars.

Robert Coles argues that national identities and political circumstances deeply impact children's consciousness, morality, sense of security, and ways of being in the world.[88] *Operation Wandering Soul* exposes the mental, psychic, and physical effects on children of a social setting in which they no longer have cultural capital unless they can enter the cycle of economic reproduction. "In the late twentieth century," write Scheper-Hughes and Sargent, "children have often been the first casualties of political disruption, war, and other forms of social disintegration."[89] Powers's child protagonists are war children, affected by both global wars and the "small wars" fought in their neighborhoods. They are stand-ins for the growing populations of displaced, orphaned, and homeless children produced by global and civil wars, genocides, poverty, famine, street violence, and drug cultures. Distant heirs of the children displaced during the early European colonizations and crusades, the migratory bands of children in *Operation Wandering Soul* belong to the new displaced populations in today's world.

If we look at Powers's intervention in light of Sharon Stephens's argument that children are "central figures—and actors—in contemporary contests over definitions of culture, its boundaries and significance," than *Operation Wandering Soul* suggests that childhood is increasingly excluded from the boundaries of cultural and political life. Increasingly pushed to the margins, abandoned in poverty, or maimed and killed in wars, children are indeed, as Scheper-Hughes and Sargent insist, the perennial losers in the aggressive restaging of the new world order. However, Powers's stories insist in every instance on the agency of children, even in the face of death. This insistence counters the narrative of mere exclusion by showing agency and resilience as the very forces that demand inclusion. This is why spectrality is central to Powers's project: it complicates narratives of disappearance and insists on returns while never losing sight of the ongoing mortgaging of the future.

First published in the early nineties, *Operation Wandering Soul* foreshadows a time when the global politics of childhood is marked by an accelerated decline of social concern for children. Postindustrial consumer societies have displaced children to the margins, if not to outright zones of abandonment in urban ghettos, shantytowns, or war zones.[90] The novel's anticipated future foreshadows the masses of maimed, abandoned, starving, and murdered children in the new wars in Afghanistan and Iraq. It foreshadows the new armies of child soldiers that emerge at a time when political, ethnic, and religious conflicts generate new war zones around the globe. Sharon Stephens writes, "As representatives of the contested future and subjects of cultural policies, children stand at the crossroads of divergent cultural projects. Their minds and bodies are at stake in debates about the transmission of fundamental cultural values."[91]

Powers portrays a centuries-long history that has failed to protect childhood as a space for the transmission of cultural values. It is a history that has systematically denied specific rights to children. While there is an emergent consciousness of this legal and ethical concern, movements in global politics toward the protection of children remain slow and controversial. *Operation Wandering Soul* appeared in print not long after the United Nations established the first legally binding Convention on the Rights of the Child in 1989. The United States was the only industrialized country that refused to sign on.[92] Hardly any of the rights spelled out in the fifty-four articles are protected in the United States today. Powers stages the apocalyptic exodus of children as a response to a system of neoliberal capitalism that treats nonproductive "Others," including disenfranchised children, as dispensable parasites, that is, a form of human detritus pushed outside the boundaries of cultural, political, and economic life.

Yet if the figure of the child marks one of the culturally assigned boundaries of the human, then there is even more at stake than "a concern for 'structural' violence in reproducing a generation of children without childhood."[93] If children are also carriers of—to use Derrida's term—a culture's "memory of the future," the exodus of children figures as a threat to global memories of the future of humankind, or to what Crapanzano calls the "world-maintaining responsibility or capacity."[94] What then is the status of Powers's imaginary ethnography of a future at risk?

The apocalyptic vision of the final disappearance of children places Powers's novel squarely in the anthropological tradition of "salvage ethnographies" concerned with witnessing a "vanishing race." Yet the particular "vanishing" addressed in *Operation Wandering Soul* has become more global and apocalyptic, raising the specter of the vanishing of the human species, emblematized by the figure of the disappearing child. At the same time, however, the novel is also a spectral ethnography in which disappearances are doubled by returns. Powers explores haunting legacies and, more specifically, spectral histories in which those who have disappeared return with a vengeance in ghostly cycles of repetition. This transgenerational haunting can be grasped only from within a spectral historiography. During their apocalyptic escape over the hospital roof, Kraft keeps telling the children stories. While he feeds their "addiction to hope,"[95] he also engages in a spectral historiography that returns to and returns the ghosts of history. "For a day longer, they are certain of forever, and the night is theirs. They can see in the dark; their eyes are yet that mint."[96] Seeing in the dark also means seeing ghosts. In this respect, the stories of apocalypse, told to defer annihilation and death, are also creating a sanctuary for ghosts and their haunted histories.

The history book Kraft reads to the children ends with a final question: "Could it be that the seed of the Thousand-Year Kingdom, that troubled dream toward which the world still falters, was sown in a place possessed long ago and lost, forgotten except to fable?"[97] The positive answer "It could. All predictions are perverted remembrance"[98] would be a fitting epigraph to *Operation Wandering Soul*. It insists on the intertwinement of memory and forgetting in the formation of millennial prophesies. The latter are a manifestation of spectral histories, that is, of a haunting by what historical narratives try to forget. If predictions are indeed perverted remembrance, apocalyptic narratives only recall what the old dream of the Thousand-Year Kingdom represses, namely that it is built on a mortgaged future. *Operation Wandering Soul* suggests that what has been repressed and forgotten in old histories becomes the driving force of new cycles of repetition. Rather than merely rewriting histories, spectral historiographies seek to disrupt these cycles in order to rewrite the future.

6 Ethnographies of the Future

Personhood, Agency, and Power

in Octavia Butler's *Xenogenesis*

Out beyond our world there are, elsewhere, other assemblages of matter making other worlds. Ours is not the only one in air's embrace.[1]
—Lucretius

How would humanity's perception of the world change if we could learn from aliens? If the properties we assign to the natural world are expressions of the way we think . . . then encounters with aliens will *change* those properties.[2]
—Clifford Pickover

In the first epigraph, Lucretius envisions alien worlds in terms of differing assemblages of matter. Some two thousand years later, Clifford Pickover asserts that alien encounters affect the properties we assign to matter and the natural world.[3] Imagining alien worlds has long been in the human mind an exercise in trying to assess the properties of our Earth's matter. It has also been an exercise in imagining the existence of spiritual matter and the range of immaterial things such as the soul, the self, or personhood. My reading of Octavia Butler's *Xenogenesis*[4] is concerned with alien encounters or the extraterrestrial imaginary and what they can tell us about such issues as property and personhood. Ever since humans have gazed at the stars, the universe, the galaxies, they have doubted that they are "the only ones in air's embrace." Increasingly we have become concerned with learning from an alien world. The flourishing genre of science fiction envisions what we could learn about ourselves in imagined encounters with alien species. Yet we can hardly ignore that the shadow of a human history of colonialism, wars, and genocide falls upon our futuristic visions of alien encounters. Human history does not provide us with ample ground to hope for benign encounters with other people, let alone with other species. From their very beginnings, human space explorations have been steeped in a deeply xenophobic colonial imaginary. Yet some science fiction writers turn our xenophobic gaze back on us, stimulating a negative mirroring process that scrutinizes our history of violence from an alien perspective.

Science fiction has always been concerned with exploring alternative notions of personhood from the perspective of alien world orders and cultures. More recently, the genre also scrutinizes notions of property in alien worlds beyond the logic of late capitalism and the forces of globalization that determine living conditions on Earth. Like a seismograph, science fiction measures the boundaries of what we may conceive as the properties that define the human or the conditions under which we consider personhood. Taking liberty to use the broad connotations coagulating around "property," I expand the term beyond narrower notions of property to include the properties defining a species as well as a sense of ownership derived from an economy of belonging.

Most choices in our intellectual work bear hidden autobiographical traces. My interest in aliens goes back to a time in my childhood when my little sister, Stephanie, and I would spend hours in front of the radio listening to white noise. I told her that these strange sounds were messages sent to us by aliens. Pretending to decipher them, I invented wild stories about imminent landings and possible abductions to a land full of mysteries and wonder. We then imagined a life on other planets where adults listened to the wisdom of children, imaginary animals carried us in pouches, and flying houses took us to other stars. I recalled these fantasies during my last visits with my mother, who, in her eighties, told us she did not want to die before the arrival of aliens on Earth. She would search the sky for them, ready to welcome them in her home. "How will you communicate with aliens?" I asked, and she replied, "Just as I communicate with you!" The trace of a subtle reproach in her reply did not go unnoticed. In many ways, I had always been "alien" to her, but especially so after I had decided to remain as a "resident alien" in the United States. When I told my mother that the artist who did my book covers thought his paintings were channeled by aliens, she pleaded in her old age's childlike magic thinking, "Tell him to send them to me. Tell him I'm waiting." My mother did not hold out long enough. We buried her on September 11, 2001, the day of the attacks on the World Trade Center. The sister for whom I invented stories of aliens died more than thirty years ago, when she was seventeen years old, of a rare form of childhood cancer. The aliens in Octavia

Butler's *Xenogenesis* routinely cure human cancers by means of simple genetic adjustments. I wish my sister had found an alien healer. I dedicate this chapter to her memory and that of my mother because it was with them I used to share my alien visions.

Let me now turn to more philosophical reasons for focusing on the extraterrestrial imaginary. Narratives of science fiction explore the boundaries of the human as a species in relation to imagined species from other planets. They function, to borrow a term from Anne Balsamo, as "ethnographies of the future."[5] Why are we interested in science fiction's visions of the future, and what kind of ethnographic knowledge do they convey? And why do we so persistently link "ethnographies of the future" with alien encounters? That humans prepare for the encounter with extraterrestrials has a long history in the cultural imaginary, both in Western and non-Western cultures. What distinguishes this history in our century is not only the fact that the "impossible" has become technologically feasible[6] but also that humans for the first time have at their disposal the technological means for the destruction of their species and the planet. Environmental destruction, overpopulation, genocide, and a disproportional arsenal of weapons make the end of the human species tangible, and its imagination creates the need for survival fantasies. In their most general thrust, the latter address the dangers posed to the reproduction of the human species. Hence the politics of human reproduction has become inseparable from the danger of planetary destruction. *Xenogenesis* presupposes this irreducible intertwinement of planetary destruction and genetically engineered reproductive politics. More generally, science fiction follows two trends in figuring this linkage of planetary/human reproduction and destruction. Extraterrestrials figure either as carriers of hope for the biogenetic survival of humans and their planet or as the harbingers of planetary destruction. Fantasies of transspecies reproduction generally evolve within this larger framework. To the extent that extraterrestrials interfere in planetary reproduction by becoming sexual or merely reproductive partners of humans, they threaten the boundaries of the human species. The general ambivalence toward extraterrestrials in contemporary millennial fantasies also determines their specific status and appeal as sexual partners. Since such millennial fantasies are often but thinly disguised heirs to the colonial imaginary, they figure the aliens either as horrifying kidnappers or as supreme seducers with superhuman sexual powers. Their politics of transspecies reproduction is simply presupposed.

Anthropologist Marilyn Strathern's *Reproducing the Future: Anthropology, Kinship and the New Reproductive Technologies* reflects a fundamental trend at the heart of futuristic thinking that bears not only upon the reproductive politics in much contemporary science fiction but also upon reproductive politics more generally. Strathern's provocative title highlights the tendency to deploy an ethnographic imaginary of the future through new politics and technologies of reproduction. Octavia Butler is no exception. Her imagined communities of humans and the alien species of the Oankali in *Xenogenesis* deal with transspecies reproduction, genetic engineering, and alternative kinship arrangements. At the same time, however, Butler casts her futuristic vision as a historical allegory that reflects upon issues of colonialism, imperialism, racism, ecology, and alternative forms of economy and kinship.

Issues of kinship, genealogy, reproduction, and the boundaries of the human inevitably raise the vexed question of personhood. The latter, in turn, is intimately tied to property, if only because Western philosophies and cultures have established and in colonial contexts imposed onto non-Western cultures a long tradition of relating personhood to self-ownership. Moreover, recent developments in reproductive technologies make it possible to think of ownership in relation to genetic material. At stake are not only the patenting of genes and genetically engineered organisms but also the question of who exerts agency in the growing field of "assisted reproduction." Testifying to irreversible changes in the cultural and biological organization of our planet, millennial fantasies about artificial and alien or transspecies reproduction highlight the challenges posed by current biopolitics to the ethical principles of human cultures.

While science fiction deals with the kidnapping and impregnation of humans by aliens, imposed genetic manipulation, and alien-directed gene trade, the more tangible nightmares take place closer to home—as we have experienced, for example, at my home university, the University of California, Irvine, when in 1994 a scandal of major proportions erupted when whistleblowers uncovered the illegal swapping of experimentally inseminated eggs and frozen embryos without knowledge or consent of the involved patients.[7] Dr. Ricardo H. Asch, Dr. Jose P. Balmaceda, and Dr. Sergio C. Stone, three internationally reputed physicians and genetic researchers, were accused of having taken eggs and embryos from clients undergoing IVF treatments and given them to other women without consent or knowledge of the parties involved. Finally, John and Deborah Lynn Challender, a couple who had used the clinic for treatment of infertility, came forward with allegations that the doctors had removed Deborah's eggs and implanted them in a woman who bore twins. In 1995, Asch was lambasted on the *Oprah Winfrey Show* as the perpetrator of "high-tech baby kidnapping" and "biomedical rape."[8] This illegal transaction led to one of the biggest medical scandals in U.S. history, and in the ensuing legal debates, bitter controversies were fought over issues of property and personhood. Most prominently, it raised the questions of who owned the embryo that was transplanted without consent and who owned the child that was later born to the uninformed recipient couple. We witnessed a nightmarish "gene trade," in which the notion of human agency and personhood was subjected to utter commodification. Or, as Mary Dodge and Gilbert Geis show in *Stealing Dreams: A Fertility Clinic Scandal*, "Asch, variously described as saintly and highhanded, had a laissez-faire attitude about his client's 'biological property' and was dismissive of the Challenders' and others' fierce feelings for their eggs and embryos."[9] This case is relevant because it demonstrates with utter clarity that in the politics of technologically assisted reproduction, issues of property and personhood are inseparably intertwined.

The case also indicates the cultural anxieties about the new reproductive technologies that provide the cultural context for Butler's very different vision of her imagined alien species' politics of transspecies reproduction. Butler's aliens, the Oankali, define themselves as "gene traders" of a different kind, as space nomads who over millennia travel throughout the galaxy, temporarily settling down on a particular dying planet. There they restore and diversify its life through the trading and mixing of genetic material from their own and other alien species. The Oankali live in a harmonious ecology with their immediate environment and the galaxy at large. They adhere to a "precapitalist" economy of ecological exchange and live in tribal kinship arrangements, transitioning periodically from sedentary to nomadic lifestyles.

In this respect, Butler's futuristic alien world functions as a historical allegory that builds on the juxtaposition of the precapitalist ecologies of indigenous cultures on the one hand and the introduction of slave economies and the imposition of race in the name of economic exploitation on the other. Within this allegory, however, Butler uses a futuristic vision of innate technologies of biogenetic engineering to unsettle the familiar binary opposition between nature and technology. Genetic information and exchange inform the Oankali's entire world. Their whole environment, including housing and spaceships, tools, and other objects, is figured as an assemblage of sentient organisms made of the same biogenetic material as the Oankali, who relate to one another through biogenetic attunement. It is in this tension between historical allegory and futuristic vision that familiar relationships between kinship, property, and personhood become unhinged from traditional philosophical contexts. While in precontact Oankali settlements these relationships are harmoniously integrated into an all-encompassing ecology, the transspecies contact with humans disrupts this ecology by introducing conflicted relations of power and domination.

At the beginning of *Dawn*, the first volume of *Xenogenesis*, the Oankali hold a group of humans in a state of suspended animation on a gigantic spaceship. Two hundred and fifty years have passed since a nuclear holocaust rendered Earth uninhabitable. Without Oankali intervention, humans would have destroyed all life on their planet. After subjecting human survivors to a reeducation program that involves transspecies reproduction, the Oankali plan to restore the Earth, which is to be inhabited by new transspecies communities. Embracing biogenetic diversity as a superior value, the Oankali attempt to continually diversify their own gene pool and thus increase the complexity and differentiation of their species. In the opening scene of *Dawn*, Lilith Iyapo, the main character, awakes from her suspended animation, unaware that her captors are aliens.

Xenogenesis, the genesis of the alien, unfolds as a myth of origin. Borrowing from the biblical myth, Butler invokes the motif of genesis as a frame for her utopian figuration of a new, post-terrestrial world. Instead of the biblical expulsion from paradise because of original sin, humans in *Xenogenesis* are forced into exile from their planet because, due to what the aliens perceive as a fatal defect in their genetic makeup, they have destroyed its natural resources. Lilith, an African-American former anthropologist, figures as the ur-mother of a new transspecies world—albeit not as biblical Eve but as Talmudic Lilith, Adam's first wife, the nightly woman. Acculturated by the Oankali for a life in an extended family of humans and aliens, she is destined to bear their first transspecies children. The plot of *Dawn* is structured like a female *bildungsroman*, following its main character, Lilith's, acculturation for a life with the Oankali in an extended transspecies family in which she will take part in raising the first generation of transspecies children. The educational trajectory during this extreme cultural encounter is marked by Lilith's gradual relinquishing of her intense xenophobia and racism toward the Oankali. However, her relationship to them remains deeply ambivalent and conflicted, even as *Dawn* ends with an imminent xenogenesis: the birth of the first hybrid of Oankali and human origin.

Adulthood Rites, the second volume, focuses on the conflicts that emerge with the new kinship arrangements between humans and Oankali. The Oankali have three sexes: male, female, and ooloi. The ooloi, a "third sex" that mediates sexuality and reproduction between males and females, are also the prime gene readers and specialists in genetic engineering. They are the healers of the tribal families, collectors of genetic and historical information, and agents of transspecies seduction and bonding. Humans are divided among themselves. Adapters like Lilith consent to become part of the transspecies culture, while "resister humans" experience the takeover by the Oankali as a form of extraterrestrial colonization. The Oankali have come to the conclusion that the pervasive violence that destroys human cultures is based on a genetic defect. Hence they leave humans with the single choice of either enhanced transspecies reproduction or infertility. The resisters prefer to live in isolated forest settlements and accept imposed infertility and death rather than adapting to the Oankali's "alien" value system. The mixed "construct children," however, become rare commodities for the childless resister humans, who capture one of them, Akin. After living among and bonding with humans, Akin becomes a cultural broker for the resisters, asserting their right to freedom of choice and eventually convincing the reluctant Oankali to give humans the option to resettle on Mars with restored fertility.

Imago, the last volume, focuses on hazards in transspecies reproduction. Nikanj, the first ooloi to perform the gene trade between humans and Oankali, makes a mistake in his engineering of construct children. He creates two "construct ooloi," a combination that the Oankali have placed under a prohibition because they fear that human genes combined with the power of an ooloi as gene manipulator might turn into a deadly mix. The conflict arises over whether construct ooloi can be kept in the transspecies community or need to be exiled. Interestingly, Nikanj's mistake introduces unconscious affect into the actions of the otherwise supremely conscious Oankali. Nikanj has unconsciously created construct ooloi because its envy of the close bond between parents and their same-sex children momentarily distracted it, leading to its breaking the cultural prohibition placed on construct ooloi. Jodahs and Aaor, the two construct ooloi, function as transitional characters that negotiate the tensions between human and Oankali emotions. Both become so symbiotically dependent on having human mates that, without them, they lose their life energy and will to live. It is they who at the end of the trilogy plant the seed for a new town designed for the harmonious integration of the two species.

In fashioning encounters between human and alien species, the extraterrestrial imaginary cannot but import crucial preoccupations of the time. Octavia Butler responds to a pervasive millennial species anxiety that emerges from both the increasingly threatening ecological destruction and the new reproductive technologies. Sustainable development as well as biological and cultural reproduction figure as core issues negotiated in the transspecies communities of humans and Oankali. Inevitably, human cultural encounters raise issues of colonialism, racism, and xenophobia, as well as the historical legacies of worldwide wars and genocide. Eurocentrism and colonial racism are often translated into a "speciesism," defined by Peter Singer as "the belief that we are entitled to treat members of other species in a way in which it would be wrong to treat members of our own."[10] Contrary to the human-animal speciesism, the speciesism in relation to imagined aliens operates according to a logic of radical otherness within proximity. In order even to experience racism or xenophobia in relation to another species, there needs to be an anthropomorphic imaginary, that is, a figuration that grants enough proximity both physically and culturally. The aversive reaction to a mollusk, for example, may be phobic but not xenophobic.

The extraterrestrial imaginary in popular science fiction is often but a simple extension of the colonial imaginary into a transspecies culture. Butler, however, insists on differentiation. She figures humans as racist, sexist, xenophobic, speciesist, violent, militarist, and self-destructive, but also as "victims" of a form of extraterrestrial colonization. Initially the Oankali keep them from having a choice in restoring their biological and cultural reproduction. While most human characters perceive the Oankali as colonizers, Butler insists on the differences between human and Oankali colonization. The Oankali do not treat humans as slaves, nor do they exploit their labor or skills for proprietary purposes. Not only do they integrate humans as equal members of the new transspecies communities but they also welcome changes in their own culture and genetic material.

In human cultures, reproduction has hardly ever been a matter of mere biopolitics. Rather, it has been heavily implicated in power politics that also played into the organization of kinship relations. The imagined human reproduction with aliens highlights the ethical implications of reproductive biopolitics from a perspective that explores the boundaries of what different cultures define as human more generally. Butler figures the Oankali as owners of superior gene technologies whose mission consists of a double task. Their goal is to diversify the gene pool of both humans and Oankali, while the

humans, by contrast, perceive this engineered gene trade as an invasive mutation that heralds the end of their species. Adhering to a "genes-are-us" policy,
the humans in *Dawn* question whether their transspecies offspring would still
be human. As "gene traders," the Oankali, by contrast, pursue their politics
of reproduction within an economy of exchange. "Trading" in this context
resembles a precapitalist exchange of goods, in which genes have pure use
value. They are, in other words, free from commodification and fetishization.

Butler's insistence on the pure use value of genes also bears upon the relationship between genes and personhood. If traditional philosophical discourses have figured the "soul" as the defining property of the human, the
"genes-are-us" policy indicates a new genetic determinism that defines the
human within a new discourse of genes. Traditionally, discourses of the soul
were intimately connected to highly politicized discourses of self-ownership.
Definitions of property tended to rely on corresponding configurations of the
person who owned or was subjected to property. In his essay on John Locke,
Étienne Balibar argues that the vexed relationship between the *self* and the
own not only structures the classical theory of "personal identity" but also continues to haunt Western theories of the self and the subject, concluding that
"there is nothing natural in the identification of self and own, which is really a
norm rather than a necessity, and reigns by virtue of a postulate."[11]

If identity is relational, including the disturbing presence of otherness
within every consciousness, we may ask how this relationality operates for
transspecies generation. What happens to identity if it is subject to a perpetual process of gene manipulation and trading? Does it still make sense to
think about the ensuing changes in terms of changing identities, or is this notion inadequate to understand personhood in Oankali culture? If indeed the
Oankali had no identity in this Lockean sense, would it follow that they have
no self-ownership? Moreover, if personhood evolves within the relationship
between the individual and the community, what are we to think about the
personhood of people in slavery or other forms of oppression?

Octavia Butler establishes complex links between the gene-driven Oankali
cultural ecology and human cultures under colonialism and slavery. Despotic
rulers, colonizers, or slaveholders could own a person's body, but as long as
they did not own the soul, they could not rob their subjects of personhood.
Technologies of genetic engineering, however, come with a new threat to
self-ownership, of which the patenting of genes is only the most obvious.
What Donna Haraway calls the fetishism of genes is a more subliminal threat.
Genes belong to a culture of commodity fetishism, Haraway argues, because

at least discursively "genes displace not only organisms but people . . . as generators of liveliness."[12] For the Oankali, however, the defining property of
genes consists in facilitating change and diversification. Hence they have only
use and exchange value and become disconnected from issues of ownership.
Neither the ownership of genes nor self-ownership is ever a cultural issue for
the Oankali.

If we read the Oankali's world as a historical allegory, we are of course
reminded that genes as an object of commodity fetishism are part and parcel
of a Western notion of genetics that is deeply implicated in the logic of late
capitalism. Over and above this discourse of a genetic consumer culture, Butler places the emphasis of cultural tensions between humans and Oankali
over the discourse of genes on the fact that genetics played a crucial role in
the racial history of slavery and colonialism. Many of these racial tensions are
also played out over issues of self-ownership. It is the humans who insist on
personhood in terms of self-ownership, because in human cultures it is slavery
that has most violently disrupted the connection between personhood and
self-ownership. It is under slavery that humans have witnessed the ultimate
conflation of personhood and property. This is why Butler's historical allegory
can be read as a vision of alien contact that rejects the history of the West precisely in its intimate connection between property and personhood. The issue
of self-ownership is inextricable from the violent histories that have led the
planet to the brink of destruction. In indigenous preindustrial, precapitalist,
and precontact communities, in which the self is predominately communal
and relational, self-ownership becomes an issue only under conditions of captivity or slavery. In the wake of Western histories of colonialism and slavery,
however, self-ownership becomes increasingly a social, economic, and legal
value. Colonizing processes and related oppressive and exploitative economic
conditions, moreover, generate concomitant psychic processes of subjugation
that are often experienced as a disowning of the self. This is why Western
philosophies and psychologies have tended to tie the psychic dimension of
self-ownership to issues of freedom and free will, often shifting the emphasis
away from the material and economic conditions that enable the latter in the
first place.

In Octavia Butler's trilogy, self-ownership emerges as a psychic legacy of
violent human histories. For the human characters, their material conditions
of self-ownership in the transspecies communities are inseparable from their
psychohistorical experience of violent human communities in which self-
ownership was tantamount with freedom from bondage. Human characters

therefore import issues of self-ownership into the new transspecies communities. Aaor, a transspecies character in *Imago*, speaks for the human need to
claim self-ownership and freedom. "When you have Human mates . . . you
have to remember to let them be Human. . . . Sometimes they need to prove
to themselves that they still own themselves. . . . "[13] For the human characters,
"owning oneself" has an external cultural aspect and an internal psychic one.
Self-ownership may mean freedom from Oankali domination as well as control over one's memories and inner life. In *Xenogenesis*, human self-ownership
is threatened on both accounts. Not only do the humans feel colonized by the
Oankali but they are also, in contrast to the Oankali, not in control of their
memories, affects, or actions. They are, in other words, creatures endowed or
cursed with an unconscious. "I am, but I do not have myself" is, according to
anthropologist Helmuth Plessner, the fundamental psychic condition of the
human.[14] Or, as Freud argues, humans are not master in their own house but
driven by unconscious memories, desires, fears, and traumatic bodily inscriptions.[15] From the perspective of the Oankali, things appear in a different light.
For them, the new kinship arrangement with humans does not belong to an
economy of property. Moreover, they perceive the lack of total memory recall
as a mere deficiency in the human genetic makeup.

The superior access to memory and genetic information further enforces
the power differential between the two species. Able to tap into their own as
well as others' genetic memories, the Oankali can gather more information
about humans than the humans themselves. With their access to all genetically stored memory and affect, they can even penetrate the unconscious.
Though this raises deep fears in humans, the construct children savor such
symbiotic merging, practicing willful osmotic assimilation and taking pleasure
in shaping themselves after human fantasies.[16] "Being oneself" is not bound
to identity but to conditions of continual change, often osmotic in response to
the needs or fantasies of others. As one of the characters says in a conversation
about construct children, "I remembered being their age and having a strong
awareness of the way my face and body looked, and of that look being *me*. It
never had been, really."[17] Personhood, in other words, is not identitarian but
relational in a radical sense.

In questions of personhood, identity, and relatedness, most humans follow
a narrow identity politics, whereas the Oankali are radical subjects-in-process.
For them, being oneself does not preclude mutations through sexual reproduction with other species. Rather than preserving biogenetic identity, the
Oankali seek survival by increasing the complexity of their gene pool. Ulti-

mately, humans and aliens in Butler's fiction clash over radical differences in their reproductive politics and concomitant anxieties about the survival of a race or a species. Reproductive politics as a site for the enactment of power and domination between species recalls once again the history of slavery and colonialism. In the process of colonial invasions, for example, forced sterilization, genocide, and deicide were often the most radical manifestations of a pervasive politics of reproduction aimed at the destruction of the other's culture, language, and means of reproduction. In a master-and-slave economy, the reduction of human beings to personal property granted the exploitation of their labor as well as sexual and reproductive powers. In their imagined encounters with aliens, fantasies of transspecies reproduction stage a related form of power politics.

Xenogenesis figures human survival as a drama of forced transspecies reproduction. Butler links this alien reproductive politics intertextually with the biblical myth of an exile from paradise. The biblical exile marks a transition from "nature" and natural innocence to sexual reproduction that follows the first "bachelor's birth" of Eve from Adam's rib. Dawn marks a new transition from "natural" sexual reproduction to genetically engineered reproduction with different species. As supreme geneticists, the ooloi as a third sex also mediate sexual intercourse and reproduction between male and female partners. As facilitators of sex, reproduction, and genetic enhancement, the ooloi gain an inordinate power over humans. As one of the characters says about Lilith's ooloi mate, Nikanj, "It knows everything that can be learned about you from your genes. And by now, it knows your medical history and a great deal about the way you think. It has taken part in testing you."[18] For humans, ooloi biochemical seduction is highly ambivalent because, bound to the mediation by ooloi, sexual desire and pleasure are biologically triangular. Although humans gain, as Lilith asserts, more intimacy and closeness with ooloi than they ever have in human sexual encounters,[19] they nonetheless resist the intrusion into knowledges and internal feeling states that are, in Westernized human cultures, highly private. Humans fear a "chemical bondage" to the ooloi, who, after all, control not only sexual pleasure but also the access to other human mates.[20] The Oankali culture thus also challenges a long Western history of cultural production of subjectivity based on privacy, individualism, interiority, and monogamous, heteronormative familial kinship arrangements. While humans would be able to find models of human cultures that are closer to the Oankali in preindustrialized indigenous communities, the human characters carry with them the psychic legacy of values internalized during a long history of Western colonial and imperial global culture, which ended in a nuclear apocalypse. It is this legacy of colonialism, racism, and the systematic domination and exploitation of humans by other humans that introduces power, domination, and warfare in the transspecies communities.

In spite of the bitter and seemingly irresolvable conflicts that mark the transspecies communities, Donna Haraway reads Xenogenesis emphatically as an ethnographic exploration of utopian personhood. As Haraway points out, Lilith's child is "the child of five progenitors, who come from two species, at least three genders, two sexes, and an indeterminate number of races."[21] From a perspective of postmodern theories, the Oankali follow a radical politics of hybridity instead of a politics of identity, adhering to a fluid economy and a practice of systematic deterritorialization at both a genetic and planetary level. Just as they diversify their genetic material in gene trades with other species, they also disseminate it across other planets, seeking to induce the emergence of new life. Oankali politics of reproduction is thus based on emergence and mutation. Yet since total control over emergence is impossible, this politics opens the door for surprises, conflict, and mistakes, as well as power struggles. From the outset, Oankali and humans clash over reproductive politics. The human characters import their legacy of "terrestrial" racism according to which "miscegenation" is always already discursively mediated through a tropology of monstrosity. These conflicts need to be assessed from a postcolonial perspective that traces the effects of human histories of colonialism and racism into the projected future. During the pregnancy with her first child conceived by an Oankali, Lilith says, "But it won't be human. . . . It will be a thing. A monster."[22] As opposed to the Oankali's integrative ethics of diversification, Lilith's attribution of monstrosity to her own transspecies child presupposes that the exclusionary preservation of human genetic identity is the only value. It presupposes, in other words, a value system still wedded to colonial and racist notions of miscegenation. Butler's technique of oscillating narrative perspectives between the incompatible ethics of the two species creates a pointed ambiguity, leaving the central ethical problem—namely, the question of violence and domination—and the central epistemological problem—defining the boundaries of the human—open until the very end.

Butler uses a polyphonic variety of agonistic narrative voices from human, Oankali, and transspecies characters to address these issues. The use of genetic technologies is at the center of pronounced clashes over agency in sexuality, reproduction, and self-definition. While the Oankali perceive their interventions as the salvage and enhancement of an otherwise doomed species, the humans see the Oankali as genetic colonizers who use them, in Lilith's words, as "captive breeders." Lilith's very use of the term "captive breeders" invokes both the history of slavery and the Nazi experiments with female reproduction and genetic manipulation. But the narrative leaves no doubt that the reaction of the human figures remains bound to their pervasive terrestrial paranoia toward otherness and difference. They simply transfer the racism that generated their histories of colonialism, slavery, war, and genocide onto the Oankali. This speciesism blinds them to crucial differences in both Oankali cultural politics and psychic makeup. Within their new transspecies communities, the Oankali integrate humans as equal members of their kinship arrangements. Yet for the human characters, Oankali colonialism with a difference is a form of colonialism nonetheless.

Ultimately, Butler contrasts two forms of domination, namely the racism of humans and the biogenetic colonialism of the Oankali. Her overarching perspective, however, becomes gradually more biased toward the aliens, rejecting the racist politics of a "pure species"[23] propagated by human characters. Narrative strategies focusing on both the Oankali culture of emotions and the transitional emotional space of the transspecies generation gradually attune readers to an alien culture of feeling and relating. Initially, we see the Oankali through Lilith's aversive reactions to their radical alterity. Increasingly, however, more complex transspecies language games evolve to negotiate difference. The fact that the Oankali are able to acquire human languages through accessing the totality of information stored in human cells grants them a hegemonic hold on diverse histories and cultures of human knowledge. Information is not enough, however, for meaningful attunement and communication. In many ways, the two species remain foreign to each other despite the Oankali's almost total informational access. Even the use of a common language is limited by cultural difference. While the Oankali easily master scores of human languages, language for them has an entirely different status and remains subordinate to immediate access. They use it like a prosthetic device to compensate for what they perceive as human communicative incompetence. The most radical differences reside in a different emotional cathexis of language and speech. The Oankali tend to reduce language to a mere carrier of information, ignoring its performative dimension as well as its affective cathexis. As the Oankali's "native informant," Lilith experiences a form of "social death"[24] in response to the withdrawal of all familiar rules of sociality, communication, and emotion. Rebelling against her captivity among the Oankali, Lilith invokes the social death her own ancestors experienced under slavery.[25] Yet her impassioned rebellion clashes with the Oankali's systematic refusal of open confrontation. Faced with uncontrolled human emotions, the Oankali simply induce deep sleep as a therapy.

This strategy produces a curious effect, sustaining a pointed ambivalence within the futuristic vision. Again and again we are confronted with difficulties of emotional attunement. For better or worse, humans seem to remain fixated on familiar communicative values and affects, even when they appear deficient in light of superior technologies of communication. The two most basic human expressions of emotion are a case in point. The Oankali lack what Plessner defines as the fundamental anthropological universals, laughter and tears.[26] "Inhuman" in this very archaic sense, in that they neither laugh nor cry, the Oankali induce a social death that exceeds the withdrawal of rules and customs to include the primordial expressions of human emotion. If we agree with Plessner that laughter and tears emerge at the limits of language and consciousness, the Oankali do not need to laugh or cry because for them emotion, consciousness, and the body are in complete synchrony. We soon learn, however, that the Oankali possess a vast range of emotions, including ease, joy, attachment, and love as well as grief, mourning, and utter loneliness. They convey emotions either through direct biochemical exchange of information or through the coded body language of their sensory tentacles. Of secondary order, spoken language becomes central only in transspecies exchanges.

This bias puts alien corporeality at the center of communicative difference. The Oankali's body language generates one of the most distressing experiences of radical alterity for the human characters. Neither the biochemical exchange of information nor the Oankali body language is immediately accessible to humans. Initially it is the Oankali's corporeal difference that presents the greatest barrier for transspecies attachment and reproduction. A minimum of corporeal similarity seems to be a precondition for any meaningful imagined transspecies relationship. Philosopher Hans Blumenberg, however, argues that of all the probabilities of astronautic experience, corporeal similarity is least expectable.[27] On the other hand, a minimum of corporeal affinity or at least possibility of connection seems to be a condition of imagined cultural contact with extraterrestrials. We cannot altogether escape a certain "anthropomorphization" of extraterrestrials whenever we envision a meaningful contact with them. The "embodiments" that science fiction imagines for extraterrestrial species serves as a prime matrix for projection and transference. The naïve notions of the "little green men with huge heads" might

indicate how narrowly we draw the boundaries within which we imagine unknown species. Nonanthropomorphized radical alterity of an intelligent species seems unimaginable, or at least unfit for good fiction. This tells us more
about our relationship to alterity in general than we might at first assume.
Butler solves this narratological challenge by endowing the alien characters
themselves with techniques of anthropomorphization. As highly superior ma-
nipulators of the genetic code, they are able to manipulate their own bodies
and temporarily to assimilate them to the shapes of human bodies. They use
such manipulation within a communicative pragmatics as a mode to facilitate
cultural and later sexual contact. The first Oankali appears for Lilith in the
shape of a "shadowy figure of a man, thin and long-haired."[28] Only in full light
does she perceive the difference: "What had seemed to be a tall slender man
was still humanoid, but it had no nose—no bulge, no nostrils—just flat, gray
skin."[29] Instead of human sensory organs, Jdahya has long tentacles that embody his anthropomorphized body language and convey his focus of attention
as well as his emotions. Asked whether he is male or female, Jdahya answers,
"It's wrong to assume that I must be a sex you're familiar with . . . but as it happens, I'm male."[30]

We must recall here that within postmodern imagination—both literature
and theory—we already have a convention for exceedingly strange humanoid
figures. One of Samuel Beckett's characters, the Unnamable, for example,
imagines himself as a constantly mutating shape and laconically asks, "Why
should I have a sex, who have no longer a nose?"[31] Within theory, Deleuze
and Guattari's "organless bodies" also mutate permanently, manifesting themselves in ever new shapes. But there is a crucial difference in the figuration or
imagination of alternative bodies that has to do with generic conventions. A
science fiction character resists our receptive disposition to translate his figuration as an alternative body *image* or phantasm as we are inclined to do with
the figures of Beckett or Deleuze and Guattari. The corporeal figuration of an
extraterrestrial requires a different "willing suspension of disbelief" precisely
because, within the generic conventions of science fiction, we perceive the
radically alien as an "imagined reality." Unlike scientific or philosophical notions of extraterrestrial life, science *fiction* is not bound to notions of a "cosmic
realism"[32] and thus unavoidably generates a kind of "literary realism" at the
level of narration. This is an aesthetic paradox of sorts, since other genres can
much more easily shed realist conventions precisely because they are *fictions*
of an alien world. Despite the radical experimentalism of its imagined worlds,
science fiction remains therefore bound to more conventional narrative

techniques. While writers such as Beckett or Deleuze and Guattari invite us
to imagine humans with distorted body images or philosophical concepts of
a "body without organs," Butler entices us to imagine an encounter with real
embodiments of alien corporeality. For Lilith, the contact with beings like
Jdahya is unfathomable because of

> his alienness, his difference, his literal unearthliness . . . she tried to
> imagine herself surrounded by beings like him and was overwhelmed by
> panic. As though she had suddenly developed a phobia—something she
> had never before experienced. But what she felt was like what she had
> heard others describe. A true xenophobia—and apparently she was not
> alone in it.[33]

Fixation on corporeal similarity in alien encounters thus produces xenophobia and racism. At a biopolitical level, the panicked reaction to the Oankali's
"alien" bodies also invokes fear related to the current biogenetic reconcep-
tualization of the human body. The unity of soma and psyche endows the
Oankali's bodies with a plasticity and fluidity that transcends the body as an
identitarian construct. This fluidity is enhanced by their ability to adapt os-
motically to their environment. Butler thus links the radical constructivism
of postmodern concepts of the body with a biogenetic concept according to
which corporeality emerges from and is continually reorganized through genetic information. For the Oankali, such genetic information is not "exterior," because as gene readers they do not need any additional information
technology. Human readers, however, are bound to read Butler's text from
the perspective of their own embeddedness in an expansive information technology and ecology. In an ecology based on new information technologies,
the boundaries of human corporeality have become tenuous, because the
exteriority of uncontrollable information that ties our bodies to new information technologies has reorganized the human organism, turning humans into
sublime cyborgs. If we recall that Freud defined the ego as the projection of
the body's surface, we realize how profoundly the new information technologies affect the boundaries of subjectivity. Perhaps Richard Doyle is right when
he argues that contemporary subjectivity is no longer organized according to
notions of subject position and the boundaries of the body but according to
a continual "becoming" in the sense of Deleuze and Guattari.[34] The exteriority of information and information technologies affect the bodies of those
exposed to them. The subjectivity of this "postmodern subject" has shifted

from a Cartesian epistemology to an epistemology of radical exteriority. Or, as Richard Doyle formulates it, "I think therefore I am has turned into 'I'm abducted, therefore I am.'"[35]

For the Oankali, by contrast, genetic information is not "exterior," since they transmit genetically encoded knowledge with their sense organs. In their transspecies contact, however, the Oankali must take into account human communicative incompetence. Just as they simulate a corporeal similarity to interact with humans, they also simulate human speech and communication. This simulation, however, is haunted by subliminal tensions between two radically different cultural and ethical codes. Above all, this tension concerns the use of rhetoric. To humans, the language games of the Oankali appear strange because they lack the very tools of rhetoric. Marked by a bare literality, their enunciations are free of images, metaphors, and tropes, but at the same time also free of displacement, concealment, and double meaning. They do not know lies or deceit, nor do they know an imaginary in a human sense; they lack stories, perhaps even dreams, and, as I argued, a dynamic unconscious. The Oankali's world is a world without fiction, art and artifice, without refinement and ornamentation. To the extent that we define their language as being without depth and double meaning, we could see the Oankali as "postmodern subjects" par excellence. And yet it appears as if they are lacking something that, for humans, has always been valued as a core element of cultural life. From an Oankali perspective, this may look as if humans are not only "attached to their wounds"[36] but also attached to the prosthetic devices they have designed to cope with them.

We encounter here then another deep ambivalence in Butler's juxtaposition of the ethics and value systems of humans and Oankali. In contrast to humans, who are never the sovereign agents of their own speech, the Oankali demonstrate complete agency in their discourse. While clearly superior in their technologies of information, and therefore in their self-consciousness, the Oankali's lack of cultural objects such as literature, music, or storytelling appears, from an anthropocentric perspective, as an impoverished literalism, a lack of refinement, or, as we once used to say, cultural and psychic depth. The Oankali's biogenetic and kinship politics, combined with their superior technologies of genetic manipulation, seem to get rid of the racism that has led to the destruction of human communities. But in her depiction of the transspecies generation, Butler almost plays into a nostalgic vision that sees the lack of transparency that marks human personhood as what stimulates the riches of cultural and inner life. It is therefore precisely this use of artistic practices that the transspecies generation introduces into the cultural life of transspecies communities.

Yet it is easy to fall into the traps of an anthropocentric nostalgia for the arts, forgetting that while the Oankali do not use aesthetic objects they do know aesthetics and indeed a supreme sense of harmony and beauty. Akin, a construct human, describes, for example, the pleasures of healing: "It was almost like making music—balancing endorphins, silencing pain, maintaining sobriety. He made simple music. Ooloi made great harmonies, interweaving people and sharing pleasure."[37] Eventually, the transspecies construct generation also brings human artifacts into Oankali cultural arrangements. Discovering the art of rhetoric, simulation, and acting, construct humans become storytellers and musicians and thus introduce the human use of cultural objects into transspecies culture.

The ambivalence toward art and artifice also plays itself out in relation to the Oankali's sovereign consciousness and total mnemonic recall. They do not know the dynamic interplay between conscious and unconscious life and its vicissitudes that characterizes human cultures. As beings without interiority and an unconscious, the Oankali may well possess full control over information, memory, knowledge, and discourse within their precontact culture. However, they lose part of this sovereignty in their new transspecies encounters. They neither possess a total grasp of the cultural values and sense of being of their transspecies partners nor are they in complete control of their emotions and patterns of relating. Biochemical rather than rhetorical seduction, for example, comes to a limit when it encounters human resistance and resentment. With her figuration of the Oankali's superior genetic technologies, Butler confronts a pervasive fear in the cultural imaginary of our time, namely that our emotional and mental worlds could be reducible to biochemical and biogenetic manipulation. Such determinism would amount to an even more radical disowning of the subject than the Freudian discovery of the unconscious. The subject becomes imaginable as one that is no longer governed by unconscious drives, desires, and fears but is instead reduced to the pure materiality of a totally engineered body-mind-soul. In such a world, even the distinction between self and other or between one's own and another culture becomes an object of biogenesis.

Let me end by outlining three fundamental challenges *Xenogenesis* presents to deliberations on the futures of property and personhood. (1) Butler's imagined alien world operates on the basis of a processual organic ecology in which the binaries of mind and body, nature and culture, or nature and technology are superseded. Technology and culture are *natural* in the sense that they are organically embedded in embodied matter. Even the Oankali abodes, their spaceships, and their objects are sentient beings. Personhood, in this context, is always defined in relation to the environment rather than against it. The subject and its environment are perceived as an inseparable unit operating under the assumption that every environmental intervention produces related changes in personhood. (2) The Oankali's processual ecology leads to an allopoietic ethics and practice toward otherness and difference. Hybridity, diversity, and change are privileged over identity and sameness. The diversification of the gene pool is welcomed as a technology of expansion, enrichment, and complexification. Developed in contrast to the anthropocentric and racialized ethics of Western cultures, Butler's biocentric and transplanetary ethics offers a basis for a systemically grounded critique of racism and its epistemological and political foundations. Free from the cultural paranoia and practices of Manichean splitting, which marks an exclusionary Western ethics, the inclusionary Oankali ethics is also free from what Gregory Bateson calls destructive schismogenesis.[38] (3) Against certain trends in debates about the *posthuman*, Butler insists on reevaluating earlier, precolonial models of human communities and personhood. At the same time, she accounts for the fact that the legacies of racism and oppression left by those histories inevitably mark any encounter with a different culture or species. *Xenogenesis* is sensitive to the psychic ecologies that create conflict in cultural and transspecies encounters. The transgenerational transmission of cultural memory, trauma, psychic dispositions, and fantasies is fraught with conflict in the encounter between two species that dramatically differ in the technologies of memory and its psychic and material inscriptions. The figuration of "construct humans"—either human or alien born—serves to illustrate the ethical dilemma that inevitably ensues if cultural contact is enforced for reasons of survival.

In *How We Became Posthuman*, N. Katherine Hayles points out how strongly current cultural fantasies of the posthuman insist on values and properties of the liberal subject in the humanist tradition.[39] Octavia Butler is no exception. The staging of transcultural and transspecies conflict in *Xenogenesis* is largely organized around notions of freedom and self-ownership. Butler's science fiction, however, presents an alternative to the cultural imaginary of cyborgs and their articulation of the human in symbiotic assemblages with intelligent machines. Her extraterrestrial imaginary supersedes the cyborg imaginary in its even more radical effacement of a binary and ontologizing division between nature and technology. In the Oankali world, hyperefficient technologies of knowledge, production, and reproduction are embodied in alien beings for which gene reading and manipulation belong to the primary modes of cultural exchange, sociality, memory, and reproduction. In place of an obsolete teleological notion of progressing civilization, the Oankali's vision of the world is one of an endless—perhaps rhizomatic—differentiation and diversification of species. Instead of an individualized consciousness and autonomous will, the Oankali operate with a distributed cognition that encompasses the implicate order[40] of inner cellular and outer planetary environments. Instead of asserting mind over matter, the Oankali's mind asserts itself spontaneously as matter and materialized consciousness.

Xenogenesis organizes its vision of an alien world around the question of the boundaries of the human. The figure of the "alien" functions as an iconotrope that helps to articulate the cultural imaginary with its prominent fears and desires at the turn of the millennium. Along with cyborgs and posthumans, aliens are part and parcel of the metonymic chain of iconotropes that define the current episteme. It seems appropriate that Octavia Butler figures her aliens as gene readers. Sixty years ago, Erwin Schrödinger in his lecture "What Is Life?" predicted that the potential of the future of an organism could be read like a hieroglyph in the chromosomes of a cell.[41] German philosopher Hans Blumenberg ends his book on reading the world (*Die Lesbarkeit der Welt*) with the question of whether we humans were ever aware that with the metaphor of the "readability" of the genetic code we have become Gnostics, under the spell of a great anthropomorphic hypostasis.[42] Addressing the blasphemous and apocalyptic undercurrent of this vision, Blumenberg points out that once we are able to read the genetic code, we approach the transition from the human as reader of the world to the human as rewriter of the book of nature. The Oankali are gene readers, and yet, although they rewrite the genetic code, they do not rewrite the book of nature—at least not in their own self-understanding. Unlike humans, they refrain from committing the epistemological error of conferring a privileged ontological status onto their own species or, for that matter, onto entities instead of relationships. Personhood for them is inconceivable in terms of entities. Unlike human epistemologies that embrace deterministic thinking and a splitting of symbiotic wholes (ecosytems) or processes into supposedly independent units or "things," their epistemology is not one of biosocial imperialism. Rather, they see the biosocial imperialism of humans as a genetic defect that translates into a pervasive thinking in hierarchies, immutable identities, and lineal causations of force and power.[43] The problem, Butler seems to suggest, does not lie in the "read-ability" or even "rewriting" of the genetic code but in an altogether different ecology of reading and writing.

For the human species, storytelling and writing have always been forms of mourning, works of memory and inscription to defer or defy death. We could even say that the very construction of personhood has been bound up with storytelling and writing. The Oankali are not mortal in any human sense and hence do not need storytelling and writing in order to defer or defy death. Nor do they need an attachment to personhood that is as individualized and bounded as it is for humans. But their sense of both personhood and species is linked in a very different way to what Achille Mbembe has called the work of death.[44] Ultimately, Butler opposes the "work of death" of the human species with the Oankali's "work of life." Humans in Butler's *Xenogenesis* are driven by a pervasive work of death expressed as racism, xenophobia, homophobia, and speciesism. After all, the trilogy opens when this work of death had re-sulted in a nuclear holocaust on Earth. The Oankali, by contrast, are figured as life crafters of sorts, working toward the restoration and continual diversifi-cation of living material and life. They intervene in and attempt to undo the human work of death on a transplanetary scale. Ahajas, one of the Oankali mothers of construct children, says toward the end of the trilogy: "Our ances-tors have seeded a great many barren worlds that way. Nothing is more tena-cious than the life we are made of. A world of life from apparent death, from dissolution. That's what we believe in."[45]

The Oankali are figured here as indigenous nomads, transplanetary space travelers, who, to borrow an image from *A Thousand Plateaus*, move through itinerant territorialities, but only to embark on a galactic line of flight, a deter-ritorialization that spans the universe. They use the same deterritorializing en-ergy to operate at the molecular level, to continually transform their own tem-porary embodiments as well as those of their environment. Inviting—indeed celebrating—the continual mutation of their genes, they embrace otherness, difference, and heterogeneity, infusing the galaxies with a monumental state of eternal becoming that humans would once have called miscegenation.

As Donna Haraway has argued, *Xenogenesis* is survival fiction, but at stake is not a mere survival of an identitarian species. Butler's vision is projected into a distant future after human struggles for identitarian cultures have suc-cumbed to global nuclear devastation. The Oankali, however, continue to struggle for the survival of knowledges. This struggle puts a new spin on the transcoding of colonial and extraterrestrial discourses. While humans often construct their fantasies of aliens after their fantasies about indigenous peoples, Butler's text suggests that the humans need the extraterrestrial or indigenous knowledges in order to survive by undoing their work of death. The trilogy ends with an allegory of new life. Jodahs, the first construct ooloi, performs the "seeding" of a new genetically engineered town,[46] based on an ecological vision of a thoroughly sentient environment, that is as genetically and emotionally attuned to its inhabitants as they are to it. This ending highlights the diametrical opposition between Butler's fantasy of the Oankali's culture of gene readers and engineers of genetic diversification and the proprietary logics of the Human Genome Diversity Project. Genes, for the Oankali, cannot be owned, commercialized, monopolized, or patented by individuals or corporations. Genes cannot become fetishized objects of value in a consumer culture. Life, for the Oankali, is a common property that cannot be owned and needs to be protected from pillaging and destruction. This is the ethics on the basis of which the Oankali life crafters oppose their "work of life" to what they perceive as the human's "work of death." It is an ethics that resembles the ethics of the first people on Earth, which included the integration and protection of other species and the galaxy in their cosmologies. Through the detour of an extraterrestrial imaginary, Butler draws on indigenous knowledges that have survived repression and marginalization. The Oankali's use of their own indigenous knowledge to undo the work of death prepares, Butler seems to suggest, a new ground for the working through of the devastating legacy of colonialism and genocide. In this sense, *Xenogenesis* indeed bears traces of a utopian ethnography of the future.

Part III
Coda

Cosmographical Meditations on the Inhuman
Samuel Beckett's *The Lost Ones*

The soul is transferred to a quite different standpoint, so to speak, and from it sees all objects differently.[1]
— Immanuel Kant, *Anthropology from a Pragmatic Point of View*

Abstraction is not a negation of form: it posits form as folded, existing only as a "mental landscape" in the soul or in the mind, in upper altitudes.[2]
— Gilles Deleuze, *The Fold*

The wretchedness of the soul rubbed raw by the tiderace of matter.[3]
— Jean-François Lyotard, *The Inhuman*

The effect of this climate on the soul is not to be underestimated.[4]
— Samuel Beckett, *The Lost Ones*

I n his short piece "Scapeland,"[5] included in *The Inhuman*, Jean-François Lyotard philosophizes on imaginary land- and soulscapes: uninhabitable spaces envisioned along the lines of a Western philosophy of space ranging from Aristotle to Kant and beyond. He quotes Kant's reflection, included above as an epigraph, upon the transference of the soul to a standpoint of difference. Lyotard calls this condition of the soul *vesania*, or systematic madness.[6] Such "madness" emerges from a radical encounter with otherness in which one loses all familiar ground, categorical frameworks, or modes of perception. It is a form of fundamental disorientation not unlike the "social death"[7] one suffers during the initial encounters of radical otherness in certain fieldwork experiences.[8] It is such a condition, one might argue, that Samuel Beckett's

The Lost Ones induces in its readers, albeit in a form far more radical than the one envisioned by Kant and Lyotard.

The Lost Ones opens like a play with stage directions for an eerie scene, evoking an abstract notion of space resonating with Dante's *Purgatorio*:

> ABODE WHERE LOST bodies roam each searching for its lost one. Vast enough for search to be in vain. Narrow enough for flight to be in vain. Inside a flattened cylinder fifty metres round and sixteen high for the sake of harmony. The light. Its dimness. Its yellowness.[9]

Minutely constructed according to geometrical shapes and measurements, this space is populated by an abject group of two hundred languishing and vanquished remnants of humans whose culture seems to be organized according to an elusive order, if not an unfamiliar harmony the principles of which have yet to be discovered. Dejection, futility, and a sense of loss pervade the mood in the cylinder. Did Beckett have the old Christian definition of the human as "a village of 200 souls"[10] in mind when he populated his abode with 200 humans at their vanishing point? Their naked bodies—only "flesh and bone subsist"[11]—roam in futile search, some in perpetual motion, some climbing a ladder, others sedentary and immobile. The cylinder measures "some twelve million [centimeters] of total surface,"[12] contains niches and alcoves, sunk as cavities in the wall above "an imaginary line running midway between floor and ceiling."[13] The abode is described by an anonymous disembodied voice committed to using scientific observation, recording spaces and movements, harmony and its disruptions. The flattened cylinder, we read, is "fifty meters round and sixteen high for the sake of harmony."[14] (What harmony, we wonder?) The ladders, sole remaining objects in the abode, "are propped against the wall without regard to harmony."[15] Harmony seems to be generated by irregularity rather than symmetry. The niches and alcoves, we are told, "are disposed in irregular quincunxes roughly ten meters in diameter and cunningly out of line. Such harmony only he can relish whose long experience and detailed knowledge of the niches are such as to permit a perfect mental image of the entire system. But it is doubtful that such a one exists."[16]

Who speaks about this distant abode and its mysterious location in an unknown space? The ominous, virtually untranslatable French title of Beckett's piece is *Le dépeupleur*. Who is this *dépeupleur* who, by virtue of his appearance in the title, marks a central perspective in Beckett's text? Alain Badiou describes him as a *singularizer*, someone who functions as a defining other, arguing that each searcher is on a quest to find his or her *dépeupleur*: "It is everyone's proper other, one who singularizes and rips one out of anonymity."[17] If Badiou were right, the title would refer to an anonymous Other, one who never receives an incorporation as a character in Beckett's imaginary world. But one could also see the *dépeupleur* as one who "de-peoples," who orphans a place—as the equally ominous German translation *Der Verwaiser* suggests. Finally, we could see him as the anonymous narrator who functions not as a character but as a virtual organizer of this posthuman space, suggesting perhaps that the space and its population have a particular virtuality of their own, imagined into existence as it were by the organizer's computing eye. Necessary to conceive the harmony of the cylinder's construction, the computing eye is attuned to a virtual order invisible to the *eye of flesh*. Beckett, in fact, plays with distinct layers of virtuality. As the author, the one who authorizes the piece, he projects the abode as the virtual artifice of a closed cylinder, suspended in a "vast space of time impossible to measure."[18] In addition, he chooses a disembodied narrative voice that is figured as a computing eye able to perceive and record an order that is invisible to material eyes.

In the vein of current philosophical thought, one could therefore see Beckett's abode as a virtualization of the posthuman. In contrast, for example, to narratives of science fiction that figure the posthuman in the mode of a presumed reality of the future, Beckett insists on a future that is merely virtual in the sense that it is presented as the effect of a thought experiment. To the extent that one could perceive the lost ones as the last humans and the narrative agency as already posthuman, the thought experiment posits itself within a transitional space between the human and the posthuman. Many markers in the text evoke the sense of an ending, if not a future that announces the end of the human as we know it. "It is perhaps the end of their abode."[19] "It is perhaps the end of all."[20] "But enough will always subsist to spell for this little people the extinction soon or late of its remaining fires."[21] Moreover, the piece ends with a glimpse of the last state of the cylinder and the end of the "little people":

Hushed in the same breadth the faint stridulence mentioned above whence suddenly such silence as to drown all the faint breathings together. So much roughly speaking for the last state of the cylinder and of this little people of searchers one first of whom if a man in some unthinkable past for the first time bowed his head if this notion is maintained.[22]

What, then, does this apocalyptic vision convey of a posthuman people whose unthinkable past might have been that of mankind? Describing this utterly foreign life world in a tone oscillating between quasi-objective observation and philosophical reflection, the narrative agency is figured as that of a cultural outsider, an ethnographer of sorts, albeit one who, while recording an other culture, entirely depends upon his own perceptions and inferences. The "little people" neither seem to use a spoken or written language nor do they seem aware of or affected by an observer's presence. They either languish in supreme indifference or implode in rare outbursts of sudden violence. The narrative agency, as we have seen, presumes a total vision of the cylinder that escapes its inhabitants. David Porush identifies the narrative voice as an "omniscient intelligence" that has imagined the cylinder into being,[23] and Hugh Kenner speaks of "the voice from universal space."[24] To be perceived, the harmony of the cylinder's construction would, as we read, require an observer capable of projecting a perfect mental image of the entire system. The narrator thus projects the cylinder as a voluminous yet virtually closed system whose "perception" depends upon a faculty of holistic vision requiring a virtual (posthuman?) eye rather than a corporeal eye pertaining to an embodied agency. Moreover, perception is not facilitated by solid objects but by virtual frontiers: "The bed of the cylinder comprises three distinct zones separated by clear-cut mental or imaginary frontiers invisible to the eye of flesh."[25] Space thus is "de-composed" into a virtual space with virtual boundaries yet as rigorously conceived as any material space with solid frontiers.

It is a disembodied narrative voice that alone displays the vision attuned to this space, recording the scene in sequential aperçus. Rather than developing a quasi-realistic ethnography of the lost ones' alien culture, this voice presents us with a sequence of serial aperçus that view the cylinder from alternating perspectives. These aperçus cast brief spotlights onto different levels of abstraction such as spatial organization and cultural code, as well as different temporal frames culminating in an aperçu of the cylinder's last state. Instead of supplementing one another to form an integrated account of the lost ones' spatiotemporal and cultural organization, these aperçus convey the tentative mode of an observer who not only underscores his dependence on speculation but also doubts the very viability of the words and notions at his disposition. The narrative thus retains the lost ones' irreducible otherness, exhibiting but a series of hypothetical concretizations of a culture that is already cast in a mode of virtuality in the first place. In this vein, the narrative proceeds from a "first aperçu of the abode"[26] to a "first aperçu of the climbers' code,"[27] and ends with an aperçu of "the last state of the cylinder."[28]

At the beginning of the text, the recording voice is attuned to vision, describing the consequences of the dim, yellow light for the "searching eye."[29] Next, the voice attunes itself to touch and sound, describing the consequences of the cylinder's climate for the skin. Exposed to a temperature that oscillates between extremes of hot and cold in a rhythm of about four seconds, the skin shrivels, causing bodies to "brush together with a rustle of dry leaves."[30] As the skin is reduced to sensations caused by involuntary contact or the impact of temperature, the ear is reduced to diminished sounds, numbed by a floor and walls of solid rubber. The tactile and the auditory converge in the "thud of bodies striking against one another,"[31] accompanied by the "silence of the steps,"[32] the "rustling of nettles,"[33] and the "indescribable sound of a kiss."[34]

Later the "soul" is introduced by "the effect of the climate on the soul."[35] The soul suffers less than the skin, we hear, but then the voice immediately displaces its attention onto the skin, which "continues none the less feebly to resist,"[36] more efficiently so than the eye, which succumbs to "nothing short of blindness."[37] This displacement, however, follows the logic of a gaze that perceives the soul in its inscriptions on the body. The feeble resistance of the skin is matched by a feeble resistance of the soul,[38] in which we detect a "slight taint of pathos" in the remainder of the human ("stirrings still").[39] It is this feeble resistance that inserts a vibration of difference into the cylinder's order of things and into the narrator's order of words and phrases. And it is in relation to this vibration of difference that the narrative voice becomes less secure, and more tentative in speculation, tone, and choice of words. While observation seems virtually infallible, simply recording the certitudes of the cylinder, interpretation and language are prone to human error and to the erosion or obsolescence of familiar notions. And even the cylinder's certitudes are imbued with mystery: "For in the cylinder alone are certitudes to be found and without nothing but mystery."[40]

The text's holistic vision or "central computing eye"[41] also becomes the organizing principle for a syncretistic reading that follows the textual and figural movements through space and language as well as the mystery of its certitudes. After all, even as it is organized as a central computing eye, the narrative voice in The Lost Ones is not the voice of a cyborg, or an artificial intelligence that generates the data in the cylinder. Beckett, in fact, seems to use this voice to tease out the paradox of an ineradicable enmeshment without reducing the radical difference between the compilation of data and the recording of the soul's stirrings. In "Can Thought Go On Without a Body?" Lyotard notes, "If you think you're describing thought when you describe a selecting and tabulating of data, you're silencing truth. Because data aren't given, but givable, and selection isn't choice. Thinking, like writing or painting, is almost no more than letting a givable come towards you."[42] For Beckett's narrator, however, the division between a cold tabulation of data and an artistic hospitality to animated truth no longer holds. This narrator is first and foremost a poet of the unknowable, of a presence that can be grasped viscerally and witnessed but not yet, if ever, understood. A poetics of minute recording seems to be the only mode to speak about this alien world. Cold data becomes animated by a vision that traces alien life where it seems most inconceivable. In this respect the abode can be seen as an experimental system par excellence in which the narrator records life like an ethnographer who at every step resists the temptation to reduce the alien to the familiar. As an imaginary ethnography that displays a vision of the future, The Lost Ones exhibits an ethics of generative epistemological doubt that opens itself to irreducible otherness by approaching it through approximation, attunement, and mindful speculation. This ethics requires a methodology and voice in which the discursive accumulation and recording of data is translated into animated figuration. Poetry alone seems adequate to a witnessed alien form of life that bears enough traces of the familiar to solicit human response and compassion, yet ultimately escapes familiar categories of comprehension.

In Discours, figure, Lyotard insists that in literary language the relationship between discourse and figure cannot be reduced to purely linguistic operations because it is also generated under the impact of the primary process.[43] Primary process is driven by the force of affect and desire, inscribing the stirrings of the soul into the very forms of discourse and figuration. In The Lost Ones, the operations of the primary process seem to infiltrate those very descriptions of the cylinder that seem to be, on the surface, "coldly intent on all these data and evidences."[44] Beckett even teases his readers by mocking the cold distance of objective observation through insertions of barely perceptible errors and contradictions into the data, recognizable only to those readers who enter the narrator's game of mathematics, geometry, and computation. These mathematical errors are the analogue to the narrator's many ungrammatical sentences, signaling not only the bold use of poetic license from linguistic or scientific codification but also the operation of a primary process sensibility that dedifferentiates language and its rules for purposes of poetic recomposition.

Relying on the traces of affect and desire, this technique prepares the ground for the intense affective cathexis elicited by Beckett's text. Mediated by the poetic voice, the subliminal inscription of affect onto the body of language exerts an intense appeal to the senses, evoking visualizations of bodies moving through or frozen in space, tactile sensations of heat and cold, sounds of clashing bodies and rustling dried skin. The choice of a narrative voice that operates as a computing eye creates a particular compression of discourse and figuration in which the figurative force of words and the rhythmical force of syntax convene to generate an appeal that transcends the visual sense, encompassing sound, touch, and smell. This intricate interplay between discourse and figure can be grasped only if one is attentive to the condensations, displacements, repetitions, ruptures, and folds that organize the computing eye, signaling both the operation and the scrupulous artistic recrafting of the primary process in Beckett's poetic language.

Far from being reduced to the distance of a cold recording of data, the narrative voice becomes, on the contrary, highly sensitive and attuned to, if not intensely invested in, the culture of the "little people" it bespeaks in its discourse. Accordingly, the migration of the searchers and climbers is embedded in a rudimentary narrative, reflecting upon existential conditions such as a passion to search, endurance of privation, abandonment beyond recall, and horror of contact. At the same time, the narrative also records primordial manifestations of affect and instinctual behavior such as sudden surges of violence or occasional impulses to copulate. The most remarkable remainder of human life in the cylinder, however, is an unfathomable resilience that fuels the lost ones' persistent attachment to minimal forms of being. It is the visual and sensual order of the cylinder that conveys its emotional attunement to existential human remainders, establishing a distinctly compassionate mood even within the poetic abstractions of a detached tone of voice that records, in a mode of measured objectivity, this cosmic universe of lost souls. At times, it even seems as if this narrator, fearful of an all-too-human pathos, needs to guard himself against an excess of attunement:

And the thinking being coldly intent on all these data and evidences could scarcely escape at the close of his analysis the mistaken conclusion that instead of speaking of the vanquished with the slight taint of pathos attaching to the term it would be more correct to speak of the blind and leave it at that.[45]

Objectivity, then, is posited in the text as a necessary yet ultimately unattainable goal. Objectivity is necessary to remain mindful of the pitfalls of anthropocentric reductions, but it is unattainable because the remainder of the human is all too pervasive and ever prone to attaching a "slight taint of pathos" to words and images. Reading *The Lost Ones* therefore requires a careful attunement to the particular nuances of voice and timbre created by the minute vibrations of difference. To return to the epigraph drawn from Kant, it is as if the act of reading transfers the soul to the narrator's alien vision, displacing the reader into an utterly foreign space that radically decomposes, transforms, and then reconfigures familiar modes of perception. This transmission of *vesania*, in turn, generates as a paradoxical effect the emergence of singular intensities, if not the sudden eruption of affect.

The resistance of the soul as the remainder of the human thus displays an obstinate resilience in a discourse focused on recording a vanishing and vanquished world. Remainders of human pathos cling to vision as much as to words. Periodically, the rhythms and movements of bodies and words are transformed into a verbal still life of sorts, fixing the imaginary eye on a "picturesque detail,"[46] thus causing the emergence of a scene of eerie beauty and terror. Imagine sedentary searchers flattening themselves with their backs to the wall while a young woman with white hair, eyes closed in abandonment, mechanically clasps to her breast "a mite" who strains away.[47] Imagine "the woman vanquished," squatting against the wall with her head between her knees, her legs in her arms and her red hair, tarnished by the light, hanging to the ground.[48] Imagination dead imagine.[49] If a "slight taint of pathos" attaches to the voice that records these visions, it is because without it the text would be empty, inhuman. Bizarre, if not exotic, these scenes bespeak, as the narrator suggests, the condition of the human at its ultimate vanishing point.

In "Can Thought Go On Without a Body?" Lyotard generates a different, albeit related, vision of the human from the vantage point of postmodernism's cultural imaginary with its survival myths and related efforts to create an artificial intelligence able to operate without a body. Lyotard argues that in order to survive the extinction of the planet—perhaps in the wake of a nuclear if not solar explosion—such a human intelligence will have to carry the force of desire within it on its interstellar voyage. But then he adds, "It isn't any human desire to know or transform reality that propels this techno-science, but a cosmic circumstance."[50] Does cosmic circumstance propel the emergence of the posthuman? Critics have already imagined the narrative agency in *The Lost Ones* to figure as a disembodied artificial intelligence. One could indeed envision the narrator as inhabiting a posthuman space, looking back at the last vanquished humans secluded in a cylinder that is, like the nautilus Roland Barthes envisions in *Mythologies*, organized according to a "self-sufficient cosmogony, which has its own categories, its own time, space, fulfillment and even existential principle."[51] Yet somehow all these attempts at allegorizing this alien Beckettian world seem too referential and literalist, reducing both its mystery and unique poetic depth. Beckett creates a virtual world emerging from a uniquely human imagination, albeit one incommensurable with anything we know.

No wonder, then, that *The Lost Ones* commands such an intense hold on a cultural imaginary haunted by the viable end of the human species and a related philosophical thought bent on exploring the boundaries between the human and the posthuman. As always, Beckett draws on a rich arsenal of philosophical histories, transforming their distilled core elements into an alchemy of poetic abstraction. In one of *The Lost Ones'* most extensive intertextual plays, Beckett constructs the transitional space between the human and the posthuman according to a familiar cosmogony in Western literature, Dante's *Purgatorio*. The miniature cosmos of the cylinder with its caverns, for example, forms a distant echo of the cornices of Dante's purgatory. Plunged in an intense gloom, the cylinder exudes a sensation of yellow, "not to say of sulphur,"[52] invoking the threat of hell to be faced by lost ones who are but remainders of human bodies and soul. In this context, Beckett's insistence on the soul resonates with the hope of a beyond—an afterlife that succeeds the purgatory—yet the narrative agency relegates such hope to the "amateurs of myth."[53] At the center in Dante's *Purgatorio* is the fourth cornice, where the "lost ones" are punished for gloominess and indifference—the "defects" of love. As in the *Purgatorio*, in the cylinder "gloominess and indifference" periodically lead to "zeal and fervent affection." Every so often, some of Beckett's vanquished resurrect to perform vain attempts at copulation, almost as if their bodies continued involuntarily to perform the action of a memory or instinctual impulse encoded from time immemorial. As we recall from Dante, love can be of two sorts: natural or of the soul. While natural love, for Dante, is unerring, love of the soul may err with respect to object or degree. Beckett's lovers are caught in desiccated bodies whose "hampering effect on the work of love"[54] condemns them to perform a grotesque spectacle of "making unmakable love."[55] This is the spectacle in which the body and the skin converge with the soul:

> This desiccation [effect of the climate on the skin] of the envelope robs nudity of much of its charm as pink turns grey and transforms into a rustling of nettles the natural succulence of flesh against flesh. . . . The spectacle then is one to be remembered of frenzies prolonged in pain and hopelessness long beyond what even the most gifted lovers can achieve in camera.[56]

Beckett's lovers err in both object and degree. The meetings between objects become indeterminate, contingent upon movements through space, man and wife coming together without their knowledge, only "in virtue of the law of probabilities."[57] The chance encounters between futile lovers who "search again neither glad nor even sorry"[58] produce the "same vivacity of reaction as to the end of the world."[59]

The temporal ambiguity of this phrase—stronger even in the French "une fin du monde"—is crucial because it leaves in suspense whether the end has already happened or is pending, or whether, as the French version seems to suggest, this particular end may merely be one of several. Presupposing the end of the world—past or future—the searchers are on a quest, "darkward bound."[60] Prone to myth, they cling to the hope sustained from "time immemorial"[61] by rumor of a way out beyond which "the sun and other stars would still be shining."[62] "So much for the inviolable zenith where for amateurs of myth lies hidden a way out to earth and sky."[63] This phrase, too, insists on ambiguity. Does the "way out to earth" suggest that the "little people" were suspended in space, somewhere above the Earth as if in a futuristic artificial satellite world, an interstellar nautilus that may once have functioned as a galactic version of Noah's ark? The privation in the cylinder would then not only be the tangible material dearth of floor space[64] but also, at a more subliminal level, nothing less than the deprivation of a cosmos—an inhabitable universe bound by constellations and nourished by a sun. In this sense, the quest of these "amateurs of myth"[65] is cosmological—a residue of an "old craving"[66] that disrupts in irregular fits their blind crawling in search of nothing, or, *if this notion were maintained*, the "all of nothing."[67]

Beyond the end of the world as we know it, the lost ones populate this "all of nothing" in futile quest or abandonment. We find "this little people of searchers"[68] left in an "abandonment beyond recall,"[69] gravitating motionless toward an unthinkable future when "dark descends and at the same instant the temperature comes to rest not far from the freezing point."[70] This vision of a posthuman apocalypse keeps the reader suspended in this "all of nothing," attuning her to the condition of the vanquished who await the cylinder's eventual depopulation as suggested by the *dépeupleur*.

In 1965, one year before the composition of *The Lost Ones*, Beckett wrote *Imagination Dead Imagine*, a three-page piece he insisted was a novel. "No trace anywhere of life,"[71] this piece begins, and there too the narrator designs a highly artificial space, a vault, three feet in diameter and three feet in depth. Lying on the ground are two white bodies, each in a semicircle. The light, without any visible source, is of a glaring white, casting no shadows, exuding a strong heat until it changes in pauses of varying length to complete darkness with temperatures approaching the freezing point. Countless rhythms mark these passages from white and heat to black and cold, enclosing the two bodies in absolute stillness. "Hold a mirror to their lips, it mists,"[72] we read. And then: "They might well pass for inanimate but for the left eyes which at incalculable intervals suddenly open wide and gaze in unblinking exposure long beyond what is humanly possible."[73]

Once again we are returned to the question, What do these posthuman worlds that Beckett designs tell us? Are they alien worlds bespeaking a condition beyond what is humanly possible yet resonant of an order of the human remembered from time immemorial? Does Beckett write some unfathomable history of the future, some imaginary ethnography of the posthuman? "Leave them there, sweating and icy, there is better elsewhere,"[74] the narrator says of the two bodies in the vault. Then he continues:

> No, life ends and no, there is nothing elsewhere, and no question now of ever finding again that white speck lost in whiteness, to see if they still lie still in the stress of that storm, or of a worse storm, or in the black dark for good, or the great whiteness unchanging, and if not what they are doing.[75]

What are the philosophical and epistemological implications of such visions of an ending, and what do they contribute to a contemporary archaeology of thought on the human and posthuman? Beckett's scene recalls a solar storm raging before the solar explosion invoked in Lyotard's vision of the posthuman. It also recalls Foucault's copiously cited conclusion at the end of *The Order of Things*, published in 1966, the same year as *The Lost Ones*:

> As the archeology of our thought easily shows, man is an invention of re-
> cent date. And one perhaps nearing its end. If those arrangements were to
> disappear as they appeared, if some event of which we can at the moment
> do no more than sense the possibility—without knowing either what its
> form will be or what it promises—were to cause them to crumble . . . then
> one can certainly wager that man would be erased, like a face drawn in
> sand at the edge of the sea.[76]

The recent invention and possibly pending erasure of man in the vast expanse
of the universe's history introduces a notion of scale that resonates with Beckett's "archeology of thought." Beckett's scale extends from the microscopic
to the planetary, from the "white speck lost in whiteness"[77] to the space beyond the cave where "the sun and other stars would still be shining."[78] We are
confronted with a poetic vision suggestive of miniature thought and minimal
thought. Yet it is a minimalism that enfolds magnitude, a "white speck lost in
whiteness" that enfolds the implicate order of planetary thought, a posthuman compression of cosmic vision. It is miniature in its scrupulous attention
to detail—the white speck lost in whiteness—an attention so scrupulous that
it perceives more than meets the "eye of flesh." It is minimal in its faithfulness
to an ever-increasing scarcity of parameters, its movement toward reduction
and compression: the "all of nothing." It is planetary thought in the emergence of a vast expanse from minute detail, cosmic in this thought's invest-
ment in a universe *in which the sun and other stars would still be shining.*

If a "slight taint of pathos" attaches to this reading—as it does to Beckett's
(and, for that matter, to Lyotard's and Foucault's) vision of the posthuman—it
is because the affects inscribed in Beckett's voices are contagious, soliciting a
transference that must first absorb and then move through them. Beckett engineers the emergence of soulscapes out of the void of his virtual *scapelands*:
imaginary, alien, and vanishing spaces that are evoked through words that
grasp the effects of unearthly light, inconceivably foreign sounds, and unbear-
ably extreme temperatures on body and soul. Beckett's language generates
textual vision with the craft of a theatrical lighting engineer. Understanding
light's function in transcoding body and soul and in producing minute vibrations of difference, he generates light effects from within language. The narrator's eye, whose power of perception surpasses that of "the eye of flesh," seems
able to sustain a vision of the lost ones in the dark, almost as if they were endowed with bioluminescence or an imaginable psychic equivalent of it. This

may be an effect of the poetic force of Beckett's language, which generates a sense of the paradoxical resilience of light, as if the trace of a memory of luminescence will forever remain inscribed in the final dark as the last memory trace of past human life.

These vibrations of difference that produce the light effects in Beckett's visual universe also register in the depth and scale of poetic language. Understanding the function of timbre, Beckett generates a voice that pulverizes language until its particles aggregate in unforeseeable ways. It is a pulverization, we could argue in a Deleuzian vein, that dissolves the molar organization of language in order to generate molecular language effects that resonate with the dissolution of molar forms in the cylinder and the simultaneous persistence of life at a molecular register.[79] These pulverizing operations of difference recall the Kantian experimental displacement of the soul from the *sensorium commune*, alluded to in the epigraph, which Lyotard calls *vesania*, or systematic madness. The effects of this induction of *vesania* are subtle and transformative. It is not that we are made to see what the text evokes visually, to hear the sounds it describes, or to feel the temperatures. Rather, Beckett's language breaks through the familiar registers of vision, sound, and touch, allowing us to see or hear something we have never seen or heard before. In Deleuzian fashion, we could almost say that we are made to hear with the eye and see with the ear of a schizo.

This induction of a systematic madness—to return to Lyotard's phrase—requires a subliminal transference between text and reader. It involves a process that resembles Paul Klee's notion of artistic vision referred to in *Discours, figure*: "to see with one eye, to feel with the other."[80] At the level of sound, it also resembles what Lyotard says about the "internal ear," that it registers the "unthought of the ear."[81] The fact that Beckett induces the emergence of an internal ear and eye not through the art forms primarily attuned to these sense organs but through language is crucial. Literature as the sole artistic medium that participates in all senses allows for a transference that transforms their very relationship, thus inscribing itself simultaneously into body and soul. The sensual effects of vision and sound that Beckett evokes might be invisible and inaudible, but they are imaginable, and the very act of imagining them transforms the available registers. The immateriality of textual vision, sound, and touch has material corporeal effects. Lyotard, however, is also right in asserting that "reading is understanding/hearing [*entendre*] and not seeing."[82] We do not see what the text describes, but its visions and sounds decompose and retune our modes of perception, while the timbre of voice assumes nearly a tactile quality, touching us at the level of something that seems utterly familiar but has never been thought—an "unthought known."[83]

While Beckett's technique presupposes the dedefinition and dedifferentiation of the familiar orders of the *sensorium commune*, it also depends upon the minute vibrations of difference that introduce negentropy into an otherwise entropic universe.[84] While "amateurs of myth" may simply remain caught up in the phantasm of a vanishing world or the myth of a way out, Beckett's text induces a larger vision, attuned to the emergence of difference and negentropy. Vanishing in Beckett is tied to and inseparable from emergence. The decomposition of a familiar world releases the unthought, however painful its emergence. The failing vision of "the eye of flesh" becomes the precondition for the emergence of an immaterial, not to say inward, gaze able to perceive invisible harmonies and dissonances. Dedifferentiation of familiar boundaries, categories, words, and worlds generates the emergence of differentiation at a different scale, as if the human is perceived from a macroscopic or microscopic distance that dissolves the units of body and mind. We witness a compression of dedifferentiation and differentiation in a vision highly sensitized to minute detail and minimal difference, or the production of molecular language effects, a technique that defines the signature of Beckett's work. It is this compression that generates the emergence of what Lyotard calls an event. An event, for Lyotard, presupposes an indeterminacy that facilitates the emergence of an unthought. What he says in "Scapeland" about the freeing of landscape from definition—note *dépaysant* and *dépeupleur*—is true for Beckett's freeing of human abodes as well: "Indeterminacy exercises a gentle violence over the determinate, so as to make it give up its QUOD. And it is not I, nor anyone, who begets this non-place."[85]

Such "gentle violence over the determinate" marks Beckett's texts throughout. Form, grammar, and semantics no longer domesticate the matter of language; they no longer make it consumable by subjecting it to the prerogatives of understanding. Lyotard says the desire simply to wander through a landscape authorizes "a transfer of material powers to scents, to the tactile quality of the ground, of walls, of plants."[86] Beckett performs such a transfer of material powers to language, rendering its very materiality tactile, sonorous, and visual, thus producing effects in language that touch those able to receive it at a molecular level of sensation. Literary form itself is no longer instrumental but material in Beckett's texts, and its materialization causes an estrangement similar to the one Lyotard calls an intimist exoticism.[87] The uncanny quality of Beckett's texts results from the paradoxical use of such estrangement to evoke the most intimately familiar abyss of the human. As a result, these texts generate a mood that is at once utterly strange and utterly familiar—intimist exoticism. "States of mind are states of spiritual matter,"[88] says Lyotard. Beckett's skill in generating abstraction out of utmost concretion and vice versa always aspires—like his characters—to transcend the outmoded binary division of mind and matter that has often been so abused to demarcate the boundaries of the human.

Beckett's explorations of human liminality may well have been the true inspiration of Lyotard's vision of the "inhuman" in "Scapeland." Lyotard seems to credit Beckett when he describes the face in a photograph of Beckett at eighty as a landscape "parched with drought, the flesh defied. And in the wrinkles, in the creases where the pupils flash with anger, a cheerful incredulity. So the mummy is still alive. Just."[89] Referring to the "MELANCHOLIA of all landscapes," Lyotard says they leave the mind desolate, exposing the "wretchedness of the soul rubbed raw by the tiderace of matter."[90] Like Lyotard, Beckett invokes philosophical discourses of the soul to explore the condition of the posthuman. However, while Beckett invokes the soul throughout *The Lost Ones*, it is not without also recalling the "slight taint of pathos" that inevitably attaches to the use of the term. Drawing on posthumanist French philosophers and writers ranging from Deleuze and Derrida to Lyotard who invoke the soul in their mapping of the posthuman, Beckett constructs the soul of the lost ones as a site of a transference between the human and its other. One can hardly avoid recalling the infamous history of Western discourses that constructed the soul as the site of the most unabashed ethno- and anthropocentrism, used to expel indigenous peoples from the community of humans along with animals. Mindful of this history, Lyotard defines the making of humans—their "soul-making"—as a process of violent domestication.

The bodies of Beckett's lost ones seem to bear the traces of such violence. However, Beckett also invokes the soul of the vanquished as a last site of resilience. The soul with its resilience seems to be a testing ground for the last remainders of humane reflexes under the experimental conditions of a closed cylinder: the abode of vanquished humans. Lyotard coins the word *l'immonde*[91] to speak of a place that causes the "inhuman" condition of "little sensations"[92] (a term Lyotard borrows from Cézanne) to which affect is reduced in states of "inner desolation."[93] The lost ones' "abandonment beyond recall"[94] is reminiscent of such inner desolation. However, the insistence on minute vibrations of difference[95] in Beckett signals that "little sensations" may also emerge from the resilience of life under the conditions of *l'immonde*, an "unworld." "Unworlding" might be another term to invoke the vanishing and vanquishing of the lost ones, including the contraction of their inner spaces to little sensations that manifest as the last but most resilient stirrings of the soul.

These inner spaces with their little sensations and vibrations of difference that reach beyond conscious perception, involving the undoing of the boundaries of self, make Beckett's "little people" seem as if they emerged from an "unthought known," creating a mood utterly strange yet strangely familiar. In order to inhabit these spaces, one needs to traverse the boundaries of consciousness and thought, opening them toward the unthought. "The unthought hurts because we're comfortable in what's already thought,"[96] Lyotard affirms. Pain is endemic to Beckett's world. It is endemic to his vanquished characters languishing in their abandonment beyond recall, or in the disembodied narrative voices obsessively trying to think the unthought. Pain afflicts his actors when they are forced to inhabit bodies pushed beyond known postures,[97] and even his readers when they try to attune themselves to his alien imaginary worlds.

Encountering the unthought requires either a loss of self or an expansion of self to a different scale that enfolds the inscriptions of sensations into our bodies—sensations that have never been registered at the level of conscious thought and that are therefore operative as an "unthought known." "The self is left behind," Lyotard writes, "sloughed off, definitely too conventional, too sure of itself and over-arrogant in the way it puts things into scale."[98] As the self vanishes, emotions devolve into sensations and intensities. Relationality shrinks to minimal reflex. Fraternity, the narrator notes for example, is an outlived sentiment as foreign to the lost ones "as to butterflies."[99] In this sense, Beckett's text is about scale too. The microscopic perception and planetary vision used to create an experimental imaginary world are matched by a micropsychology that explores the "soul" in its raw states, its intensities, without the support of a scaffold or armor for the self. Raw souls appear off-scale and thrust into cosmic abandonment.

Lyotard links these states with a new understanding of poetry or the poetic, one marked by an "implosion of forms themselves."[100] Rather than generating alternative "ways of worldmaking,"[101] Beckett's poetry engages in unmaking the world, or, as I called it earlier, "unworlding." In this very process, he generates not an alternative world but a new way of being in the world and in language. Beckett's language implodes the mind along with the forms it harbors to organize its perceptions according to codes and laws. *L'immonde*, *l'informe*, and the "inhuman" are terms Lyotard uses to refer to these states of dedifferentiation, disinformation, or dissolution of the self. But with Beckett we must be careful to avoid confusing the *informe* with the undifferentiated or the unformed. Beckett's *informe* is an implosion of form generated from within the symbolic order of language, in fact, unthinkable from without.

At the same time, *The Lost Ones* projects an imaginary world made of words that create the effects of an implosion of the self and the very forms of self-organization. Nobody reveals with more clarity than Beckett that such implosion of forms is possible only through a most rigorous and refined shaping and crafting of what one could call, with Lyotard, the matter in thought.[102] But it is a highly artificial and artistic shaping that reaches beyond both the descriptive and the categorical. Undoing the very conventions through which we organize our perception of the world, this "poetry" exposes us to an ontological abyss, generating the vertiginous mental spirals, the delirious void so familiar to Beckett's readers. Far from being presymbolic or prelinguistic, this artistic practice or poetics continues to rely entirely on craft, even while undoing the history of its conventional uses. Beckett's poetics renews the texture of the written word, the architecture of space, and the intricacies of coloration and timbre. "How could we capture the breath of wind that sweeps the mind into the void . . . if not in the texture of the written word?"[103] asks Lyotard. How could we capture that "white speck lost in whiteness" invoked at the end of *Imagination Dead Imagine* if not in the texture of Beckett's writing or the architecture of his theater? Poetry, Lyotard insists, must emerge from the superplenitude of the void, "otherwise it is merely a staging [*mise en scène*] and a mobilization [*mise en oeuvre*] of the powers of language."[104]

Lyotard links this poetic state with infancy and its modes of exchange with the world:

A baby must see its MOTHER's face as a landscape. Not because its mouth, fingers and gaze move over it as it blindly grasps and sucks, smiles, cries and whimpers. Not because it is "in symbiosis" with her. . . . We should assume, rather, that the face is indescribable for the baby. It will have forgotten it, because it will not have been inscribed. . . . This mother is a mother who is a timbre "before" it sounds, who is there "before" the coordinates of sound, before destiny.[105]

At the end of Beckett's "Fizzle 6" we read, "For an instant I see the sky, the different skies, then they turn to faces, agonies, loves, the different loves, happiness too, yes, there was that, too, unhappily. . . . No but now, now simply stay still, standing before a window, one hand on the wall, the other clutching your shirt, and see the sky, a long gaze, but no, gasps and spasms, a childhood sea, other skies, another body."[106] The "childhood sea" that emerges in many of Beckett's texts when their narrators' strive for the end is one of those soulscapes that create the "unworld" (*l'immonde*). The coordinates of "the real" dissolve into a resonance of something that can be recalled only in the vagueness of a timbre, or a mood.

The figure of the child occupies a central place in both Beckett's and Lyotard's thinking about the human. The very terms "human" and "inhuman," Lyotard argues, must oscillate between native indetermination and instituted or self-instituting reason. The notions of the *immonde*, the *informe*, and the "inhuman" (*inhumain*) are, for Lyotard, intimately tied to the notion of the infant (*enfant*). Immonde, informe, "inhuman," and "infant" are, for Lyotard, metonymically aligned on a chain that facilitates the transcoding of the political, the cultural, the psychological, and the aesthetic. "Native indetermination," by contrast, seems constrained, "forced" into a development "where it is not mankind which is at issue, but differentiation."[107] This stance against determination, differentiation, and development is the core of Lyotard's politics and poetics. "'Development' is the ideology of the present time,"[108] he writes, "development is the very thing which takes away the hope of an alternative to the system from both analysis and practice."[109] Tapping into the resources of native indetermination is, for Lyotard, accordingly, the only form of resistance we have left. "What else remains as 'politics' except resistance to this inhuman? And what else is left to resist with but the debt which each soul has contracted with the miserable and admirable indetermination from which it was born and does not cease to be born? —which is to say, with the other inhuman?"[110] "It is the task of writing, thinking, literature, arts to venture to bear witness to it [this debt to childhood],"[111] writes Lyotard at the conclusion of his introduction to *The Inhuman*. What he propagates, then, is a poetics and politics of indeterminacy that draw on the unformulated, the undifferentiation, nonconceptuality, and indetermination of the earliest modes of a child's exchange with the world as a resource that allows one to resist the ideologies, constraints, and impositions of the symbolic order.

Conceiving his model of the "inhuman" as a form of radical antihumanism, Lyotard proclaims our very need to interrogate the "value of man."[112]

His notion of the human coincides with philosophical notions of the subject in which an infant is not yet a subject until it enters the symbolic order. If humans were born human, Lyotard argues, it would not be possible to educate them. It is then the institutions of culture that make humans human. In this sense, literature, as Lyotard conceives it, would be writing *against culture* rather than a form of *writing culture*.[113] Beckett's work, however, would seem to render such a clear-cut opposition obsolete. Doesn't Lyotard, despite his deep suspicion of the ideologies of conventional categorization, import here a deeply Western categorization of the subject into his model — a categorization that posits infancy as a prehuman phase? In such a model, the human proper presupposes acculturation and the entry into the symbolic order. A broader notion of the subject (and the human), however, would include infants more productively, allowing one to rethink the dynamic between the presymbolic and the symbolic in less-exclusive or less-antagonistic terms. Beckett systematically collapses and reorganizes the boundaries between the presymbolic and the symbolic, between differentiation and dedifferentiation, or, for that matter, between *discours* and *figure*. Aren't the boundaries between the two spheres so malleable that maintaining a rigidly antagonistic distinction between them feeds precisely into the notion of linear development that Lyotard wants to resist? And finally, doesn't the notion that infants are not yet human repeat the fallacy of a dated historical model that relegates infants as well as indigenous peoples to "prehistory."

To do justice to Lyotard, we need to view his concept of the "inhuman" in light of the ambiguous status he accords to the child in relation to culture. He distinguishes the inhumanity of the system (or the symbolic order in Lévi-Strauss's terms) from the inhumanity of infants that results from what he calls a native lack. It is in this latter sense that he can say that what is proper to humankind is inhabited by the inhuman. Because of his use of two diametrically opposite notions of the inhuman, the boundary between the human and the inhuman oscillates for Lyotard. Precisely because the infant is not yet granted the status of human, it is "eminently the human"[114] in a different sense. "Hostage of the adult community,"[115] the child calls on that community to become more human. If the designations of human and inhuman oscillate between "native indetermination" and "instituted reason,"[116] one may indeed conclude that all education is inhuman because it does not happen without constraint or terror. Yet such a perspective requires that one view the processes that induce differentiation in the child's development exclusively under the perspective of constraint. Considering development to be the true ideology

of the time—regardless whether it applies to capitalist economy or child development—Lyotard aims his critique of postmodernism at a "metaphysics
of development,"[117] that is, at development without finality or a value system
attached to it. In a similar vein, Lyotard rejects, at the theoretical level, conceptualization and the construction of theoretical systems (grand narratives)
because of the constraints they impose, which, in turn, he once again views
in terms of totalization.

This is where Beckett's work assumes a more radical dimension. Moved
beyond good and evil or beyond familiar polarities more generally, differentiation and dedifferentiation emerge in Beckett's imaginary worlds from within a
process of continual semiosis in which they are distinct yet inseparable. Without differentiation, infants would remain in a desolate state of native lack.
Without differentiation, the "little people" in the cylinder would be frozen in
the monotonous indifference of mere entropy. Vibrations of difference and
picturesque details such as, for example, the two vanquished women (one
with white hair, the other with red hair), or the mite that strains away from his
mother's dried breast, would become unthinkable. Without differentiation,
infants would never be completely born, hovering like so many of Beckett's
characters in a psychic limbo beyond life and death. Finally, without dedifferentiation they would, like other Beckett characters, approach a state of soul-
less automata, deprived of the pleasures and pains of drives and desires. A perspective that highlights the ambivalence of both constructive and destructive
potentials of early differentiation does not ignore the power relations involved
in, nor the constraints and terrors of, education. Rather, such a perspective
resists the temptation to ontologize domination as a human condition. In the
same vein, it also resists the temptation to reduce the structural ambivalence
of differentiation to a mere ideology of development.

Politics is, for Lyotard, the resistance to the inhuman of a systemic development that follows the internal logic and dynamic of the system alone. He
considers such resistance a "debt to childhood"[118] and calls upon literature
and philosophy to provide a thinking *from the outside* able to bear witness
to this debt. One would hope that, in fulfilling this function, literature and
philosophy also take part in a process of differentiation not entirely bound
up with power, constraint, and terror. Just as the human and the inhuman in
Lyotard's sense, differentiation thus has a double side as well. It is not only
a tool of adults for "holding the child's soul hostage," as Lyotard says, but
also one for freeing the infant from the bondage of its early dependency. The
infant's gradual attunement to differentiation would, for Lyotard, already be

too bound up in constraints because it would impose determination upon the indeterminate. But where would we be without the "form-giving" experience that differentiates perception and the "word-forming experience"[119] that induces differentiation into the infant's use of sounds? Wouldn't we resemble the lost ones in their wordless search?

Beckett's work bears witness to the ambivalence of indetermination, the ontological abyss, and the emergence of productivity that are linked to the indeterminate. His texts and plays expose the constraints and traps of conceptualization as well as the hegemony of a "spirit of system."[120] They also expose the wretchedness of the undifferentiation that comes with an "incomplete birth."[121] Without acculturation, differentiation, and the impositions of form we would be suspended, like the unnamable and all his imaginary clones, in an abysmal void free from the constraints of manifestation perhaps but also deprived of an inhabitable world. In contrast to Lyotard, Beckett exposes the irresolution between the two modes of being as a curse that threatens any viable ontology. "De-composed" and suspended in virtual space seems, in fact, to be a condition that Beckett envisions as a symptom of our impending posthuman time.

Lyotard invokes Kant's notion of the *sensus communis* not only in reference to the inhuman but also in his concept of aesthetics. He opposes an unmediated "community of feeling"[122] to theories of aesthetic communication, arguing that the *sensus communis* is anterior to and can therefore not be reduced to communication and pragmatics. As Lyotard reminds us, Kant attributes aesthetic feeling to the inscription of artistic/literary form on the subject. Drawing on this Kantian notion in his theory of the sublime, Lyotard argues that the feeling of the sublime resists immediate communicability and is therefore compatible with the formless, the *informe*. But we recall that, for Lyotard, the *informe* is modeled on the indifferentiation of the infant. There are, in other words, multiple resonances that link Lyotard's theory of the inhuman with his aesthetics of the sublime. A text like Beckett's *The Lost Ones* requires a notion of aesthetic experience much broader than conscious communication and aesthetic judgment. The most subliminal forms of aesthetic experience are, as Christopher Bollas has shown, intimately related to the "unthought known," that is, the mnemonic traces of undifferentiation in infancy.[123] This is precisely why literature and the arts are capable, through subliminal processes of transference, of bearing witness to the early cultural imprints on the subject. At the same time, they are also capable of helping us overcome some of the constraints imposed at the time. Seen in this way, we could even say that literature contributes to loosening the bonds that would otherwise keep us hostage to our early cultural formation.

In the act of reading *The Lost Ones*, literary transference operates via the processing of new effects never before seen, heard, or understood. The alien textual world of the cylinder creates its own reference; its object is not identifiable. It also creates its own addressee: a reader's disconcerted body, invited to stretch its sensory capacities beyond measure.[124] At the same time, however, this world would not be able to touch or move us if it did not appeal to an "unthought known." We attune ourselves to Beckett's worlds on the basis of a faint recognition of undifferentiated visual, sonorous, and tactile spaces that have left their imprint on our bodies before they encountered words and meaning, order and form, sound and sense, touch and smell. The transformation of written signifiers into sensations and moods operates via a transference that engages what Lyotard defines as the boundaries of the human, stretching them into the area of the *informe*, the infant, and the inhuman.

If this reading has highlighted the resonance between Beckett's post-human world of "little people" and Lyotard's prehuman world of infants—a resonance that supersedes their ideological difference concerning the status of differentiation—it is because both Beckett and Lyotard draw on a "polyaesthetics"[125] that engages the body's primordial inscriptions. Both are interested in the processes of transference that engage these inscriptions and transform their immaterial effects on the soul. Beckett returns to the primordial as the last remainder of the human, as that which subsists throughout time and space immemorial and continues to imprint the soul. Lyotard writes, "The 'soul' has at its disposal the only language. The body is a confused speaker: it says 'soft', 'warm', 'blue', 'heavy', instead of talking straight lines, curves, collisions and relations."[126] Perhaps this vision of a body language may suggest why the inseparable linkage between the concrete and the abstract in Beckett's work exerts such a strong appeal. "Abstraction is not a negation of form: it posits it as folded, existing only as a 'mental landscape' in the soul or in the mind, in upper altitudes," writes Deleuze in *The Fold*.[127] Beckett uses his imaginary geographies of straight lines, curves, collisions, and relations less as a geometrical discourse to map out an alien space than as a language of the soul to map out a soulscape hitherto unknown to humans. The alien space of the cylinder with its virtual boundaries, its ruptures and folds, its passages, niches, and alcoves, its vaults, caves, and crypts, becomes a space of transference in which the immateriality of the soul is affected by the immateriality of the lines, curves, collisions, and relations generated by Beckett's words.

In "Deconstructing the Machine: Beckett's *The Lost Ones*," David Porush perceives the cylinder as an enormous cybernetic machine controlled from some outside source. There is, however, a ghost (or a soul) in the machine, because, as Porush asserts, "In order to understand some of the quirks and paradoxes in style and expression in Beckett's prose, *the machines of the cylinder and the text itself must be understood as ones that do not work.*"[128] While they do not work as machines, they work at a different level—that of the literary or aesthetic—as spaces that facilitate the emergence of hitherto unimagined visions and sensations that exert a unique appeal to the senses and generate an intense cathexis. Like the cylinder, Beckett's language contains niches and alcoves, and like the skin of the lost ones, it contains recesses and folds from within which we witness vibrations of difference in words and images. These vibrations open up a space for the emergence of the unthought (the *impense*) in the form of an imaginary posthuman from which we may finally intuit the vast expanse of the human to come *if that notion were maintained*. This is perhaps the most subliminal transformational use of literature—a form of "soul-making" that continually reconfigures the boundaries of the human and its primordial imprints.

Notes

Introduction

1. Derrida, "This Strange Institution Called Literature," 73.

2. Saer, *El concepto de ficción*. The term "speculative anthropology" is also discussed in Riera, *Littoral of the Letter*, 75–100.

3. Jacqueline Rose, *The Last Resistance* (London: Verso Press, 2007).

4. Schwab, *Mirror and the Killer-Queen*.

5. Rheinberger, *On Historicizing Epistemology*.

6. My arguments are developed in a dialogical relation with Fischer, *Emergent Forms of Life*.

7. Derrida, *Of Grammatology*, and Kubler, *Shape of Time*.

8. Rheinberger, "Man weiß nicht genau."

9. Fischer, *Emergent Forms of Life*.

10. Wittgenstein, *Philosophical Investigations*, no. 241.

11. Rheinberger, *Toward a History of Epistemic Things*, 28. Emphasis mine.

12. We recall that Adorno put forth a similar claim when he argued that literature figuratively anticipates the conceptual knowledge of philosophy.

13. Christopher Bollas calls these forms of unconscious knowing "the unthought known" (*Shadow of the Object*, 101).

14. Grace, *Baby No-Eyes*.

15. The notion of polytemporality and its relevance in narratives of modernity is analyzed in Latour, *We Have Never Been Modern*, 75.

16. For a more detailed analysis of this dynamic, see Schwab, *Haunting Legacies*.

17. For a more detailed discussion of the unconscious transference of literary knowledge, see Schwab, "Words and Moods."

18. Luhmann, *Liebe als Passion*.

19. On the "holding environment," see Winnicott, *Holding and Interpretation*; on the "word-forming experience," see Bollas, *Shadow of the Object*.

20. Hanne, *Power of the Story*.

21. Ibid., 2.

22. See Mbembe, "Necropolitics."

23. For a detailed analysis of these processes, see Schwab, "Cultural Texts and Endopsychic Scripts."

24. Iser, *Die Appellstruktur der Texte*.

25. Though a proper noun, Saer does not capitalize *colastiné* in *The Witness*.

26. For a discussion of "bizarre objects," see Bion, *Learning from Experience*, 11, 25, 58.

27. For a detailed discussion, see my *Subjects without Selves*, "Words and Moods," and "Cultural Texts and Endopsychic Scripts."

28. See Ehrenzweig, *Hidden Order of Art*, 123. For a detailed discussion of literature's impact on reorganizing the boundaries of subjectivity, see Schwab, *Subjects without Selves*.

29. See Bion, *Attention and Interpretation*, 42.

30. See Bollas, *Shadow of the Object*. See also my "Words and Moods," and "Cultural Texts Endopsychic Scripts."

31. Derrida, "This Strange Institution Called Literature," 42.

32. Rheinberger, *Toward a History of Epistemic Things*, 224.

33. Wittgenstein, *Tractatus Logico-Philosophicus*, 18–19: "That the world is my world appears in the fact that the boundaries of language (the only language I understand) indicate the boundaries of my world."

34. For a detailed analysis, see Schwab, "Words and Moods."

35. Kristeva, *Revolution in Poetic Language*, 25.

36. Derrida, "This Strange Institution Called Literature."

37. Jacques Derrida, "Freud and the Scene of Writing," in *Writing and Difference* ["Freud et la scène de l'écriture," in *L'écriture et la différence*].

38. Ibid., 199 ["La *structure* de l'*appareil* psychique sera *représentée* par une machine d'écriture . . . quel appareil il faut créer pour représenter l'écriture psychique," 297].

39. Ibid., 201 ["l'essence même du psychisme," 299].

40. Ibid., 212 ["la conscience est . . . surface offerte au monde extérieur," 314].

41. Ibid. ["ce travail d'écriture qui circule comme une énergie psychique entre l'inconscient et le conscient," 314–15].

42. Ibid., 216.

43. Ibid., 214 ["Celle-ci a laissé une trace travailleuse qui n'a jamais été *perçue*, vécue dans son sens au présent, c'est-à-dire au conscient," 317].

44. Ibid., 209 ["L'expérience inconscient . . . n'emprunte pas, produit ses propres signifiants, ne les crée certes pas dans leur corps mais en produit la signifiance," 311].

45. Derrida, "This Strange Institution Called Literature," 35.

46. Ibid.

47. Ibid., 36.

48. Ibid., 43.

49. Ibid.

50. Ibid.

51. Michael Fischer, "Autobiographical Voices (1, 2, 3) and Mosaic Memory: Ethnicity, Religion, Science (An Inquiry into the Nature of Autobiographical Genres and Their Uses in Extending Social Theory)," in *Emergent Forms of Life*, 179.

52. Derrida, "This Strange Institution Called Literature," 34.

53. Winnicott, "Location of Cultural Experience," 8.

54. Fischer, *Emergent Forms of Life*, 180.

55. I am using the term "ethnography of the future" in reference to Balsamo, "Reading Cyborgs Writing Feminism," 148. See also Strathern, *Reproducing the Future*.

56. Derrida, "This Strange Institution Called Literature," 38.

57. Fischer, *Emergent Forms of Life*, 317.

58. Derrida, "This Strange Institution Called Literature," 42.

59. Literature provides the generative matrix of an experimental system that can be used and reshaped individually according to a reader's taste, ideology, and literary or theoretical preconceptions. In addition, readers also color the experience of literature with internal clusters of unconscious ideas. These processes also operate on the collective level, forming something akin to clusters of attitudes and values that inform perception and affect and provide the basic structures in the cultural imaginary. Just as persons receive and harbor clusters of unconscious ideas, so, I believe, do cultures. They may materialize as ingrained cultural ideologies or as shared cultural phantasms, or they may be elaborated creatively in myths, literature, and related arts.

60. Graves, *Greek Myths*, 21. For a discussion of Graves's use of the term "iconotropy," see also Bollas, *Being a Character*, 219.

61. Certeau, *Heterologies*.

62. Wiggins, *John Dollar*, 189.

63. Bhabha, *Location of Culture*, esp. p. 54.

64. Stephens, *Children and the Politics of Culture*.

65. Scheper-Hughes and Sargent, *Small Wars*.

66. Beckett, *Lost Ones*, 38 [*Le dépeupleur*: "Entre les extrêmes qui contiennent la vibration l'écart n'est guère plus de deux ou trois bougies," 34].

67. Ibid., 43 ["distinctes aux frontières précises mentales ou imaginaires puisque invisibles à l'œil de chair," 38].

68. Ibid., 8.

69. Ibid., 38 ["un faible grésillement d'insecte qui est celui de la lumière elle-même," 34].

70. Ibid., 39. ["l'être pensant venu se pencher froidement sur toutes ces données," 35].

71. Lyotard, *Inhuman*, 182.

1. Another Writing Lesson

1. Lévi-Strauss, *Tristes tropiques*, 411 [*Tristes tropiques*: "Qu'ai-je appris d'autre, en effet, des maîtres que j'ai écoutés, des philosophes que j'ai lus, des sociétés que j'ai visitées et de cette science même dont l'Occident tire son orgueil, sinon des bribes de leçons qui mises bout à bout, reconstituent la médiation du Sage au pied de l'arbre?" 475].

2. Derrida, *Of Grammatology*, 120 [*De la grammatologie*: "ethnocentrisme *se pensant* au contraire comme anti-ethnocentrisme, ethnocentrisme dans la conscience du progressisme libérateur," 175].

3. Lévi-Strauss, "Á propos de 'Lévi-Strauss dans le XVIIIe siècle'": "M. Derrida manie le tiers exclu avec la delicatesse d'un ours."

4. Derrida, *Of Grammatology*, 124 ["qu'on peut isoler la valeur esthétique," 181].

5. Lévi-Strauss, *Tristes tropiques*, 295 ["épisode grotesque," 338].

6. Ibid. ["Dans la littérature de voyage, de telles circonstances annoncent une attaque imminente," 338].

7. Ibid., 296. ["l'aventure," 296].

8. Ibid. ["Seul, sans doute, il avait compris la fonction de l'écriture. Aussi m'a-t-il réclamé un bloc-notes et nous sommes pareillement équipés quand nous travaillons ensemble. Il ne me communique pas verbalement les informations que je lui demande, mais trace sur son papier des lignes sinueuses et me les présente, comme si je devais lire sa réponse. Lui-même est à moitié dupe de sa comédie; chaque fois que sa main achève une ligne, il l'examine anxieusement comme si la signification devait en jaillir, et la même désillusion se peint sur son visage. Mais il n'en convient pas; et il est tacitement entendu entre nous que son grimoire possède un sens que je feins de déchiffrer; le commentaire verbal suit presque aussitôt et me dispense de réclamer les éclaircissements nécessaires. Or, à peine avait-il rassemblé tout son monde, qu'il tira d'une hotte un papier couvert de lignes tortillées qu'il fit semblant de lire et où il cherchait, avec une hésitation affectée, la liste des objets que je devais donner en retour des cadeux offerts," 340].

9. Quoted in Derrida, *Of Grammatology*, 123.

10. Ibid., 124 ["la catégorie esthétique," 181].

11. Homi K. Bhabha, "Of Mimicry and Man: The Ambivalence of Colonial Discourse," in *Location of Culture*, 85–92.

12. I think that the chief's response to the anthropologist presents an interesting instance that illuminates a condition under which a colonial subject or a subaltern subject can not only speak but also "talk back." See Spivak, "Can the Subaltern Speak?"

13. Bhabha, *Location of Culture*, 85.

14. Ibid., 86.

15. Fiorini, "Naming Game."

16. "It would be more accurate to presume . . . that Levi-Strauss' 'chief' was play-ing an entire act of imitating the Whiteman. Evidently, here the mimesis of the act is more than simply an exercise in mystification, where the Nambikwara 'chief,' who alone had achieved the understanding of graphic representation, duped everyone present. By assuming the perspective of the Whiteman, the Nambikwara 'chief' was not only acting in lieu of the foreigner, but also defining his own position viz a viz [sic] the distribution of the goods in relation to the latter's alterity. . . . In sum, the mimesis performed by the 'chief' did not only comprise the alienation of his people (as well as the outsiders) by his mediation of the distribution, but it also embodied the alienation of his own role as a vehicle and instrument of an outsider, the White-man, Levi-Strauss himself" (Fiorini, "Naming Game").

17. Ibid.

18. See Barthes, *Roland Barthes by Roland Barthes*, 152.

19. I use "literature" here in a very broad sense that includes the performative use of signs for the purpose of irony, play, and metacommunication.

20. See also Dissanayake, *Homo Aestheticus*.

21. Lévi-Strauss, *Tristes tropiques*, 296 ["Cette comédie se prolongea pendant deux heures. Qu'espérait-il? Se tromper lui-même, peut-être; mais plutôt étonner ses compagnons, les persuader que les marchandises passaient par son intermédi-aire, qu'il avait obtenu l'alliance du blanc et qu'il participait à ses secrets," 340].

22. Greenblatt, *Marvelous Possessions*.

23. Lévi-Strauss, *Tristes tropiques*, 296f ["Nous étions en hâte de partir, le mo-ment le plus redoutable étant évidemment celui où toutes les merveilles que j'avais apportées seraient réunies dans d'autres mains. Aussi je ne cherchai pas à approfon-dir l'incident," 340].

24. Ibid., 297 ["Le séjour avorté, la mystification dont je venais à mon insu d'être l'instrument, avaient créé un climat irritant; au surplus, mon mulet avait de l'aphte et souffrait de la bouche," 340].

25. Ibid. ["Le soleil descendait sur l'horizon, je n'avais plus d'arme et je m'attendais tout le temps à recevoir une volée de flèches," 341].

26. Gregory Bateson, "Style, Grace, and Information in Primitive Art," in *Steps to an Ecology of Mind*, 128–56. See also Bollas, *Shadow of the Object*. The formation of a cultural unconscious and the transmission of cultural values, tastes, and even tacit codes begin with the earliest times of the acculturation of infants. What Bollas says about the unthought knowledge that we accumulate before the acquisition of language proper therefore also applies to cultural knowledge. In this sense, a tacit, or "unthought," knowledge operates at the level of the cultural imaginary and of cultural and intercultural transference.

27. I use the term in the sense of Bollas, *Being a Character*.

28. Butler and de Zegher, *On Line*, 195.

29. Ibid.,194.

2. Traveling Literature, Traveling Theory

1. Calvino, *Invisible Cities*, 138f [*Le città invisibili*: "Il Gran Kan possiede un atlante i cui disegni figurano l'orbe terracqueo tutt'insieme e continente per continente, i confini dei regni più lontani, le rotte delle navi, i contorni delle coste, le mappe delle metropoli più illustri e dei porti più opulenti. . . . L'atlante raffigura anche città di cui né Marco né i geografi sanno se ci sono e dove sono . . . delle città che ancora non hanno una forma né un nome. . . . Nelle ultime carte dell'atlante si diluivano reticoli senza principio né fine, città a forma di Los Angeles, a forma di Kyoto-Osaka, senza forma," 144–46].

2. Marco Polo, *Il Milione*.

3. Calvino, *Invisible Cities*, 137 ["Mi sembra che tu riconosci meglio le città sull'atlante che a visitarle di persona," 145].

4. Ibid., 139 ["finché ogni forma non avrà trovato la sua città, nuove città continueranno a nascere," 146].

5. Ibid. ["comincia la fine delle città," 146].

6. See Rieff, *Los Angeles*.

7. I am referring mainly to the Winnetou series *Winnetou and Old Shatterhand* and *Der Schatz im Silbersee*. For an English translation, see May, *Winnetou*.

8. Buck, *Peony*.

9. For a detailed discussion of Germany's transgenerational legacy, see Schwab, *Haunting Legacies*.

10. See Mitscherlich, *Inability to Mourn*.

11. See Fanon, *Black Skin, White Masks*.

12. Edward W. Said, "Traveling Theory," in *World, Text, and Critic*, 227–47.

13. From an interview we learn that the cast always had trouble finding gas. See Kaplan and Ottinger, "*Johanna d'Arc of Mongolia*: "The gas stations were secret because the military was worried about sabotage" (18).

14. See Clifford and Marcus, *Writing Culture*.

15. See, for example, Budick and Iser, *Translatability of Cultures*.

16. Winnicott, "Location of Cultural Experience."

17. Bhabha, *Location of Culture*.

18. I use the term in the sense developed in Abraham and Torok's theory of the transgenerational phantom (*Shell and the Kernel*). See also Grand, *Reproduction of Evil*.

19. See Rheinberger, "Man weiß nicht genau."

3. Restriction and Mobility

1. Douglas, *Natural Symbols*, 189.

2. Clifford, *Predicament of Culture*, 110.

3. Franz Kafka, "The Wish to Be a Red Indian," in *Complete Stories*, 390. For the original, see "Wunsch, Indianer zu werden," in *Franz Kafka: Erzählungen* (Frankfurt: Fischer, 1996), 34–35.

4. It is important to consider that in the German original Kafka emphasizes the wish to "become" an Indian (Indianer zu werden). This notion of becoming is lost in the authorized English translation but important for my reading of the text.

5. Görling, *Heterotopia*, 13.

6. See Charles Baudelaire, "The Assassin's Wine," in *Flowers of Evil*, 142f. See also Walter Benjamin, "The Paris of the Second Empire in Baudelaire," in *Writer of the Modern Life*, 46–133. And see Buck-Morss, "Flâneur."

7. Greenblatt et al., *Cultural Mobility*, 1–23.

8. See Roger Caillois, "Le fantastique naturel," in *Cases d'un échiquier*, 61–73. See also Caillois, *Anthologie du fantastique*.

9. Kafka, *Complete Stories*, 390.

10. Franz Kafka, "Reflections for Gentlemen-Jockeys," in *Complete Stories*, 389 ["Neid der Gegner," 18].

11. Ibid., 390 ["dem ewigen Händeschütteln, Salutieren, Sich-Niederbeugen und In-die-Ferne-Grüßen," 18].

12. Deleuze and Guattari, *Anti-Oedipus*.

13. Deleuze and Guattari, *Kafka*.

14. Godzich, *Culture of Literacy*, 132.

15. Jameson, "Third-World Literature."

16. Aijaz Ahmad, "Jameson's Rhetoric of Otherness and the National Allegory," in *In Theory*, 95–122.

17. Homi K. Bhabha, "How Newness Enters the World: Postmodern Space, Postcolonial Times and the Trials of Cultural Translation," in *Location of Culture*, 212–235.

18. Said, *Freud and the Non-European*, 7–8.

19. Among the anthropologists it is Michael M. J. Fischer who has most scrupulously traced such an emergence. See his *Emergent Forms of Life* and *Anthropological Futures*.

20. Silko, *Storyteller*, 54–62.

21. Ibid., 62.

22. Ibid., 54.

23. Gerald Vizenor's manifesto for a postmodern Native American literature can be seen as paradigmatic of this position in which he polemicizes against the pressure of the publication industry and the market toward confining Native American writing to the conventions of literary and magic realism (*Narrative Chance*).

24. Asad, "Concept of Cultural Translation."

25. Walter Benjamin, "The Task of the Translator," in *Illuminations*, 69–82.

26. Crapanzano, "Hermes' Dilemma," 51.

27. Hayles, *How We Became Posthuman*, 132.

28. Abish, *How German Is It*.

29. Abish, *Alphabetical Africa*.

30. See my *Subjects without Selves* and *Mirror and the Killer-Queen*.

31. Bhabha, *Location of Culture*, 1–18.

32. Lévi-Strauss, "Race and Culture."

33. Herman Melville, "The Metaphysics of Indian-Hating," in *Confidence-Man*, 192–202.

4. *The Melancholic Cannibal*

1. Saer, *Witness*, 35 [*El entenado*: "No sabe nunca cuando se nace: el parto es una simple convención. Muchos mueren sun haber nacido; otros nacen apenas, otros mal, como abortados," 35].

2. Derrida, " 'Eating Well.' "

3. See Sigmund Freud, "Formulations on the Two Principles of Mental Functioning" (1911), in *SE* 12:213–26, and "A Metapsychological Supplement to the Theory of Dreams" (1917), in *SE* 14:217–35. "Reality testing" is, according to Freud, acquired during the process of differentiation between the internal and external worlds. This differentiation emerges gradually from the increasing ability to separate inner and outer experiences as well as the ability to say no (function of judgment). Freud saw reality testing as one of the functions of the ego.

4. Lestringant, *Cannibals*, 6.

5. Ibid., 7.

6. García-Moreno, "Indigestible Other," 585.

7. Saer, *Witness*, 128 ["Lo exterior era su principal problema. No lograban, como hubiesen querido, verse desde afuera. Yo, en cambio, que había llegado del horizonte borroso, el primer recuerdo que tengo de ellos es justamente el de su exterioridad," 120].

8. Jacques Lacan has argued that the act of mirroring serves a crucial function in the ontological formation of children and sets the stage for the differentiation of self and other in later life. Disruptions in this process are responsible for various psychological disorders, including psychosis in some cases (Jacques Lacan, "The Mirror Stage as Formative of the *I* Function, as Revealed in Psychoanalytic Experience," in *Écrits*, 3–9). For a more encompassing discussion of the mirror phase, see also Winnicott, *Playing and Reality*.

9. Saer, *Witness*, 109 ["para mí no había más hombres sobre esta tierra que esos indios y . . . desde el día en que me habían mandado de vuelta yo no había encontrado, aparte del padre Quesada, otra cosa que seres extraños y problemáticos a los cuales únicamente por costumbre o convención la palabra hombres podía aplicárseles," 103].

10. As Peter Hulme has argued in *Colonial Encounters*, the term also relates to the linguistic morphology of the word "Carib."

11. Michel de Montaigne, "Of cannibals," in *Complete Essays*, 150 [*Essais*: "J'ai eu long temps avec moy un homme qui avoit demeure dix ou douze ans en cet autre monde qui a este decouvert en nostre siecle," 251].

12. Ibid., 152 ["Ils sont sauvages, de mesmes que nous appelons sauvages les fruicts que nature, de soy et de son progrez ordinaire, a produicts: là où, à la verité, ce sont ceux que nous avons alterez par nostre artifice et detournez de l'ordre commun, que nous devrions appeller plutost sauvages," 254].

13. Saer, *Witness*, 26 ["la certidumbre de una experiencia común desaparecía y yo me quedaba solo en el mundo para dirimir todos los problemas arduos que supone su existencia," 27].

14. Ibid., 45 ["eterno extranjero," 45].

15. Ibid., 143 [*"Def-ghi* se le decía a las personas que estaban ausentes o dormidas; a los indiscretos, a los que durante una visita, en lugar de permanecer en casa ajena un tiempo prudente, se demoraban con exceso; *def-ghi* se le decía también a un pájaro de pico negro y plumaje amarillo y verde que a veces domesticaban y que los hacía reír porque repetéia algunas palabras que le enseñaban, como si hubiese hablado; *def-ghi* llamban también a ciertos objetos que sa ponían en lugar de una persona ausente y que la representaban en las reuniones . . . le decían *def-ghi*, de igual modo, al reflejo de las cosas en el agua, una cosa que duraba era *def-ghi*," 133].

16. Ibid., 144 ["porque me hacéian compartir, con todo lo otro que llamaban de la misma manera, alguna esencia solidaria," 134].

17. Ibid. ["De mí esperaban que duplicara, como el agua, la imagen que daban de sí mismos, que repitiera sus gestos y palabras, que los representara en su ausencia y que fuese capaz, cuando me devolvieran a mis semejantes, de hacer como el espía o el adelantado que, por haber sido testigo de algo que el resto de la tribu todavía no había visto, pudiese volver sobre sus pasos para contárselo en detalle a todos," 134].

18. Blumenberg, *Legitimacy of the Modern Age*.

19. Simard, *La réduction*.

20. Saer, *Witness*, 139 ["la sensación antigua de nada, confusa y rudimentaria," 130].

21. Ibid., 138 ["reencontrar . . . el de una experiencia antigua incrustada más allá de la memoria," 128].

22. Ibid., 139 ["se comían entre ellos," 129].

23. Ibid., 138 ["ellos no había otro modo de distinguirse del mundo," 129].

24. See Bollas, *Shadow of the Object*.

25. Saer, *Witness*, 139 ["Pero, sobre todo, lo que venían trayendo del pasado, la sensación antigua de nada, confusa y rudimentaria, había quedado en ellos como su verdadera forma de ser. Si es verdad, como dicen algunos, que siempre queremos repetir nuestras experiencias primeras y que, de algún modo, siempre las repetimos,

la ansiedad de los indios debía venirles de ese regusto arcaico que tenía, a pesar de haber ambiado de objeto, su deseo," 130].

26. Ibid., 140 ["el más antiguo, el más adentrado, el deseo de comerse a sí mismos," 130].

27. See Freud's *Totem and Taboo* and *Civilization and Its Discontents*.

28. Mahler, Pine, and Bergman, *Psychological Birth of the Human Infant*.

29. Saer, *Witness*, 35 ["No se sabe nunca cuando se nace: el parto es una simple íconvención. Muchos mueren sin haber nacido; otros nacen apenas, otros mal, como abortados. Algunos, por nacimientos sucesivos, van pasando de vida en vida, y si la muerte no viniese a interrumpirlos, serían capaces de agotar el ramillete de mundos posibles a fuerza de nacer una y otra vez, como si poseyesen una reserva inagotable de inocencia y de abandono," 35].

30. Regarding the reflections that follow here, see Appadurai, *Modernity at Large*, 139–58.

31. Appadurai sees this primordialism operate also in the antimodern religious, fundamentalist, or racist and ethnocentric mass movements.

32. Saer, *Witness*, 152 ["sequedad," 142].

33. Ibid., 49 ["como si la culpa, tomando la apariencia del deseo, hubiese sido en ellos contemporánea del pecado. A medida que comían, la jovialidad de la mañana iba dándole paso a un silencio pensativo, a la melancolía, a la hosquedad," 48].

34. Ibid., 133 ["y todo lo que creo saber de ellos me viene de indicios inciertos, de recuerdos dudosos, de interpretaciones, así que, en cierto sentido, también mi relato puede significar muchas cosas a la vez, sin que ninguna, viniendo de fuentes tan poco claras, sea necesariamente cierta," 124].

35. Ibid., 111 ["el mundo entero, hasta la más modesta de sus presencias, se presenta, para el que lo atraviesa, como un lugar desierto y calcinado," 105].

36. I use the term "crypt" in the sense developed in Abraham and Torok, *Shell and the Kernel*.

37. See Kristeva, *Black Sun*.

38. See Görling, *Heterotopia*.

39. Ibid., 234.

40. Saer, *Witness*, 167 ["El único justo, es el saber que reconoce que sabemos únicamente lo que condesciende a monstrarse," 155].

41. Wiggins, *John Dollar*, 11.

42. Ibid., 189

43. Ibid., 8.

44. Ibid., 3.

45. Interestingly, one of Marianne Wiggins's recent books is an imaginary biographical novel of Edward Curtis, titled *The Shadow Catcher*.

46. Wiggins, *John Dollar*, 7.

47. In the sense defined by Homi K. Bhabha in "Of Mimicry and Man: The Ambivalence of Colonial Discourse," in *Location of Culture*, 85–92.

48. Wiggins, *John Dollar*, 7.

49. Ibid., 9.

50. Ibid., 86.

51. Ibid., 106.

52. Ibid., 97.

53. Ibid., 182.

54. Ibid.

55. Ibid., 183f.

56. Ibid., 187.

57. See Ulnik, *Skin in Psychoanalysis*.

58. Wiggins, *John Dollar*, 188.

59. The scene in which the girls devour the remains of their fathers is a rewriting of Freud's fantasy of the cannibalistic devouring of the father by the horde of brothers. See Freud, *Totem and Taboo*.

60. Wiggins, *John Dollar*, 58.

61. Abraham and Torok, *Shell and the Kernel*, 127 [*L'écorce et le noyau*: "Absorber ce qui vient à manquer sous forme de nourriture, imaginaire ou réelle, alors que le psychisme est endeuillé, c'est refuser le deuil et ses conséquences, c'est refuser d'introduire en soi la partie de soi-même déposée dans ce qui est perdu, c'est refuser de savoir le vrai sens de la perte, celui qui ferait qu'en le sachant on serait autre, bref, c'est refuser son introjection," 261].

62. Ibid., 130 ["Tous les mots qui n'auront pu être dits, toutes les scènes qui n'auront pu être remémorées, toutes les larmes qui n'auront pu être versées, seront avalés, en même temps que le traumatisme, cause de la perte. . . . Dans la crypte repose . . . les moments traumatiques—effectifs ou supposés—qui avaient rendu l'introjection impraticable. Il s'est créé ainsi tout un monde fantasmatique inconscient qui mène une vie séparée et occulte," 266].

63. Ibid., 129 ["fausses incorporations," 264].

64. Ibid., 129f ["Il [le repas imaginaire] rappelle le repas funéraire qui doit avoir même finalité: la communion alimentaire entre les survivants. Elle peut vouloir dire: à la place de la personne du défunt, c'est notre présence mutuelle que nous introduisons dans nos corps sous forme de nourriture assimilable; quant au défunt, c'est dans la terre que nous le déposerons et non pas en nous-mêmes. La nécrophagie, enfin, toujours collective, se distingue également de l'incorporation . . . Elle [l'absorption réelle de la dépouille] aura pour effet d'exorciser le penchant, qui pourrait naître avec le décès, d'une incorporation psychique," 265].

65. Wiggins, *John Dollar*, 184.

66. Ibid., 175.

67. Ibid., 214.

68. I use the term "transcoding" here in the sense developed in Jameson, *Political Unconscious*.

69. Wiggins, *John Dollar*, 194.

5. War Children in a Global World

1. Nancy Scheper-Hughes and Carolyn Sargent, "Introduction," in *Small Wars*, 9

2. Sharon Stevens, "Introduction," in *Children and the Politics of Culture*, 6.

3. Powers, *Operation Wandering Soul*.

4. Postman, *Disappearance of Childhood*.

5. Sommerville, *Rise and Fall of Childhood*; Winn, *Children Without Childhood*; Gilmour, *Innocent Victims*; Vittachi, *Stolen Childhood*; Allsebrook and Swift, *Broken Promise*; and Garbarino et al., *Children in Danger*.

6. Powers, *Operation Wandering Soul*, 349.

7. Ibid., 328.

8. Ibid.

9. Frank, *Anne Frank*, 264.

10. See Strathern, *Reproducing the Future*.

11. Robert Coles quoted in Stephens, *Children and the Politics of Culture*, 3.

12. My use of the term "thinking the future" casts Powers's novel as an imaginary "ethnography of the future" as defined, for example, by Marilyn Strathern and Michael M. J. Fischer.

13. Rieff, *Los Angeles*.

14. Powers, *Operation Wandering Soul*, 3.

15. Ibid.

16. Ibid.

17. Ibid., 249.

18. Ibid., 28.

19. Ibid., 147.

20. Ibid., 133.

21. Ibid., 54.

22. See Emmanuel Levinas, "Ethics and the Face," in *Totality and Infinity*, 194–201.

23. Powers, *Operation Wandering Soul*, 159.

24. Ibid., 72–73.

25. Ibid., 23.

26. Ibid., 229.

27. Ibid.

28. Ibid., 218.

29. Ibid., 219–20.

30. Ibid., 218.

31. The Children's Crusade occurred in 1212, not long before the advent of the Pied Piper in 1284.

32. See "What Happened to These Children?" *Saturday Evening Post*, December 24, 1955. See also a comprehensive summary of the different hypotheses of the origin of the legend at http://en.wikipedia.org/wiki/The_Pied_Piper_of_Hamelin.

33. Powers, *Operation Wandering Soul*, 178.

34. Ibid., 182.

35. Ibid., 187.

36. Stites, "Bordercrossings," 113.

37. Ibid.

38. Stites, "Bordercrossings," 113.

39. Powers, *Operation Wandering Soul*, 31–32.

40. Ibid., 33.

41. Ibid., 262.

42. Ibid.

43. Ibid., 263.

44. Ibid.

45. Ibid., 264.

46. Ibid., 349.

47. Ibid., 263.

48. Ibid., 274.

49. Ibid.

50. Ibid., 276.

51. With Los Angeles as the local ethnographic setting, Powers has chosen the metropolis commonly labeled as the city of the future. Childhood provides a perfect lens through which to scrutinize how the aftershocks of Western expansionism mark contemporary L.A. culture with rampant economic devastation, filling the city's most vulnerable centers with the victims from cultures or countries that have fallen prey to multinational corporate market laws. South Central L.A. now harbors a diverse urban ghetto population made up of children from America's most disenfranchised. This legacy of colonialism and imperialism now determines the face and the fate of the City of Angels—a city that, according to the narrator, harbors a state of "emergency gone quotidian" (*Operation Wandering Soul*, 20).

The adaptive response to such a state of emergency is an emotional economy in which one can survive only with a technique of instant repression. Daily disasters are mentally filtered out before they can even "touch" one. If employed on a daily basis as a standard filter of perception, the protective psychic barrier—Freud's *Reizschutz*—loses its adaptive function. Meant to ward off exceptional overstimulation, this psychic barrier now works unilaterally to numb the senses and emotions, creating the state of indifference that prevents intervention, protest, or simply immediate emotional involvement. Emergency becomes a matter of statistics. This is why "stats," as the narrator calls them, play such a central role in *Operation Wandering Soul*. Statistical data are scattered across the various stories, as if to restore a manageable context to the catastrophe and thus to reverse emotional depletion. Confronting us with heart-wrenching statistics of decline, Powers doubles the voice of the Pied Piper, who predicted the decline of medieval Hamelin, only to mock readers with the narrator's rhetorical question: "Who at this late date would dare to be so medieval as to dispute statistics?" (ibid., 220).

"Ten American children are killed each day by handguns alone" (ibid., 135).

"One in five American schoolchildren has possessed a gun. On any given day, one hundred thousand come to school armed" (ibid., 336).

52. Ibid., 271.

53. Ibid.

54. This doubling or simulation of voices resonates with other patterns of doubling and replacing voices throughout the novel. One example is Joleene's use of the simulated voice of her fetish doll to replace her own voice.

55. See Mbembe, "Necropolitics."

56. Powers, *Operation Wandering Soul*, 253.

57. Ibid., 289.

58. Ibid., 290.

59. Ibid.

60. Ibid., 304.

61. Ibid.

62. Ibid., 306.

63. Ibid., 290.

64. Ibid., 76.

65. Ibid.

66. This connection between mortality and the endless productivity enabled by literature is best analyzed in the last chapter of Iser, *Fictive and the Imaginary*.

67. Kermode, *Sense of an Ending*.

68. Robbins, "'When Do You Think the World Will End?'"

69. The narrator sarcastically calls this evacuation a "picnic on the parade ground of apocalypse" (Powers, *Operation Wandering Soul*, 39).

70. Ibid., 46.

71. Ibid., 330.

72. Ibid., 215.

73. Ibid., 221.

74. Ibid., 222.

75. Ibid., 223.

76. Ibid., 225.

77. I use the term here in the sense defined in Lecercle, *Philosophy of Nonsense*.

78. Powers, *Operation Wandering Soul*, 344.

79. Ibid., 247f.

80. Ibid., 349.

81. See, for example, the postmodern apocalypse featured in Pynchon's *Gravity's Rainbow* with its masculinist myth of the Rocket.

82. Powers, *Operation Wandering Soul*, 348.

83. Ibid., 121.

84. Ibid., 350.

85. Ibid., 282.

86. Ibid., 283.

87. Stephens, *Children and the Politics of Culture*, 21.

88. See Scheper-Hughes and Sargent, *Small Wars*, 2.

89. Ibid., 24.

90. Ibid., 10, 389–412. I am using the term "zones of abandonment" in the sense defined in Biehl, *Vita*.

91. Stephens, *Children and the Politics of Culture*, 23.

92. The only other country was Somalia.

93. Scheper-Hughes and Sargent, *Small Wars*, 15.

94. Vincent Crapanzano, "World-Ending," in *Imaginative Horizons*, 194.

95. Powers, *Operation Wandering Soul*, 335.

96. Ibid., 348.

97. Ibid., 187.

98. Ibid., 188.

6. *Ethnographies of the Future*

1. Quoted in Pickover, *Science of Aliens*, 61.

2. Ibid., 60.

3. Clifford Pickover is a researcher at the IBM Thomas J. Watson Research Center.

4. Octavia Butler's *Xenogenesis* is a trilogy composed of *Dawn, Adulthood Rites*, and *Imago*. These novels will be cited separately in this chapter. New editions of *Xenogenesis* changed the title to *Lilith's Brood*.

5. Balsamo, "Reading Cyborgs Writing Feminism," 148

6. See Blumenberg, *Die Vollzähligkeit der Sterne*, 351.

7. See http://today.uci.edu/news/release_detail.asp?key=73. See also http://64.233.161.104/u/isearch?q=cache:icnxeIxAiVoJ:www.uci.edu/fc/press_releases/1995/0516.html+asch+balmaceda+stone&hl=en&ie=UTF-8.

8. Maranto, "Test-Tube Treachery."

9. Ibid.

10. Quoted in Nash, *Rights of Nature*, 138.

11. Balibar, "My *Self* and My *Own*," 41.

12. Haraway, *Modest_Witness*, 135.

13. Butler, *Imago*, 172.

14. Plessner, "Die anthropologische Dimension der Geschichtlichkeit," 160.

15. Freud makes such statements in various places. See, for example, *Freud Reader*, 656.

16. Butler, *Imago*, 89.

17. Ibid., 90.

18. Butler, *Dawn*, 20.

19. Butler, *Imago*, 147.

20. In this vein, the "tasting" of humans with tongues and tentacles serves both to create intimacy and to collect genetic information. Genetic research as a kind of intimate "fieldwork" is "natural" for the Oankali because they know neither a separation of body and mind nor one of nature and culture. Emphasizing the ethnographic implications of *Xenogenesis*, Haraway concludes, "Anthropologists of possible selves, we are technicians of realizable futures. Science is culture" (*Modest_Witness*, 230). But what kind of anthropology, culture, and especially "realizable future" are at stake here? Butler's "imagined community" of humans and aliens unfolds as a drama of forced reproduction.

21. Haraway, *Modest_Witness*, 227.

22. Butler, *Dawn*, 246.

23. Ibid., 245.

24. For a definition of the concept of "social death," see Erdheim and Nadig, "Ethnopsychoanalyse."

25. See Patterson, *Slavery and Social Death*.

26. Plessner, "Die anthropologische Dimension der Geschichtlichkeit."

27. Blumenberg, *Die Vollzähligkeit der Sterne*, 353: "Denn spezifische Leibgleichheit ist etwas, was unter allen Wahrscheinlichkeiten astronautischer Erfahrung am wenigsten zuverlässig erwartet werden darf."

28. Butler, *Dawn*, 9.

29. Ibid., 11.

30. Ibid.

31. Beckett, *Unnamable*, 23.

32. Blumenberg, *Die Vollzähligkeit der Sterne*, 537.

33. Butler, *Dawn*, 22.

34. Richard Doyle, "The Sublime Object of Biology," in *On Beyond Living*, 1–24.

35. Doyle, *Wetwares*, 198.

36. See Wendy Brown, "Wounded Attachments," in *States of Injury*, 52–76.

37. Butler, *Adulthood Rites*, 272.

38. Gregory Bateson, "Culture Contact and Schismogenesis," in *Steps to an Ecology of Mind*.

39. Hayles, *How We Became Posthuman*, 283–291.

40. See Bohm, *Wholeness and the Implicate Order*, 140–213.

41. Schrödinger, *What Is Life?*.

42. Blumenberg, *Die Lesbarkeit der Welt*, 383.

43. See Wilden, *System and Structure*, 210.

44. Mbembe, *On the Postcolony*, 173–211. See also Mbembe, "Necropolitics."

45. Butler, *Imago*, 138.

46. "I sorted through the vast genetic memory that Nikanj had given me. There was a single cell within that great store—a cell that could be awakened from its stasis within yashi and stimulated to divide and grow into a kind of seed. This seed could become a town or a shuttle or a great ship. . . . I took the remaining mass—the seed—still within my body to the place the humans and the visiting families had agreed was good for people and towns. . . . Here the town could grow and always have the companionship of some of us. It would need that companionship as much as we did during our metamorphoses. . . . 'This could be a good place,' one of our elders commented. . . . I chose a spot near the river. There I prepared the seed to go into the ground. . . . I planted it deep in the rich soil of the riverbank. Seconds after I had expelled it, I felt it begin the tiny positioning movements of independent life" (Butler, *Imago*, 219–20).

Coda

1. Kant, *Anthropology from a Pragmatic Point of View*, 110.

2. Deleuze, *Fold*, 35.

3. Jean-François Lyotard, "Scapeland," in *Inhuman*, 186 [*L'inhumain*: "De l'esprit râpé par le raz de matière," 197].

4. Beckett, *Lost Ones*, 52 [*Le dépeupleur*: "L'effet de ce climat sur l'âme n'est pas à sous-estimer," 46].

5. Lyotard, *Inhuman*, 190.

6. Ibid., 182.

7. In general, "social death" is a term used to describe the condition of people who are denied the status of being fully human. Used by theorists like Zygmunt Bauman and Orlando Patterson or historians of the Holocaust, social death describes conditions such as racial exclusion, persecution, slavery, and apartheid. In addition, encounters with otherness that undermine the familiar parameters of orientation in the world may induce mental states that resemble social death.

8. See Patterson, *Slavery and Social Death*. See also Erdheim and Nadig, "Grössenphantasien und sozialer Tod."

9. Beckett, *Lost Ones*, 7.

10. *The Tormont Webster's Illustrated Encyclopedic Dictionary* (Boston: Houghton Mifflin, 1987), 1586.

11. Beckett, *Lost Ones*, 9 ["Ainsi subsistent chair et os," 9].

12. Ibid., 7 ["quelque quatre-vingt mille centimètres carrés de surface totale," 7].

13. Ibid., 11 ["une ceinture imaginaire courant à mi-hauteur," 10].

14. Ibid., 7 ["cinquante mètres de pourtour et seize de haut pour l'harmonie," 7].

15. Ibid., 9 ["s'appuient contre le mur de façon peu harmonieuse," 9].

16. Ibid., 11f ["Elles sont disposées en quinconces irréguliers savamment désaxés ayant sept mètres de côté en moyenne. Harmonie que seul peut goûter qui par longue fréquentation connaît à fond l'ensemble des niches au point d'en posséder une image mentale parfaite. Or il est douteux qu'un tel existe," 11].

17. Badiou, *Beckett*, 49: "C'est l'autre propre de chacun, celui qui le singularise, qui l'arrache a l'anonymat." English translation mine.

18. Beckett, *Lost Ones*, 35 ["un temps très long impossible à chiffrer," 31].

19. Ibid., 7 ["Leur séjour va peut-être finir," 7].

20. Ibid., 8 ["Tout va peut-être finir," 8].

21. Ibid., 15 ["Mais il en restera toujours assez pour abolir chez ce petit peuple à plus ou moins longue échéance jusqu'au dernier vestige de ses ressorts," 14].

22. Ibid., 62f ["Se tait du même coup le grésillement d'insecte mentionné plus haut d'où subitement un silence plus fort que tous ces faibles souffles réunis. Voilà en gros le dernier état du cylindre et de ce petit peuple de chercheurs dont un premier si ce fut un homme dans un passé impensable baissa enfin une première fois la tête si cette notion est maintenue," 55].

23. Porush, *Soft Machine*, 158. Porush overlooks, however, the fact that the voice posits itself in many instances as unknowing, hesitant, and reduced to speculation when it comes to interpreting as opposed to merely observing the culture of the little people, even when it comes to the appropriate use of language and categorical attributions.

24. Kenner, *Samuel Beckett*, 17.

25. Beckett, *Lost Ones*, 43 ["Le fond du cylindre comporte trois zones distinctes aux frontières précises mentales ou imaginaires puisque invisibles à l'œil de chair," 38].

26. Ibid., 13 ["un premier aperçu du séjour," 12].

27. Ibid., 27 ["un premier aperçu du code des grimpeurs," 24].

28. Ibid., 62 ["le dernier état du cylindre," 55].

29. Ibid., 8 ["pour l'œil qui cherche," 7].

30. Ibid. ["se frôlent avec un bruit de feuilles sèches," 8].

31. Ibid., 9 ["du choc des corps entre eux," 8].

32. Ibid. ["le silence des pas," 8].

33. Ibid., 53 ["un froissement d'orties," 47].

34. Ibid., 8f ["Un baiser rend un son indescriptible," 8].

35. Ibid., 52 ["L'effet de ce climat sur l'âme," 46].

36. Ibid. ["continue néanmois de se défendre," 46].

37. Ibid., 53 ["la cécité effective," 46].

38. Ibid., 52.

39. This formulation plays with the title of another piece by Beckett.

40. Beckett, *Lost Ones*, 42 ["Car seul le cylindre offre des certitudes et au-dehors rien que mystère," 38].

41. See Deleuze and Guattari, *Thousand Plateaus*, 233.

42. Lyotard, *Inhuman*, 18 ["Quand on croit décrire la pensée sous la forme d'une sélection des données et de leur articulation, on tait la vérité: les données ne sont pas données, mais donnables, et la sélection n'est pas une choix. Penser comme écrire ou peindre n'est presque que laisser venir du donnable," 26–27].

43. Lyotard, *Discours, figure*, 311.

44. Beckett, *Lost Ones*, 39 ["se pencher froidement sur toutes ces données et évidences," 35].

45. Ibid. ["Et pour l'être pensant venu se pencher froidement sur toutes ces données et évidences il serait vraiment difficile au bout de son analyse de ne pas estimer à tort qu'au lieu d'employer le terme vaincus qui a en effet un petit côté pathétique désagréable on ferait mieux de parler d'aveugles tout court," 35].

46. Ibid., 30 ["Détail pittoresque," 27].

47. Ibid. ["un bambin," 241].

48. Ibid., 56. ["la vaincue," 49].

49. I return later to this resonance with Beckett's piece of the same title. See Beckett, *Imagination Dead Imagine*, in *Complete Short Prose of Samuel Beckett*, 182–85.

50. Lyotard, *Inhuman*, 22 ["ce n'es pas le désir humain de connaître et de transformer la réalité qui meuve la technoscience, mais une circonstance cosmique," 30].

51. Roland Barthes, "The Nautilus and the Drunken Boat," in *Mythologies*, 65 ["Nautilus et le bateau ivre," in *Mythologies* (Paris: Éditions du Seuil, 1957): "une sorte de cosmogonie fermée sur elle-même, qui a ses catégories propres, son temps, son espace, sa plénitude, et même son principe existentiel" 80].

52. Beckett, *Lost Ones*, 36 ["pour ne pas dire de souffre," 32].

53. Ibid., 21 ["des amateurs du mythe," 19].

54. Ibid., 53 ["la gêne qui en découle pour l'amour," 47].

55. Ibid., 37 ["faire l'infaisable amour," 33].

56. Ibid., 53 ["Ce dessèchement de l'enveloppe enlève à la nudité une bonne partie de son charme en la rendant grise et transforme en un froissement d'orties la succulence naturelle de chair contre chair. . . . Le spectacle est curieux alors des ébats qui se prolongent douloureux et sans espoir bien au-delà de ce que peuvent en chambre les amants les plus habiles," 47].

57. Ibid. ["en vertu de la loi des probabilités," 47].

58. Ibid., 55 ["se remettent à chercher ni soulagés ni même déçus," 48].

59. Ibid., 54f ["la même vivacité de réaction comme à une fin de monde," 48].

60. Ibid., 20 ["le noir les attende," 18].

61. Ibid., 17 ["tout temps," 16].

62. Ibid., 18 ["brilleraient encore le soleil et les autres étoiles," 17].

63. Ibid., 21 ["Voilà pour ce zénith inviolable où se cache aux yeux des amateurs de mythe une issue vers terre et ciel," 19].

64. Ibid., 60.

65. Ibid., 21 ["des amateurs du mythe," 19].

66. Ibid., 31 ["fièvre oculaire," 28].

67. Ibid., 32 ["le rien tout entier," 28].

68. Ibid., 63 ["ce petit peuple de chercheurs," 55].

69. Ibid., 60 ["l'abandon sans retour," 53].

70. Ibid., 62 ["le noir se fait en même temps que la température se fixe dans le voisinage de zéro," 55].

71. Samuel Beckett, *Complete Short Prose of Samuel Beckett*, 182.

72. Ibid., 184.

73. Ibid.

74. Ibid., 185.

75. Ibid.

76. Foucault, *Order of Things*, 387.

77. Beckett, *Complete Short Prose of Samuel Beckett*, 185.

78. Beckett, *Lost Ones*, 18 ["brilleraient encore le soleil et les autres étoiles," 17].

79. See Gilles Deleuze and Félix Guattari, "The Social Field" and "The Molecular Unconscious," in *Anti-Oedipus*, 273–296.

80. Lyotard, *Discours, figure*, 228. My translation.

81. Lyotard, *Inhuman*, 172.

82. Lyotard, *Discours, figure*, 217.

83. I borrow this term and the concept from Bollas, *Shadow of the Object*. See also my discussion of the relevance of this concept for literary studies in Schwab, "Words and Moods."

84. See also Porush's reading of the cylinder as an entropic space in *The Soft Machine*. My reading differs from Porush's in emphasizing the negentropic forces that render the space more complex and ultimately more interesting.

85. Lyotard, *Inhuman*, 184 ["Douce violence que l'indétermination exerce sur le déterminé, pour qu'il lâche son QUOD. Et ce non-lieu, ce n'est pas moi qui l'engendre, ni personne," 195].

86. Ibid., 186 ["une passation des pouvoirs matériels, aux odeurs, à la qualité tactile du sol, des murs, des végétaux," 196].

87. Ibid. ["exotisme intimiste," 197].

88. Ibid. ["États d'âme sont états de matière spirituelle," 197].

89. Ibid., 185 ["craquelé par l'aridité, un défi à la chair. Et dans les rides, sous les plis où les prunelles s'exaspèrent, l'incredulité gaie. La momie vit donc encore. Quelque peu," 195].

90. Ibid., 185, 186 ["MÉLANCOLIE de tous les paysages. . . . l'esprit râpé par le raz de matière," 196, 197].

91. Ibid., 187 ["l'immonde," 197].

92. Ibid. ["petites sensations," 197].

93. Ibid. ["La désolation du dedans," 197].

94. Beckett, *Lost Ones*, 60 ["l'abandon sans retour," 53].

95. Ibid., 38.

96. Lyotard, *Inhuman*, 20 ["Le non-pensé fait mal parce qu'on est bien dans le déjà pensé," 28].

97. See the theatrical conception developed for Beckett's theater by Michael Fox. Fox also develops a similar argument in his unpublished work on Beckett.

98. Lyotard, *Inhuman*, 187 ["Le soi déposé derrière, en défroque, trop convenu décidément, trop sûr de soi et arrogant dans sa mise à l'échelle," 197].

99. Beckett, *Lost Ones*, 21 ["qu'aux papillons," 19].

100. Lyotard, *Inhuman*, 189 ["l'implosion des formes mêmes," 199].

101. Goodman, *Ways of Worldmaking*.

102. Lyotard, *Inhuman*, 38 ["la matière dans la pensée," 47].

103. Ibid., 188 ["comment pointer autrement que dans la texture d'écrit, sur les indices scripturaux, le souffle qui happe l'esprit au gouffre," 198].

104. Ibid. ["sinon elle n'est que la mise en scène et en œuvre des pouvoirs de la langue," 199].

105. Ibid., 189 ["Un bébé, la face de sa MÈRE doit être un paysage. Ce n'est pas parce qu'il y promène sa bouche, ses doigts, son regard, empoignant ou tétant un peu tout à l'aveuglette, extasié, pleurant, grognon. Ce n'est pas non plus parce qu'il est 'en symbiose' avec elle… Il faudrait plutôt songer à l'indescriptible de cette face pour l'enfant. Il l'aura oubliée, parce qu'elle n'aura pas été inscrite… Cette mère serait le timbre, 'avant qu'il sonne, 'avant les coordonnés du son, avant le destin," 199–200].

106. Samuel Beckett, "Fizzle 6," in *Complete Short Prose of Samuel Beckett*, 238f.

107. Ibid., 6.

108. Ibid.

109. Ibid., 7.

110. Ibid.

111. Ibid.

112. Ibid., 1.

113. I use this term in the sense of Clifford and Marcus, *Writing Culture*. See also Schwab, "Literary Transference and the Vicissitudes of Culture."

114. Lyotard, *Inhuman*, 4 ["éminemment l'humain," 11].

115. Ibid. ["l'otage de la communauté adulte," 11].

116. Ibid. ["l'indétermination native . . . la raison instituée," 12].

117. Ibid., 6.

118. Ibid., 7. ["cette dette envers l'enfance," 15].

119. Christopher Bollas uses these terms in *The Shadow of the Object*.

120. This is a core term in Beckett's *The Unnamable*.

121. See Mahler, Pine and Bergman, *Psychological Birth of the Human Infant*, and my chapter on *The Unnamable* in *Subjects without Selves*, 132–71.

122. Lyotard, *Inhuman*, 117 ["une communauté sentimentale," 128].

123. Bollas, *Shadow of the Object*, and Schwab, "Words and Moods."

124. This final turn of my reading echoes Lyotard's reading of Michael Snow's *La region centrale*. See Lyotard, "Unconscious as Mise-en-scène," 96–98.

125. This is Lyotard's term.

126. Lyotard, *Discours, figure*, 38.

127. Deleuze, *Fold*, 35.

128. Porush, *Soft Machine*, 161.

Bibliography

Abish, Walter. *Alphabetical Africa*. New York: New Directions, 1974.

———. *How German Is It (Wie Deutsch Ist Es)*. New York: New Directions, 1979.

Abraham, Nicolas, and Maria Torok. *L'écorce et le noyau* is the French original of *The Shell and the Kernal. The Shell and the Kernel: Renewals of Psychoanalysis*, vol. 1. Edited and translated and edited by Nicholas T. Rand. Chicago: University of Chicago Press, 1994.

Ahmad, Aijaz. *In Theory: Classes, Nations, Literatures*. New York: Verso, 1994.

Allsebrook, Annie, and Anthony Swift. *Broken Promise: World of Endangered Children*. New York: Hodder Arnold, 1989.

Appadurai, Arjun. *Modernity at Large: Cultural Dimensions of Globalization*. Minneapolis: University of Minnesota Press, 1996.

Asad, Talal. "The Concept of Cultural Translation in British Social Anthropology." In *Writing Culture: The Poetics and Politics of Ethnography*, edited by James Clifford and George Marcus, 141–64. Berkeley: University of California Press, 1986.

Badiou, Alain. *Beckett: L'increvable désir*. Paris: Hachette, 1995.

Balibar, Étienne. "My *Self* and My *Own*: One and the Same?" In *Accelerating Possession: Global Futures of Property and Personhood*, edited by Bill Maurer and Gabriele Schwab, 21–44. New York: Columbia University Press, 2006.

Balsamo, Anne. "Reading Cyborgs Writing Feminism." In *The Gendered Cyborg: A Reader*, edited by Gill Kirkup, Linda Janes, Kath Woodward, and Fiona Hovenden, 148–58. New York: Routledge, 2000.

Barthes, Roland. *Mythologies*. Translated by Annette Lavers. New York: Hill and Wang, 1972.

———. *Roland Barthes by Roland Barthes*. Translated by Richard Howard. New York: Farrar, Straus, and Giroux, 1977.

Bateson, Gregory. *Steps to an Ecology of Mind*. Chicago: University of Chicago Press, 1972.

Baudelaire, Charles. *Flowers of Evil*. Translated by Keith Waldrop. Middletown, Conn.: Wesleyan University Press, 2007.

Beckett, Samuel. *The Complete Short Prose of Samuel Beckett, 1929–1989*. Edited by S. E. Gontarski. New York: Grove Press, 1997.

———. *Le dépeupleur*. Paris: Éditions de Minuit, 1970.

———. *The Lost Ones*. Translated by Samuel Beckett. New York: Grove Press, 1972.

———. *The Unnamable*. New York: Grove Press, 1958.

Benjamin, Walter. *Illuminations*. Edited by Hannah Arendt. Translated by Harry Zohn. New York: Schocken Books, 1968.

———. *The Writer of the Modern Life: Essays on Charles Baudelaire*. Edited by Michael W. Jennings. Translated by Howard Eiland, Edmund Jephcott, Rodney Livingstone, and Harry Zohn. Cambridge, Mass.: Harvard University Press, 2006.

Bhabha, Homi K. *The Location of Culture*. New York: Routledge, 1994.

Biehl, João. *Vita: Life in a Zone of Social Abandonment*. Berkeley: University of California Press, 2005

Bion, Wilfred R. *Attention and Interpretation*. London: Tavistock, 1970.

———. *Learning from Experience*. Northvale, N.J.: Aronson, 1994.

Blumenberg, Hans. *Die Lesbarkeit der Welt*. Frankfurt: Suhrkamp, 1981.

———. *Die Vollzähligkeit der Sterne*. Frankfurt: Suhrkamp, 1997.

———. *The Legitimacy of the Modern Age*. Translated by Robert W. Wallace. Cambridge, Mass.: MIT Press, 1985.

Bohm, David. *Wholeness and the Implicate Order*. London: Routledge, 1980.

Bollas, Christopher. *Being a Character: Psychoanalysis and Self Experience*. New York: Hill and Wang, 1992.

———. *The Shadow of the Object: Psychoanalysis of the Unthought Known*. New York: Columbia University Press, 1987.

Brown, Wendy. *States of Injury*. Princeton: Princeton University Press, 1995.

Buck, Pearl S. *Peony*. New York: Bloch, 1990.

Buck-Morss, Susan. "The Flâneur, the Sandwichman and the Whore." *New German Critique* 39 (1986): 99–140.

Budick, Sanford, and Wolfgang Iser. *The Translatability of Cultures: Figurations of the Space Between*. Stanford: Stanford University Press, 1996.

Butler, Octavia. *Adulthood Rites*. New York: Warner, 1988.

———. *Dawn*. New York: Warner, 1987.

———. *Imago*. New York: Warner, 1989.

Butler, Cornelia H., and Catherine de Zegher. *On Line: Drawing Through the Twentieth Century*. New York: Museum of Modern Art, 2010.

Caillois, Roger. *Anthologie du fantastique*. Paris: Gallimard, 1966.

———. *Cases d'un échiquier*. Paris: Gallimard, 1970.

Calvino, Italo. *Invisible Cities*. Translated by William Weaver. New York: Harcourt, 1997.

———. *Le città invisibili*. Torino: Einaudi, 1972.

Certeau, Michel de. *Heterologies: Discourse on the Other.* Translated by Brian Massumi. Minneapolis: University of Minnesota Press, 1986.

Clifford, James. *The Predicament of Culture: Twentieth-Century Ethnography, Literature, and Art.* Cambridge, Mass.: Harvard University Press, 1988.

Clifford, James, and George E. Marcus. *Writing Culture: The Poetics and Politics of Ethnography.* Berkeley: University of California Press, 1986.

Crapanzano, Vincent. "Hermes' Dilemma: The Masking of Subversion in Ethnographic Description." In Clifford and Marcus, *Writing Culture,* 51–76.

——. *Imaginative Horizons: An Essay in Literary-Philosophical Anthropology.* Chicago: University of Chicago Press, 2004.

Deleuze, Gilles. *The Fold: Leibniz and the Baroque.* Translated by Tom Conley. Minneapolis: University of Minnesota Press, 1992.

Deleuze, Gilles, and Félix Guattari. *Anti-Oedipus: Capitalism and Schizophrenia.* Translated by Robert Hurley, Mark Seem, and Helen R. Lane. Minneapolis: University of Minnesota Press, 1983.

——. *Kafka: Toward a Minor Literature.* Translated by Dana Polan. Minneapolis: University of Minnesota Press, 1986.

——. *A Thousand Plateaus: Capitalism and Schizophrenia.* Translated by Brian Massumi. London: Continuum, 2004.

Derrida, Jacques. *De la grammatologie.* Paris: Éditions de Minuit, 1967.

——. " 'Eating Well' or the Calculation of the Subject: An Interview with Jacques Derrida." In *Who Comes After the Subject?* Edited by Eduardo Cadava, Peter Connor, and Jean-Luc Nancy, 96–119. Translated by Peter Connor and Avital Ronnell. New York: Routledge, 1991.

——. *L'écriture et la différence.* Paris: Éditions de Seuil, 1967.

——. *Of Grammatology.* Translated by Gayatri Chakravorty Spivak. Baltimore: Johns Hopkins University Press, 1974.

——. "This Strange Institution Called Literature: An Interview with Jacques Derrida." In *Acts of Literature,* edited by Derek Attridge, 33–75. New York: Routledge, 1992.

——. *Writing and Difference.* Translated by Alan Bass. Chicago: University of Chicago Press, 1978.

Dissanayake, Ellen. *Homo Aestheticus: Where Art Comes From and Why.* New York: Free Press, 1992.

Douglas, Mary. *Natural Symbols: Explorations in Cosmology.* New York: Random House, 1973.

Doyle, Richard. *On Beyond Living: Rhetorical Transformations of the Life Sciences.* Stanford: Stanford University Press, 1997.

——. *Wetwares: Experiments in Postvital Living.* Minneapolis: University of Minnesota Press, 2003.

Ehrenzweig, Anton. *The Hidden Order of Art: A Study in the Psychology of Artistic Imagination*. Berkeley: University of California Press, 1967.

Erdheim, Mario, and Maya Nadig. "Ethnopsychoanalyse." In *Psychoanalyse: Ein Handbuch in Schlüsselbegriffen*, edited by W. Mertens, 129–35. Munich: Urban und Schwarzenberg, 1983.

———. "Gössenphantasien und sozialer Tod." *Kursbuch* 58 (1979): 115–26.

Fanon, Frantz. *Black Skin, White Masks*. Translated by Charles Lam Markmann. New York: Grove Press, 1967.

Fiorini, Marcelo. "The Naming Game and the Writing Lesson." Unpublished manuscript.

Fischer, Michael M. J. *Anthropological Futures*. Durham, N.C.: Duke University Press, 2009.

———. *Emergent Forms of Life and the Anthropological Voice*. Durham, N.C.: Duke University Press, 2004.

Foucault, Michel. *The Order of Things: An Archaeology of the Human Sciences*. New York: Random House, 1970.

Frank, Anne. *Anne Frank: The Diary of a Young Girl*. New York: Bantam, 1993.

Freud, Sigmund. *Civilization and Its Discontents*. Translated and edited by James Strachey. New York: Norton, 1961.

———. *The Freud Reader*. Edited by Peter Gay. New York: Norton, 1995.

———. *Totem and Taboo: Some Points of Agreement Between the Mental Lives of Savages and Neurotics*. Translated and edited by James Strachey. New York: Norton, 1950.

Garbarino, James, Nancy Dubrow, Kathleen Kostelny, and Carole Pardo. *Children in Danger: Coping with the Consequences of Community Violence*. San Francisco: Jossey-Bass, 1992.

García-Moreno, Laura. "The Indigestible Other: Writing, Cannibalism and Melancholy in Juan José Saer's *The Witness*." *Revista de estudios hispánicos* 37 (2003): 585–612.

Gilmour, Alan. *Innocent Victims: The Question of Child Abuse*. London: Michael Joseph, 1988.

Godzich, Wlad. *The Culture of Literacy*. Cambridge, Mass.: Harvard University Press, 1994.

Goodman, Nelson. *Ways of Worldmaking*. Indianapolis: Hackett, 1978.

Görling, Reinhold. *Heterotopia: Lektüren einer interkulturellen Literaturwissenschaft*. Munich: Fink, 1997.

Grace, Patricia. *Baby No-Eyes*. Honolulu: University of Hawai`i Press, 1998.

Grand, Sue. *The Reproduction of Evil: A Clinical and Cultural Perspective*. Hillsdale, N.J.: Analytic Press, 2000.

Graves, Robert. *The Greek Myths*: 1. London: Penguin, 1977.

Greenblatt, Stephen. *Marvelous Possessions: The Wonder of the New World.* Chicago: University of Chicago Press, 1991.

Greenblatt, Stephen, Ines Županov, Reinhard Meyer-Kalkus, Heike Paul, Pál Nyíri, and Friederike Pannewick. *Cultural Mobility: A Manifesto.* Cambridge: University of Cambridge Press, 2010.

Hanne, Michael. *The Power of the Story: Fiction and Political Change.* Providence: Berghan Books, 1994.

Haraway, Donna. *Modest_Witness@Second_Millenium.FemaleMan©_Meets Onco Mouse™: Feminism and Technoscience.* New York: Routledge, 1997.

Hayles, N. Katherine. *How We Became Posthuman: Virtual Bodies in Cybernetics, Literature, and Informatics.* Chicago: University of Chicago Press, 1999.

Hulme, Peter. *Colonial Encounters: Europe and the Native Caribbean, 1492–1797.* London: Methuen, 1986.

Iser, Wolfgang. *Die Appellstruktur der Texte: Unbestimmtheit als Wirkungsbedingung literarischer Prosa.* Konstanz: Universitätsverlag, 1970.

——. *The Fictive and the Imaginary: Toward a Literary Anthropology.* Baltimore: Johns Hopkins University Press, 1993.

Jameson, Fredric. *The Political Unconscious: Narrative as a Socially Symbolic Act.* Ithaca: Cornell University Press, 1981.

——. "Third-World Literature in the Era of Multinational Capitalism." *Social Text* 15 (1986): 65–88.

Kafka, Franz. *Franz Kafka: The Complete Stories.* Edited by Nahum N. Glatzer. Translated by Willa and Edwin Muir. New York: Schocken Books, 1946.

——. *Franz Kafka: Erzählungen.* Frankfurt: Fischer, 1996.

Kant, Immanuel. *Anthropology from a Pragmatic Point of View.* Translated and edited by Robert B. Louden. Cambridge: Cambridge University Press, 2006.

Kaplan, Janet A., and Ulrike Ottinger, "*Johanna d'Arc of Mongolia*: Interview with Ulrike Ottinger." *Art Journal* 61, no. 3 (autumn 2002): 17–21.

Kenner, Hugh. *Samuel Beckett.* Berkeley: University of California Press, 1968.

Kermode, Frank. *The Sense of an Ending: Studies in the Theory of Fiction.* Oxford: Oxford University Press, 1966.

Kristeva, Julia. *Black Sun: Depression and Melancholia.* Translated by Leon S. Roudiez. New York: Columbia University Press, 1992.

——. *Revolution in Poetic Language.* Translated by Margaret Waller. New York: Columbia University Press, 1984.

Kubler, George. *The Shape of Time: Remarks on the History of Things.* New Haven, Conn.: Yale University Press, 1962.

Lacan, Jacques. *Écrits: A Selection.* Translated by Bruce Fink. New York: Norton, 2002.

Latour, Bruno. *We Have Never Been Modern.* Translated by Catherine Porter. Cambridge: Harvard University Press, 1993.

Lecercle, Jean-Jacques. *Philosophy of Nonsense: The Intuitions of Victorian Non-sense Literature*. New York: Routledge, 1994.

Lestringant, Frank. *Cannibals: The Discovery and Representation of the Cannibal from Columbus to Jules Verne*. Translated by Rosemary Morris. Berkeley: University of California Press, 1997.

Levinas, Emmanuel. *Totality and Infinity: An Essay on Exteriority*. Translated by Alphonso Lingis. Pittsburgh: Duquesne University Press, 1969.

Lévi-Strauss, Claude. "Á propos de 'Lévi-Strauss dans le XVIIIe siècle.'" Letter addressed to the publishers of *Cahiers pour l'analyse*, no. 8.5 (October 1967): 89–90.

——. "Race and Culture." Lecture, UNESCO, 1971.

——. *Tristes tropiques*. Paris: Librarie Plon, 1955.

——. *Tristes tropiques*. Translated by John and Doreen Weightman. New York: Penguin, 1992.

Luhmann, Niklas. *Liebe als Passion: Zur Codierung von Intimität*. Frankfurt: Suhrkamp, 1982.

Lyotard, Jean-François. *Discours, figure*. Paris: Éditions Klincksieck, 1978.

——. *The Inhuman: Reflections on Time*. Stanford: Stanford University Press, 1988.

——. *L'inhumain: Causeries sur le temps*. Paris: Éditions Galilée, 1988.

——. "The Unconscious as Mise-en-scène." Translated by Joseph Maier. In *Performance in Postmodern Culture*, edited by Michel Benamou and Charles Caramello, 87–98. Madison, Wis.: Coda Press, 1977.

Mahler, Margaret S., Fred Pine, and Anni Bergman. *The Psychological Birth of the Human Infant: Symbiosis and Individuation*. New York: Basic Books, 1975.

Maranto, Gina. "Test-Tube Treachery." *Los Angeles Times Book Review*, February 1, 2004.

May, Karl Friedrich. *Winnetou*. Translated by David Koblick. Pullman: Washington State University Press, 1999.

Mbembe, Achille. "Necropolitics." Translated by Libby Meintjes. *Public Culture* 15, no. 1 (2003): 11–40.

——. *On the Postcolony*. Translated by A. M. Berrett, Janet Roitman, Murray Last, and Steven Rendall. Berkeley: University of California Press, 2001.

Melville, Herman. *The Confidence-Man*. Oxford: Oxford University Press, 2009.

Mitscherlich, Alexander and Margarete. *The Inability to Mourn: Principles of Collective Behavior*. New York: Grove Press, 1967.

Montaigne, Michel de. *The Complete Essays of Montaigne*. Translated by Donald M. Frame. Stanford: Stanford University Press, 1957.

——. *Essais, livre I*. Paris: Garnier-Flammarion, 1969.

Nash, Roderick. *The Rights of Nature: A History of Environmental Ethics*. Madison: University of Wisconsin Press, 1989.

Patterson, Orlando. *Slavery and Social Death: A Comparative Study*. Cambridge: Cambridge University Press, 1985.

Pickover, Clifford. *The Science of Aliens*. New York: Basic Books, 1998.

Plessner, Helmuth. "Die anthropologische Dimension der Geschichtlichkeit." In *Sozialer Wandel: Zivilisation und Fortschritt als Kategorien der soziologischen Theorie*. Edited by Hans Peter Dreitzel, 160–68. Berlin: Neuwied, 1972.

Polo, Marco. *Il Milione di Marco Polo*. New York: McGraw-Hill, 1977.

Porush, David. *The Soft Machine: Cybernetic Fiction*. New York: Methuen, 1985.

Postman, Neil. *The Disappearance of Childhood*. New York: Vintage, 1994.

Powers, Richard. *Operation Wandering Soul*. New York: Harper Perennial, 1993.

Rheinberger, Hans-Jörg. "Man weiß nicht genau, was man nicht weiß. Über die Kunst, das Unbekannte zu erforschen." *Neue Zürcher Zeitung*, May 5, 2007.

——. *On Historicizing Epistemology: An Essay*. Translated by David Fernbach. Stanford: Stanford University Press, 2010.

——. *Toward a History of Epistemic Things: Synthesizing Proteins in the Test Tube*. Stanford: Stanford University Press, 1997.

Rieff, David. *Los Angeles: Capital of the Third World*. New York: Simon and Schuster, 1991.

Riera, Gabriel. *Littoral of the Letter: Saer's Art of Narration*. Lewisburg, Penn.: Bucknell University Press, 2006.

Robbins, Joel. "'When Do You Think the World Will End?': Globalization, Apocalypticism, and the Moral Perils of Fieldwork in 'Lost New Guinea.'" *Anthropology and Humanism* 22, no. 1 (June 1997): 6–30.

Rose, Jacqueline. *The Last Resistance*. London: Verso Press, 2007.

Saer, Juan José. *El concepto de ficción*. Buenos Aires: Ariel, 1997.

——. *El entenado*. Buenos Aires: Folios Ediciones, 1983.

——. *The Witness*. Translated by Margaret Jull Costa. London: Serpent's Tail, 1990.

Said, Edward W. *Freud and the Non-European*. London: Verso, 2003.

——. *The World, the Text, and the Critic*. Cambridge, Mass.: Harvard University Press, 1983.

Scheper-Hughes, Nancy, and Carolyn Sargent, eds. *Small Wars: The Cultural Politics of Childhood*. Berkeley: University of California Press, 1998.

Schrödinger, Erwin. *What Is Life? The Physical Aspect of the Living Cell*. Cambridge: Cambridge University Press, 1944.

Schwab, Gabriele. "Cultural Texts and Endopsychic Scripts." *SubStance: A Review of Theory and Literary Criticism* 30, nos. 1 and 2 (2001): 160–76.

——. *Haunting Legacies: Violent Histories and Transgenerational Trauma*. New York: Columbia University Press, 2010.

——. "Literary Transference and the Vicissitudes of Culture." In *The Anthropological Turn in Literary Studies*. Edited by Jürgen Schlaeger, 115–39. Tübingen: Gunter Narr, 1996.

——. *The Mirror and the Killer-Queen: Otherness in Literary Language*. Bloomington: Indiana University Press, 1996.

———. *Subjects without Selves: Transitional Texts in Modern Fiction*. Cambridge, Mass.: Harvard University Press, 1994.

———. "Words and Moods: The Transference of Literary Knowledge." *SubStance: A Review of Theory and Literary Criticism* 26, no. 3 (1997): 107–27.

Silko, Leslie Marmon. *Storyteller*. New York: Arcade, 1981.

Simard, Jean-Jacques. *La réduction: L'autochtone inventé et les Amérindiens d'aujourd'hui*. Sillery, Qué.: Éditions de Septentrion, 2003.

Sommerville, C. John. *Rise and Fall of Childhood*. New York: Vintage, 1982.

Spivak, Gayatri Chakravorty. "Can the Subaltern Speak?" In *Marxism and the Interpretation of Culture*. Edited by Cary Nelson and Lawrence Grossberg, 271–313. Urbana: University of Illinois Press, 1988.

Stephens, Sharon. *Children and the Politics of Culture*. Princeton: Princeton University Press, 1995.

Stites, Janet. "Bordercrossings: A Conversation in Cyberspace." *Omni* 16, no. 2 (November 1993): 39–113.

Strathern, Marilyn. *Reproducing the Future: Anthropology, Kinship, and the New Reproductive Technologies*. New York: Routledge, 1992.

Ulnik, Jorge. *Skin in Psychoanalysis*. London: Karnac Press, 2008.

Vittachi, Anuradha. *Stolen Childhood: In Search of the Rights of the Child*. Cambridge: Polity Press, 1989.

Vizenor, Gerald, ed. *Narrative Chance: Postmodern Discourse on Native American Indian Literatures*. Albuquerque: University of New Mexico Press, 1989.

Webster's Illustrated Dictionary. Boston: Houghton Mifflin, 1987.

Wiggins, Marianne. *John Dollar*. New York: Harper and Row, 1989.

———. *The Shadow Catcher*. New York: Simon and Schuster, 2008.

Wilden, Anthony. *System and Structure: Essays in Communication and Exchange*. New York: Tavistock, 1972.

Winn, Marie. *Children Without Childhood: Growing Up Too Fast in the World of Sex and Drugs*. New York: Penguin, 1984.

Winnicott, D. W. *Holding and Interpretation: Fragment of an Analysis*. New York: Gove Press, 1994.

———. "The Location of Cultural Experience." In *Transitional Objects and Potential Spaces: Literary Uses of Winnicott*. Edited by Peter Rudnytsky, 3–12. New York: Columbia University Press, 1993.

———. *Playing and Reality*. London: Tavistock, 1971.

Wittgenstein, Ludwig. *Philosophical Investigations*. Translated by G. E. M. Anscombe. New York: Macmillan, 1953.

———. *Tractatus Logico-Philosophicus*. Translated by C. K. Ogden. New York: Cosimo Classics, 2007.

Index

Foucault, Michel, 169–70
Frank, Anne, 112, 115
Freud, Sigmund, 9, 11, 12, 103, 123, 126, 150; and cannibalism, 19–20, 79–80, 83, 87; on "empty screen," 28–29, 41–42; on the unconscious, 13, 152
"Freud and the Scene of Writing" (Derrida), 12

García-Moreno, Laura, 81
Geis, Gilbert, 138
gender: in Butler, 139, 140, 145, 146, 147, 149; and repression, 52; in survival narratives, 94, 95
genetic engineering, 21, 134–56
genocide, 113, 134
Germany, 48–50, 74, 116–18, 128
gift exchange, 30, 33, 42, 43
globalization: and children, 20–21, 113, 119, 120, 130, 132, 133; and culture, 61, 68–69, 73, 74, 76; and literature, 54, 68; and Marco Polo, 45, 58; and noble savage, 63; in Powers, 121; and property, 135
Golding, William, 19, 95
Gone with the Wind (Mitchell), 48
Görling, Reinhold, 63, 92, 93
Grace, Patricia, 4–5
Grapes of Wrath (Steinbeck), 48–49
Graves, Robert, 18
Greenblatt, Stephen, 39, 64
Guattari, Félix, 66, 149, 150

Hanne, Michael, 6
Haraway, Donna, 142, 146
Hayles, N. Katherine, 73, 153
Hemingway, Ernest, 48
Herodotus, 83
Heterologies: Discourse on the Other (de Certeau), 18

Holocaust, 50, 111–12, 115
How German Is It? (Abish), 74
How We Became Posthuman (Hayles), 153
human, the: in Beckett, 166; boundaries of, 136, 137, 141–42, 146, 154, 173, 180, 181; vs. the inhuman, 176; Lyotard on, 177; vs. the posthuman, 18, 167, 169. See also inhuman, the; posthuman, the
Human Genome Diversity Project, 156

identity politics, 72, 146
Il Milione di Marco Polo, 45–46, 59
imaginaries: California, 47–48; extraterrestrial, 134, 136, 141, 151, 153, 156; Mongolia, 55; postcolonial, 95. See also colonial imaginary; cultural imaginary
Imagination Dead Imagine (Beckett), 169, 175
Imago (Butler), 140, 144
Index Librorum Prohibitorum, 49
infancy, 5–6, 11, 175–78, 179, 180. See also children
information technologies, 150–51
inhuman, the, 148, 166, 173, 175–80
Inhuman, The (Lyotard), 159, 172, 173, 176
Innocent Victims (Gilmore), 110
Invisible Cities (Calvino), 16, 45, 46–47
irony, 16, 31–38, 40, 56
Iser, Wolfgang, 7

Jameson, Fredric, 68
Jews, 17, 50–53, 59–60. See also Holocaust
Johanna d'Arc of Mongolia (film), 16–17, 54–56